GENEALOGY

OF

SOME EARLY FAMILIES

IN GRANT
AND PLEASANT DISTRICTS
PRESTON COUNTY
WEST VIRGINIA

Also

THE THORPE FAMILY
OF FAYETTE COUNTY
PENNSYLVANIA

and

THE CUNNINGHAM FAMILY
OF SOMERSET COUNTY
PENNSYLVANIA

Edward Thorp King

CLEARFIELD

Originally published
1933

Reprinted
Genealogical Publishing Co., Inc.
Baltimore, Maryland
1977

Reprinted for
Clearfield Company, Inc. by
Genealogical Publishing Co., Inc.
Baltimore, Maryland
1994, 2002

Library of Congress Catalogue Card Number 77-70367
International Standard Book Number: 0-8063-0761-7

Made in the United States of America

INTRODUCTION

The beginning of this book was to have been a history of the King family in Preston County, West Virginia. After collecting data for a year it developed that the data thus far gathered would make a better Genealogy for several related families, all of whom were among the early settlers in Grant and Pleasant Districts, Preston County, W. Va. (These Districts were formed in 1852, and prior to June 20, 1863, Preston was in the state of Virginia.) Another year was spent gathering data to make more complete the families represented. The result of three years work is herewith presented by an amateur of no previous experience as a genealogist, and it is hoped that it may, in part, supplement the genealogical work already done in 1914 by Cole and Morton, and that others will take sufficient interest in the history of their respective families to continue to carry on with the genealogical records in the future.

In a work of this kind many mistakes are found and special effort was made to copy records exactly as they were found in Bibles, on tombstones or wherever the information was obtained, some of which may conflict with data found in another place. Where names and dates were not supplied space is purposely left blank for such names and dates to be filled in by those having the information, and desiring the record complete.

The writer being remote from the source of information wrote hundreds of letters and the response and assistance given was indeed encouraging and helped greatly to complete this work. I am truly grateful to those who assisted to secure data.

The index number at the beginning of each family record is for the purpose of locating the parent record of preceding generation quickly and accurately. The last figure in any index number represents the number of the child in the parent family record and the remainder of the number (excluding the last figure) represents the parent family index number.

Edward Thorp King.

Marshalltown, Iowa,
Aug. 10, 1933.

CONTENTS

CEMETERY RECORDS GRANT AND PLEASANT DISTRICTS, PRESTON CO., W. VA.

JOHN CHRISTOPHER

OF PISGAH, PRESTON COUNTY, WEST VIRGINIA
AND SOME OF HIS DESCENDANTS

1. JOHN CHRISTOPHER, according to history was "an orphan," reared by John Seaport, and inherited his farm two miles south of Pisgah, W. Va. - b. Dec. or Jan. 10, 1814- - 5 - d. Mar. 16, 1891, buried Pisgah, W. Va. - m. 1st. Mary Lawson - b. Mar. 28, 1804 - d. Sept. 11, 1854, buried on the abandoned Bricher farm two miles south of Pisgah, W. Va

    Children by first marriage:
    1. Frances A. - b. Sept. 2, 1836 - d. June 1, 1907 - m. George King.
    2. Irvin E. - b. Apr. 12, 1839 - d. July 6, 1924 - m. Mary C. King.
    3. Jehu (twin) - b. Apr. 12, 1839 - d. Feb. 24, 1916 - m. Isabelle King.
    4. Tazwell - b. Mar. 22, 1845 - d. Libby Prison, Served during Civil War with Co. H., 3rd P. H. B. Md. Inft.
    5. Marshall S. - b. May 23, 1843 - d. Sept. 20, 1854.

    John Christopher married 2nd. Aug. 8, 1858 Delila Walls - b. Sept. 26, 1834 - d. Oct. 26, 1896 buried Pisgah, W. Va. daughter of William Walls (James) and Elizabeth Morrison. (see Walls Genealogy).

    Children by 2nd marriage:
    6. Barney P. - b. July 29, 1856 - m. Jessie A. Spurgeon.
    7. Asbury Allen - b. Mar. 5, 1859 - m. Phoebe J. Cress.
    8. Sylvester H. - b. Sept. 5, 1860 - d. Mar. 16, 1932 - m. Deborah Rogers.
    9. John R. - b. Sept. 27, 1861 - m. 1st. Mary Field. 2nd. Bessie Kirby.
    10. Spencer Camden - b. Mar. 22, 1863 - d. Apr. 10, 1863.
    11. Mattie L. - b. Mar. 17, 1864 - m. 1st. John Sadler. 2nd James Cunningham.
    12. Mary Elizabeth - b. Mar. 6, 1866 - m. Ezra D. Mathews.
    13. Lazonia S. - b. Mar. 18, 1867 - m. Ann Hornby.
    14. Rufus Columbus - b. Oct. 14, 1869 - m. Jennie Gribble.
    15. Elmer Emmor - b. Dec. 14, 1871 - m. 1st. Laura Teets. 2nd. Elizabeth Shay Garner.
    16. Rosa I. - b. May 16, 1875 - m. French Greathouse.

12. IRVIN E. CHRISTOPHER (John) - b. Apr. 12, 1839 - d. July 6, 1924 - m. Dec. 2, 1867 Mary C. King - b. Aug. 19, 1847 Pisgah, W. Va. - d. Mar. 26, 1906. Both are buried Pisgah, W. Va.

- daughter of Thomas King (James) and Jane Brandon (William - Alexander).
   Children:
   1. Tekoah H. - b. Feb. 28, 1870 - m. Mary S. Greathouse.
   2. Ralph S. - b. Apr. 8, 1872 - m. Effie E. Ryan.
   3. Orpha J. - b. June 28, 1874 - m. Feb. 7, 1898 at Cumberland, Md. Dr. James A. Graham - b. April 10, 1868 in Preston County, W. Va., son of David Graham 1834 - 1892 (Samuel Sept. 3, 1799 - Oct. 16, 1881) and Martha Field 1842 - 1914. Children:
      i. Pauline Graham - b. Apr. 25, 1899 - m. HARRY B. LOSE, their children:
         a. Martha Jane Lose - b. Oct. 9, 1921.
         b. Harry Graham Lose - b. Aug. 1, 1924.
         c. Madge Lose - b. Oct. 1925 - d. Nov. 1925.
         d. James William Lose - b. Nov. 20, 1929.
      ii. James P. Graham - b. Oct. 19, 1904 - m. Gertrude McKinney. Children:
         a. James McKinley Graham - b. April 12, 1928.
         b. Jack DaCosta Graham - b. Sept. 30, 1931.
      iii. Ben Irvin Graham - b. Sept. 17, 1912.
      iv. David Field Graham - b. June 7, 1916.
   4. Minnie - b. July 17, 1876 at Pisgah, W. Va. - m. at San Francisco, Calif. Aug. 21, 1916, ARTHUR J. MEYERS - b. ———. Children:
      i. James Christopher Meyers - b. Aug. 30, 1918.
   5. Persis - b. Mar. 2, 1881 at Pisgah, W. Va. - m. July 29, 1902 at Morgantown, W. Va., JOSEPH HERBERT KASZER - b. ——— - d. ——— - buried Morgantown, W. Va., son of ————————— -. Children:
      i. Mary Christopher Kaszer - b. Sept. 15, 1903.
      ii. Herbert Earl Kaszer - b. April 14, 1911.
   6. William G. - b. Apr. 2, 1884 - d. Apr. 9, 1889, buried at Pisgah, W. Va.
   7. Daisy P. - b. Nov. 6, 1887 - m. Charles G. Ryan (see Ryan Genealogy).
13. JEHU CHRISTOPHER (John) twin to 12. Irvin - b. April 12, 1839, Pisgah, W. Va. - d. Feb. 23, 1916, buried at Pisgah, W. Va. - m. Jan. 6, 1872 at Laurel Run, near Pisgah, Isabelle King - b. Feb. 18, 1853, near St. Peter Church, in Grant District, Preston Co., W. Va. - d. Mar. 21, 1927, buried at Pisgah, W. Va., daughter of William J. King and Elizabeth H. Street (see King Genealogy).
   Children:

1. Shiloah - b. Dec. 27, 1872 at Pisgah, W. Va. - m. Mar. 21, 1894 at Pisgah, W. Va. JESSE FORMAN - b. Dec. 31, 1868, Terra Alta, W. Va. - d. Feb. 20, 1920, buried at Pisgah, W. Va. son of Samuel Forman 1843 - 1917 (Jesse) and Savilla Everly b. 1846 (Lewis) Children:
   i. Okey Fay Forman - b. Jan. 4, 1895 - m. Sadie Ryan.
   ii. Lester Ray Forman - b. Dec. 5, 1896 - m. Opal Talbert.
   iii. Erma Floe Forman - b. June 28, 1899 - m. Edward Cooley.
   iv. Vida Maude Forman - b. Mar. 4, 1901 - d. Dec. 5, 1923 - m. Thomas Robins.
   v. Samuel Jehu Forman - b. Feb. 14, 1903 -
   vi. Savilla Belle Forman - b. Sept. 3, 1905 -
   vii. Emma Grace Forman - b. Nov. 6, 1907 - m. Dewey Everly.
   viii. Mary Elizabeth Forman - b. Jan. 9, 1911 -
   ix. Jessie Beryle Forman - b. Aug. 29, 1913 -
   x. Loyal Grant Forman -b. Sept. 8, 1916 -
2. Lester - b. Feb. 13, 1874 - m. 1st. Rebecca Gribble, 2nd. Dessie Ringer.
3. Rutherford Hayes - b. Dec. 31, 1876 - d. Dec. 16, 1891, buried at Pisgah, W. Va.
4. Elizabeth J. - b. Jan. 6, 1879 - m. Nov. 15, 1917 JOHN FURMAN - b. May 14, 1888, Davistown, Greene County, Penn., son of Robert Furnam and Mary Edwards.
5. Maude - b. Sept. 30, 1880, Pisgah, W. Va. - m. Dec. 26, 1901 at Brandonville, W. Va. CLINTON GRAHAM - b. Aug. 18, 1876, Rockville, W. Va. Children:
   i. Paul Graham - b. Dec. 15, 1902 - m. Hazel Walls (see Walls Gen).
   ii. Cecil Graham - b. Nov. 2, 1904 - m. Leona Grantz.
   iii. Dallas Graham - b. Nov. 16, 1906 -
   iv. Zelda Graham - b. Feb. 9, 1909 -
   v. Isabelle Graham - b. May 12, 1912 -
   vi. Harlan Graham - b. April 6, 1915 -
   vii. Beatrice Graham - b. Jan. 1, 1917 -
   viii. Warren Graham - b. Feb. 7, 1920 -
   ix. Merwin Graham - b. July 24, 1926 -
6. Siota E. - b. Dec. 2, 1882 - d. July 11, 1898, buried at Pisgah, W. Va.
7. Sylvester - b. April 12, 1885 - d. Dec. 11, 1927 - m. Mildred Everly.
8. Hosea Thurman - b. Dec. 11, 1888 - m. Emma Ryan.

9. Guy B. - b. Oct. 25, 1892 - d. Sept. 20, 1918 - Accidently killed while serving in France during World War. Enlisted for service May 25, 1918, on duty at Camp Lee, Va., until July, 1918, in France with M. G. Company 15th Inft., - buried at Pisgah, W. Va.
10. Jehu Junior - b. Oct. 18, 1895 - d. Oct. 10, 1896, buried at Pisgah, W. Va.

17. ASBURY ALLEN CHRISTOPHER (John) - b. Mar. 5, 1859, near Pisgah, W. Va. - d. Sept. 3, 1927 - m. July 10, 1880, Phoebe J. Cress - b. Nov. 23, 1861, near Hudson, - d. Mar. 25, 1921, both are buried near Hudson, in Pleasant District, Preston Co., W. Va. - daughter of Jacob Cress, 1829 - 1908 and Lucinda Cale, 1823 - 1901.

Children:
1. Lucinda - b. Mar. 17, 1881 - m. 1st. Oct. 4, 1902, at Bruceton Mills, W. Va. JAMES A. RADABAUGH - b. Sept. 9, 1880 - d. Feb. 18, 1921, buried at Mt. Zion Cemetery, in Pleasant District, Preston Co., W. Va., son of John W. Radabaugh and Sarah Radabaugh. Children of Lucinda and James A. Radabaugh:
   i. Birdie O. Radabaugh - b. Jan. 29, 1905 - m. Floyd Harris. Children:
      a. Freda June Harris - b. June 28, 1931.
   ii. Jessie P. Radabaugh - b. May 9, 1906 - m. Wayne Bayles. Children:
      a. Willis E. - b. May 29, 1925.
      b. Everett E. Bayles - b. April 1, 1927.
   iii. Cecil F. Radabaugh - b. Feb. 9, 1908 - m. Verna Harned. Children:
      a. James E. Radabaugh - b. Jan. 31, 1928.
      b. Garel F. Radabaugh - b. Aug. 30, 1931.
   iv. Goldie M. Radabaugh - b. Aug. 30, 1909 - m. Steven Bishop. Children:
      a. Virginia M. Bishop - b. Nov. 7, 1931.
   Lucinda Christopher Radabaugh - m. 2nd. Albert B. Falkenstine.
2. Florence - b. May 17, 1884 - m. April 18, 1903, ARTHUR J. GALLOWAY - b. June 8, 1882, son of John and Liddia Galloway. Children:
   i. Hollis Galloway - b. Sept. 18, 1905 -
   ii. Carlus Galloway - b. Sept. 22, 1909 -
   iii. Delphia Galloway - b. April 10, 1912 -
   iv. Emma Jane Galloway - b. Sept. 1, 1903 -

3. Marshall R. - b. Mar. 15, 1886 - m. Josie Wolf.
4. Sanford E. - b. May 21, 1888 - m. Ethel Everly.
5. Alta M. - b. July 23, 1890 - m. June 15, 1907, near Hudson, W. Va. THOMAS H. GIBSON - b. Jan. 1, 1881, son of Nelson H. and Jennie Gibson. Children:
   i. Howard Gibson - b. Dec. 2, 1907 - m. Irene Keffover. Children:
      a. Vida Gibson - b. June 15, 1927.
      b. Harold Gibson - b. Nov. 1, 1928
      c. Juanita Gibson - b. Oct. 16.
      d. Thomas Gibson - b.
   ii. Darwin Gibson - b. Feb. 26, 1910 -
   iii. Vernal Gibson - b. June 21, 1913 - m. Fred Bishop. Children:
      a. Willis Bishop - b. April 21, 1929.
      b. Everett Bishop - b. Aug. 23, 1931.
6. Albert H. - b. May 1, 1894 - m. Osie Liston.
7. Wilbert F. - b. Oct. 1, 1896 - d. Dec. 28, 1896.
8. Hosea B. - b. Dec. 30, 1897 - m. Edna Stone.
9. Charles S. - b. Dec. 11, 1899 - m. Pearl Wolfe.
10. William H. - b. Dec. 4, 1901 - m. Alta Wilhelm.
11. Eva B. - b. Feb. 27, 1904 - m. Dec. 23, 1922, FOSTER RADABAUGH - b Aug. 26, 1900. Children:
    i. Denzil Radabaugh - b. Oct. 9, 1923.
    ii. Clifford A. Radabaugh - b. Feb. 5, 1929.
12. Wilbert F. - b. Oct. 1, 1896.

18. SYLVESTER H. CHRISTOPHER (John) - b. Sept. 5, 1860 - d. Mar. 16, 1932 - m. Deborah Jane Rogers - b. May 30, 1863, daughter of ——————
   Children:
   1. John - b. ————— - d. ————— - buried at Pisgah, W. Va.

19. JOHN R. CHRISTOPHER (John) - b. Sept. 27, 1861, near Pisgah, W. Va. - d. Apr. 7, 1933 - m. 1st. April 25, 1888, at Herring, W. Va., Mary Field - d. April 9, 1920, daughter of Richard and Lucinda Field - m. 2nd Jan. 25, 1922, Bessie Kirby - b. Sept. 4, 1888, daughter of William and Elizabeth Kirby of Burton, W. Va.
   Children by 1st marriage:
   1. Dora Anna - b. June 29, 1889 - m. 1st. Cecil Hagedorn - m. 2nd. Omer Strawser.
   2. Forest Ray - b. March 31, 1891.

3. Iva Olive - b. Feb. 12, 1894 - m. Frank Wiles.
4. Richard Graham - b. July 31, 1896 - m. Arminta Conner.
5. Goldie May - b. April 1, 1899 - m. 1st. Luther Mooney - m. 2nd. Richard Turbin.

1-13. LAZONIA S. CHRISTOPHER (John) - b. Mar. 18, 1867, at Pisgah, W. Va. - m. at Pisgah, W. Va., Oct. 23, 1887, Sarah Ann Hornby - b. July 2, 1870, daughter of Charles Hornby (Thomas) and Martha Smith (John). - Hardware Dealer living in Fairchance, Penn.

Children:

1. Florina Elsie - b. July 30, 1888 - m. May 29, 1908, DELL ROBINSON. Children:
   i. Leroy Robinson.
   ii. Sylvia Robinson.
2. Earnest Desmond - b. Jan. 8, 1890 - m. Maude Price.
3. Harvey Russell - b. June 16, 1891 - m. Helen Wilson.
4. Nellie Myrtle - b. Dec. 16, 1893 - m. Aug. 29, 1914, WALTER BALDWIN, son of John Baldwin. Children:
   i. Robert Baldwin - b. Oct. 13, 1915.
5. Nora Gay - b. Sept. 24, 1895 - d. Oct. 30, 1897.
6. Ora Belle - b. Nov. 16, 1897 - m. Dec. 31, 1919, Raymond O'Neal.
7. Goldie Virginia - b. Apr. 26, 1899 - m. Sept. 27, 1919, GILBERT COOLEY, son of Lucas Cooley - Children:
   i. Eugene Gilbert Cooley - b. Dec. 24, 1920.
   ii. Gerald Sherman Cooley - b. June 7, 1924.
8. Sadie Blanche - b. Apr. 2, 1902 - d. Dec. 5, 1904.
9. Arthur Earl - b. Apr. 20, 1904 - m. Eva May Blasey.
10. Mildred May - b. Oct. 22, 1906 - m. July 16, 1924, GERALD SWANEY - b. Nov. 28, 1904, son of Alvin Swaney. Children:
    i. Edward Ray Swaney - b. Mar. 3, 1928.
    ii. Geraldine May Swaney - b. Mar. 28, 1930.
11. Lillie Minnis - b. Oct. 13, 1908 - m. Aug. 1, 1928, SYLVESTER WILSON - b. Jan. 10, 1907, son of Sylvester Wilson and Dora Shoaf. Children:
    i. Lillie Bell Wilson - b. July 18, 1930.
    ii. Sylvia Arline Wilson - b. Feb. 20, 1932.
12. Sherman Ray - b. Nov. 18, 1911 -

121. TEKOAH H. CHRISTOPHER (Irvin - John) - b. Feb. 10, 1870 at Pisgah, W. Va. - m. at Herring W. Va. Jan. 17, 1892 Mary S. Greathouse.

Children:
1. Zeddie - b. Sept. 18, 1892 - m. Grace Arford.
2. Delphia - b. ——— - m. Edward Colebank. Children:
   i. Edward Colebank - b. ———
   ii. Della Colebank - b. ———
   iii. Frank Colebank - b. ———
   iv. Mary Colebank - b. ———
3. Della - b. ——— - m. Jules Henry. Children:
   i. Flora Henry - b. ———
   ii. Joseph Henry - b. ———
4. Zola - b. ——— - m. Howard Clayton. Children:
   i. Howard Clayton, Jr. - b. ———
   ii. Niles Gary Clayton - b. ———
5. Homer - b. ——— - m. Catherine Lyons.

122. RALPH S. CHRISTOPHER (Irvin - John) - b. April 8, 1872 m. - in Garret County, Md., Sept. 17, 1892, Effie E. Ryan - b. Oct. 18, 1875, Pisgah, W. Va. - d. Dec. 31, 1922, buried at Pisgah, W. Va., daughter of Edward D. Ryan and Elizabeth Wolfe (see Wolfe and Ryan Gen.).

Children:
1. Earl - b. Feb. 16, 1893 - m. Edna Jenkins.
2. Dayton - b. Nov. 4, 1894 - m. Merle Everly.
3. Lloyd - b. Apr. 19, 1896 - m. Joanna Jager.
4. Hattie - b. Mar. 9, 1898 - m. Lloyd O'Neal.
5. Vida M. - b. Mar. 3, 1900 - m. Charles McGill.
6. Kermit - b. Sept. 12, 1901 - m. Mary O'Neal.
7. Kenneth K. - b. June 8, 1903 - d. 1926 - m. Gerald Blackburn.
8. Ermie - b. Mar. 5, 1905 -
9. Pansy - b. Dec. 28, 1906 -
10. Mary - b. May 31, 1908 -
11. Dallas - b. Mar. 16, 1910 - d. 1927.
12. Quentin - b. April 1, 1912.
13. Una F. - b. Oct. 14, 1913.
14. Bertha - b. April 13, 1915.
15. Lola Vada - b. Nov. 19, 1916.

132. LESTER CHRISTOPHER (Jehu - John) - b. Feb. 13, 1874, Pisgah, W. Va. - m. 1st. July 7, 1899, Rebecca Gribble - b. Aug. 19, 1870 - d. Aug. 1, 1924, buried at Pisgah, W. Va., daughter of John Gribble (Archibald - John) and Lucinda Ringer. - m. 2nd. Dessie Ringer. Lived near Bruceton Mills, W. Va.

Children by 1st marriage:
1. Alva R. - b. Oct. 7, 1897 - m. Zora Everly.
2. Dana C. - b. Mar. 9, 1900 - m. 1st. Olive Swaney; 2nd. Mary Brady.
3. Harry Z. - b. Dec. 5, 1901.
4. Lucinda B. - b. Aug. 13, 1903 - m. June 16, 1930, at Kingwood, W. Va. CHARLES GALLOWAY - b. Dec. 26, 1904, Monesson, Penn., son of James Galloway (John) and Mamie Belle King (Evan - Albert F. - Thomas - James). Children:
   i. Everett Galloway - b. Mar. 16, 1930, Bruceton Mills, W. Va.
   ii. Charlotte Elaine Galloway - b. Dec. 14, 1931, Brandonville, W. Va.
5. John Jehu - b. Mar. 18, 1906 - m. Flossie Benson.
6. William Gail - b. Aug. 12, 1910 - d. Oct. 30, 1910, bur. at Pisgah, W. Va.
7. Paul - b. Jan. 10, 1913.

137. SYLVESTER CHRISTOPHER (Jehu - John) - b. Apr. 12, 1885, at Pisgah, W. Va. - d. Dec. 11, 1927, buried at Pisgah, W. Va. Lived at Pisgah, W. Va. - m. at Cumberland, Md., July 4, 1917, Mildred Everly - b. Dec. 26, 1899, Hudson, W. Va., daughter of Charles Everly (Henry - Lewis) and Cora Galloway (John).

Children:
1. Darwin - b. May 24, 1918, Pisgah, W. Va.
2. Melvin - b. Jan. 3, 1920, Pisgah, W. Va.
3. Glenavee - b. Nov. 27, 1923, Pisgah, W. Va .

138. HOSEA THURMAN CHRISTOPHER (Jehu - John) - b. Dec. 11, 1888, Pisgah, W. Va. - m. at Pisgah, W. Va., Mar. 20, 1909, Emma Ryan - b. Aug. 19, 1888, Pisgah, W. Va., daughter of Daniel Ryan and Dora Alice King (see Ryan Genealogy). Residence, Pisgah, W. Va.

Children:
1. Claude Ryan - b. Sept. 27, 1909, Pisgah, W. Va.
2. Carlus Benton - b. April 2, 1919, Pisgah, W. Va.

173. MARSHALL R. CHRISTOPHER (Asbury Allen - John) b. Mar. 15, 1886 - m. Dec. 29, 1909, Bruceton Mills, W. Va., Josie Wolf - b. April 28, 1880, Rockville - d. Jan. 21, 1931, Hudson, W. Va., bur. at Pisgah, W. Va., daughter of John A. Wolf (Augustine - Samuel) and Martha King (Alpheus - James).
Children:
1. Wilma V. - b. Oct. 21, 1910 - m. Marshall E. Graham.
Children:
    i. Evelyn J. Graham - b. July 10, 1928, Preston County, W. Va.
    ii. Evert R. Graham - b. Dec. 10, 1930, Preston County, W. Va.

174. SANFORD E. CHRISTOPHER (Asbury Allen - John) - b. May 21, 1888 - m. Jan. 4, 1911, at Bruceton Mills, W. Va., Ethel Everly - b. June 26, 1893, daughter of Fletcher Everly.
Children:
1. Virgil Wayne - b. May 6, 1912 -
2. Willard Cledis - b. Dec. 9, 1918 -

176. ALBERT H. CHRISTOPHER (Asbury Allen - John) - b. May 1, 1894 - m. Dec. 31, 1913, Osie Liston - b. May 25, 1893, daughter of John Liston.
Children:
1. Gilbert O. - b. Oct. 16, 1914 -
2. Mildred A. - b. May 3, 1920 -
3. Carlus G. - b. Oct. 19, 1924 -
4. Edward F. - b. May 12, 1927 -

178. HOSEA B. CHRISTOPHER (Asbury Allen - John) - b. Dec. 30, 1897 - m. April 2, 1918, Edna Stone - b. Aug. 3, 1899, daughter of Birdie Stone.
Children:
1. Gladys J. - b. Sept. 28, 1918 -

179. CHARLES S. CHRISTOPHER (Asbury Allen - John) - b. Dec. 11, 1899 - m. July 31, 1922, Evelyn Pearl Wolfe - b. July 19, 1905.
Children:
1. Evert Grant - b. Mar. 14, 1923 -
2. Glenna Belle - b. May 19, 1928 -

17-10. WILLIAM H. CHRISTOPHER (Asbury Allen - John) - b. Dec. 4, 1901 - m. May 30, 1923, Alta N. Wilhelm - b. Sept. 28, 1904, daughter of Authur Wilhelm (George) and Rosetta Cunningham (Robert - John).
Children:
1. Alfreda A .- b. ———

1-13-2. EARNEST DESMOND CHRISTOPHER (Lazonia - John) - b. Jan. 8, 1890 - m. Nov. 17, 1909, Maude Price - b. May 3, 1884, daughter of William Price and Elizabeth Byerley.

Children:
1. Jennie - b. Dec. 29, 1909 - m. Oct. 1, 1927, EARL EVANS WHOOLERY (William). Children:
   i. Earl W. Whoolery - b. Jan. 31, 1928.
   ii. Isamae Whoolery - b. July 11, 1930.
2. Kenneth - b. May 1, 1912, Fairchance, Penn.
3. William - b. Oct. 24, 1913, Fairchance, Penn.
4. James - b. Feb. 7, 1917, Fairchance, Penn.
5. Ray - b. May 13, 1918, Fairchance, Penn.
6. Ora - b. Sept. 22, 1919 - d. Sept. 22, 1919, bur. Fairchance, Penn.
Twin 7. Cora - b. Sept. 22, 1919 - d. Dec. 2, 1920, bur. Fairchance, Penn.
8. Grant - b. March 31, 1921, Fairchance, Penn.
9. Fred - b. March 8, 1927, Fairchance, Penn.

1-13-3. HARVEY RUSSELL CHRISTOPHER (Lazonia - John) - b. June 16, 1891 -m. Dec. 23, 1915, Helen Wilson - b. ——— daughter of Arthur Wilson.

Children:
1. Delbert - b. Oct. 14, 1916.
2. Harvey Junior - b. Sept. 21, 1918.

1-13-9. ARTHUR EARL CHRISTOPHER (Lazonia - John) - b. Apr. 20, 1904 - m. Oakland, Md., Dec. 6, 1924, Eva May Blasey - b. Mar. 19, 1910, daughter of Samuel Blasey and Luella Livingston.

Children:
1. George Edward - b. Sept. 19, 1925, Fairchance, Penn.
2. Betty Jane - b. Nov. 6, 1927, Fairchance, Penn.
3. Evelyn May - b. Mar. 1, 1930, Fairchance, Penn.

1211. ZEDDIE B. CHRISTOPHER (Tekoah H. - Irvin - John) - b. Sept. 18, 1892 - m. at Morgantown, W. Va., Dec. 26, 1913, Grace Arford - b. July 10, 1894, daughter of George F. Arford (John Calvin - Benjamin from Holland) and Adda Sharpnack (Andrew - Brownell - Thomas - John).

Children:
1. Wilford - b. July 31, 1915.
2. Paul - b. Sept. 20, 1917.
3. Zeddie B. Jr. - b. Feb. 25, 1919.
4. Helen - b. Jan. 23, 1921.

5. Mary Alice - b. May 2, 1924.
6. William Edwin - b. Sept. 18, 1926.
7. Richard - b. Feb. 17, 1929.

1215. HOMER CHRISTOPHER (Tekoah H. - Irvin - John) - b. ————— - m. Catherine Lyons - b. ———— daughter of —————
Children:
1. Martha Jane - b. ————

1321. ALVA R. CHRISTOPHER (Lester - Jehu - John) - b. Oct. 7, 1897 - m. at Uniontown, Penn., July 10, 1918, Zora Everly - b. Mar. 2, 1897, daughter of John Barton Everly - b. April 11, 1873 (John L.) and Arminta A. Yeast (William Alexander - Adam).
Children:
1. Eunice - b. Oct. 29, 1919, Clifton Mills, W. Va.
2. Wallace Glen - b. June 29, 1921, Bruceton Mills, W. Va.
3. Opal Jean - b. Oct. 15, 1922, Bruceton Mills, W. Va.
4. Donald Ray - b. Sept. 20, 1930, Bruceton Mills, W. Va.

1325. JOHN JEHU CHRISTOPHER (Lester - Jehu - John) - b. Mar. 18, 1906 - m. at Kingwood, W. Va., June 1, 1929, Flossie Benson - b. Mar. 14, 1903, Bruceton Mills, W. Va., daughter of Abraham Benson (William - James) and Maggie Belle Collins - b. Aug. 5, 1863 (Eliphalet - William).
Children:
1. Shirley Deane - b. Mar. 21, 1931, Fairchance, Penn.

* * * *

1341. Minnis Christopher - b. Mar. 28, 1898, daughter of Elizabeth Christopher (Jehu - John) - m. at Kingwood, W. Va., Sept. 20, 1924. GILBERT ROOSEVELT EVERLY - b. Sept. 11, 1903, son of James S. Everly (Henry - Lewis) and Mary Ann McNair (Andrew S.) Children:
i. Lova Lucille Everly - b. April 2, 1925, Pisgah, W. Va .
ii. Zeda Ruth Everly - b. July 20, 1926, Pisgah, W. Va.
iii. Mary Elizabeth Everly - b. Nov. 27, 1927, Bruceton Mills, W. Va.
iv. Elvidore Gilbert Everly - b. April 18, 1932, Bruceton Mills, W. Va.

SOME DESCENDANTS OF JOHN CONNOR
OF GRANT DISTRICT, PRESTON COUNTY, WEST VIRGINIA

1. JOHN CONNOR, a member of the Quaker colony in Grant District, came from the eastern part of Pennsylvania in 1776. Lived at Bruceton Mills, W. Va.
   Children:
   1. Robert - b. 1762. - single.
   2. William - b. 1765 - m. Elizabeth Forman.
   3. to 9 older children, John, James, etc.

12. WILLIAM CONNOR (John) - b. 1765 - m. Elizabeth Forman b. Feb. 12, 1769, daughter of Robert Forman, 1736 - 1812 and Mary Naylor, 1745 - 1822. Lived at Bruceton Mills, W. Va.
    Children:
    1. Robert - b. 1792 - went west.
    2. Richard - b. ——— - went west.
    3. John - b. ——— - m. ——— Glover.
    4. William C. - b. Jan. 1, 1799 - d. July 25, 1868 - m. Mary Glover .
    5. Joseph - b. ——— - m. Anne McCollum - went west.
    6. Mary - b. 1803 - m. John Rodeheaver.
    7. Jane - m. Thornton Bruley - went to Indiana.
    8. Job - b. 1809 - m. 1st. ——— Groves. 2nd Jane Martin - went west.

124. WILLIAM C. CONNOR (William - John) - b. Jan. 1, 1799 - d. July 25, 1868, buried at Brandonville, W. Va. - was justice of the peace prior to the Constitution of 1850. - Lived at Bruceton Mills, W. Va. - m. Mary Glover, daughter of Benjamin Glover.
     Children:
     1. Cyrus - b. ——— - served in the Civil War.
     2. Samuel F. - b. June 19, 1826 - m. Sophia Guseman.
     3. Hiram - b. ——— - went west.
     4. Elma - b. ——— - went to Iowa.
     5. Harmon - b. ——— - single.
     6. Lavina - b. ——— - d. July 6, 1873 - m. Oct. 23, 1856. JACOB J. GUSEMAN - b. Aug. 8, 1835, son of Jacob Guseman and Christena Wolfe. Children:
        i. John W. Guseman - b. ——— - d. Aug. 10, 1903.
        ii. Cyrus L. Guseman - b. ——— d. ———

iii. Clara Phelicia Guseman - b. ———— - d. Mar. 27,
    1896 - m. Ezra A. Feather.
iv. Theodore J. Guseman - b. ———— - m. Catherine Feather.
v. Mary Florence Guseman - b. ———— - d. May 2, 1907,
    m. Willey M. Forman.
vi. James A. Guseman - b. ———— m. Marcella McVicker.
7. Benjamin - b. ———— - d. ———— - m. Mary Feather.
8. William - b. ———— - d. ———— - m. Harriet Rodeheaver.
9. John - b. ————
10. Rhoda - b. ———— - d. ———— - m. Abraham Guseman.
11. Martha - b. ———— - d. ———— - m. Joseph Falkenstine.
12. Elizabeth - b. ———— - d. ———— m. Ezra Bishop.

1242. SAMUEL F. CONNOR (William C. - William - John) - b.
June 19, 1826 - m. June 1, 1846, Sophia Guseman - b. April 1,
1822 - d. Feb. 27, 1888, buried at Bruceton Mills, W. Va.,
daughter of Jacob Guseman and Christina Wolfe.

Children:
1. Sarah Caroline - b. June 17, 1848 - d. July 3, 1930 - single
- buried at San Diego, Calif.
2. Isaac Lee - b. Mar. 25, 1850 -
3. William Lawrence - b. June 29, 1853 - m. 1st. Lizzie Kantner. 2nd, Emma Cunningham.

12423. WILLIAM LAWRENCE CONNER (Samuel F. - William
C. - William - John) - b. June 29, 1853, Bruceton Mills, W. Va. -
Lived in Illinois, Minnesota, Missouri, Iowa, California, 1873 to
1875. - m. 1st. April, 1887, in West Virginia, Lizzie Kantner and
went to Buena Park, Calif., in 1889, where Lizzie Kantner Conner died in Feb., 1890, buired at Santa Ana, Calif. - m. 2nd. at
Bruceton Mills, W. Va., Sept. 10, 1891, Emma Cunningham -
b. Jan. 12, 1873, Bruceton Mills, W. Va. - Lived at Bruceton
Mills, W. Va., until April, 1894; in California until Feb., 1895;
from 1895 until 1907 at Bruceton Mills, W. Va. - Served as
deputy Sheriff and tax collector at Bruceton Mills, W. Va. -
Vice President of Bruceton Milling Co. - Carpenter by trade. -
Since June 29, 1907, lived in Pasadena, Calif., now residing at
329 South Marengo Ave., Pasadena, Calif. - Member First
Christian Church of Pasadena.

Emma Cunningham Conner attended the Peace Reunion of the
Blue and Gray at Gettysburg, Pa., in 1913; member of Ladies of
the Grand Army of the Republic, James A. Garfield Circle No. 55,
Dept. of Calif. and Nevada, 1914; member of Sons of Union Veter-

ans, Lucretia Garfield tent No. 19; president of Ladies of Grand Army of the Republic 1918; Division President of Sons of Veterans for Texas, Colorado, Pacific Coast States and Hawaiian Islands; member of Womans' Relief Corps, Auxiliary to John F. Godfrey Post. No. 93 Grand Army of the Republic; organized the Mother's of Defenders of the Flag and secured state Charter in 1917; was one of the committee of five to select the design for a Memorial in memory of World War heroes at a cost of $33,000.00, at the intersection of Colorado Street and Orange Grove Avenue, Pasadena, Calif., also sent in the name that was chosen for the Memorial known as Defenders' Parkway; was one of the official hostesses at the first Street Dance at Hotel Green for boys training at Camp Arcadia; was the only woman representative of all patriotic organizations to present General Pershing with an American Flag and bouquet of flowers at the time of his visit on the Pacific Coast in 1919; was one of a committee of the Patriotic Orders of Pasadena, California, that secured the lease of the old Library building at Raymond avenue and Walnut street to be used and now known as Patriotic Hall and presented at the dedication exercises a flag in the name of George M. Burlingame Auxiliary, No. 14, to Sons of Union Veterans Camp No. 36; a member of American Legion Auxiliary, South Pasadena Unit No. 140, Department of California; has letters of thanks from General Pershing; and General Foch for flag presented him while in Pasadena on his tour of the United States; other letters of thanks from Mrs. Warren G. Harding, the late Theodore and Mrs. Roosevelt, Dr. Hugo Eckner while on his tour with the Graf Zeppelin; member of War Mothers who received their Charter from Congress and was first Delegate elected to attend their first National Convention held in Philadelphia, Penn., September, 1925, but a serious automobile accident prevented her attending this convention; member of degree of Pocahontas Auxiliary to Redmen.

Children:

1. Ethel Fern - b. April 11, 1895, Bruceton Mills, W. Va. - m. at Santa Ana, Calif., June 28, 1919. CLYDE KEMP MALOY - b. July 30, 1891, at Cayuga, North Dakota, an Indian village, son of ——————. Served during World War as private 1st class 16th Co., California National Guards, Coast Artillery Corps, San Pedro, Calif.; transferred to 5th Co., U. S. Army, Fort McArthur, San Pedro; Coast Artillery School Fort Winfield Scott and Fort Miley, San Francisco, Calif.; made Electrician Sargent at Specialist school at Fort Monroe, Virginia, and assigned to 74th Railroad Artillery; sent to Camp Mills, New York, to embark for France and

sailed on the President Grant with eight other troop ships and two battle ships.

Living at 1042 West 10th St., San Pedro, Calif.   Children:

i. Sicily Ann Maloy - b. June 15, 1921, San Pedro, Calif.

2. Clarence Cunningham - b. Mar. 3, 1897 - m. Gladys Smith.

3. Manilla Eliza - b. July 14, 1898, Bruceton Mills, W. Va. - m. Wynnett Bedall - b. ———— son of ————. Children:

i. Wynnett Bedell, Jr. - b. ————

124232. CLARENCE CUNNINGHAM CONNER (William L. - Samuel F. - William C. - William - John) - b. Mar. 3, 1897, Bruceton Mills, W. Va. - Went to California in 1907 - Enlisted with National Guards April 9, 1917, served with Company I, 160th Infantry, Camp Arcadia, Calif. Transferred to Bakersfield, and later to Camp Kearney, San Diego, Calif., in fall of 1917. In July, 1918, sent to New York for further duty overseas. Motorcycle dispatch carrier while in France, was wounded in left knee by schrapnel in battle of Argonne, three months in hospital in France, arrived in New York in 1919 on U. S. S. Convalescence, sent to U. S. Hospital, Mare Island, San Francisco, later to Camp Kearney and was discharged from there. - Trade, Automobile Mechanic - m. April, 1920, Gladys Smith.

Children:

1. Clarence C., Jr. - b. Dec. 27, 1920, Pasadena, Calif.

JOHN CUNNINGHAM
OF SOMERSET (BEDFORD) COUNTY, PENNSYLVANIA
AND SOME OF HIS DESCENDANTS

1. JOHN CUNNINGHAM - b. 1774, County Down, Ireland - d. 1841, buried at Bethel Church, Paddytown, Somerset County, Penn. Emigrated to America in 1790 with his mother, Martha Reed (Read - Reid). She was born in County Down, Ireland, August, 1746, and died Dec. 18, 1806, is buried in Somerset County, Penn. John Cunningham married Jane McClintock - b. ———— - d. ————. Buried at Bethel Church, Paddytown, Somerset County, Penn., daughter of Alexander McClintock - b. in Ireland - d. 1803. Emigrated to America in 1760 with his wife, Mary Esten. Children of John Cunningham and Jane McClintock:

   1. Alexander - b. ———— 1793 - d. Nov. 7, 1879 - m. Susan Foust.
   2. William - b. ———— - d. ———— - m. Sidney Marietta
   3. Elizabeth - b. ———— - d. at age of 20.
   4. James - b. ———— - d. ———— - m. Nancy McMillan.
   Twins—(5 and 6).
   5. John - b. ———— 1806 - d. ———— 1875 - m. Elizabeth Marietta.
   6. Margaret - b. ———— 1806 - d. ———— 1896 - m. MOSES JUSTICE - b. ———— 1800 - d. Sept. ———— 1884, both are buried at New Athens, Ohio. Son of Nathan Justice and Elizabeth Boling. Children of Margaret Cunningham:
      i. Mary Justice - b. ———— 1827 - d. ———— 1886 - m. Joseph White.
      ii. Elizabeth Jane Justice - b. ———— 1829 - d. 1899 - m. George Lanning.
      iii. Margaret Justice - b. Apr. 8, 1831 - d. Mar. 19, 1870 - m. Daniel Eicher.
      iv. Phoebe Justice - b. ———— 1835 - d. Aug. 1867 - single.
      v. John Justice - b. ———— 1835 - d. Mar. ———— 1873 - m. Adaline Wood.
      vi. Martha Justice - b. ———— 1838 - d. ———— 1876 - single.
      vii. James Justice - b. Nov. 15, 1843 - d. Oct. ———— 1918 - m. Elizabeth Widdows.
      viii. Viola Justice - b. ———— 1848 - d. Nov. ———— 1881 - m. John Howell.
   7. Robert - b. Oct. 31, 1808 - d. June 7, 1889 - m. 1st. Sarah Pinkerton, - m. 2nd. Nancy Lambert.

8. Jennie - b. ———— - d. ———— - m. Thomas Hannah.
9. Martha - b. ———— - d. ———— - m. James Bays.
10. Mary - b. ———— - d. ———— - m. JACOB GOWER -
    b. ———— - d. ———— 1863, both are buried at Bethel
    Church, Somerset County, Penn. Son of ————. Children:
    i. John Gower - b. ———— - d. ———— 1870 - m. Lucinda
       Silbaugh.
    ii. Simon Gower - b. May 5, 1834 - d. Dec. 4, 1915 - m.
        Alzina M. Newcomb.
    iii. Margaret Jane Gower - b. Sept. 12, 1836 - d. Dec. 27,
         1899 - m. Samuel S. Robinson.
    iv. James Franklin Gower - b. ———— 1840 - d. Jan. 11, 1906
        - m. Amanda or Matilda McClintock, daughter of
        Stephen McClintock (Robert - John - Alexander) and
        Laura Kinsinger.
    v. Jesse Gower - b. Dec. 25, 1846 - d. ———————— - m. Emily
       Abney.
11. Eston - b. ———— 1813 -d. May 23, 1886 - m. Rachel Mc-
    Clintock.

11. ALEXANDER CUNNINGHAM (John) - b. Oct. 31, 1793 - d.
    Nov. 7, 1874 - m. Susan Foust - b. 1803 - d. Aug. 19, 1882, lived
    near Berlin in Brothers Township, Somerset County, Pa.
    Children:
    1. Mariah - b. ———— d. ———— - m. 1st. John Wheeler,
       - m. 2nd John Miller. Children:
       i. Elsie - b. ———— - m. Dan Heinbaugh.
       ii. Samuel - b. ———— - d. ————
       iii. Abie - b. ———— - d. ————
       iv. William - b. ————
    2. One girl died young.
    3. One boy died young.
    4. Catherine - b. ———— - d. ———— - m. SAMUEL YARD
       of Westmoreland County, Penn., and later went to Indiana.
       Children:
       i. Steve Yard - b. ———— - m. ————
       ii. John Yard - b. ———— - m. ————
       iii. (daughter) - b. ————
    5. George - b. ———— 1838 - d. Aug. 9, 1914 - m. Sarah King.
    6. Rebecca - b. July 22, 1840 - d. ———— - m. JOSEPH HOS-
       TETLER - b. ———— - d. May 13, 1898. Children:
       i. Albert Hostetler - b. ———— - m. Lena McClintock.
       ii. Susan Hostetler - b. ———— - m. Ed Kregar.

    iii. Almira Hostetler - b. ————— - m. John Smucker.
    iv. Edward Hostetler - b. ————— - m. Flora Kregar.
    v. Robert Hostetler - b. ————— - m. Ada Styres.
    vi. John Hostetler - b. ————— - m. Minnie Moon.
  7. Harrison - b. ———— - d. ———— - m. Allila Bear.
  8. James C. - b. ———— - d. ———— - m. —————
  9. Bruce - Died at age of three.

12. WILLIAM CUNNINGHAM (John) - b. ———— - d. ————
    - m. Sidney Marietta - b. ———— - d. ———— - daughter of
    George Marietta.
        Children:
    1. Thomas - b. ———— - d. ———— - m. Harriett Buttermore.
    2. Austin - b. ———— - d. ———— - m. —————
    3. John - b. ———— - d. ———— - m. —————
    4. George - b. ———— - d. ———— - m. —————
    5. Caroline - b. ———— - d. ———— - m. CLARK COLLINS
    - b. ———— son of —————. Children.
      i. Elmer Collins - b. —————
      ii. Annie Collins - b. ———— - m. ———— Ways.
      iii. Emmett Collins - b. —————
      iv. William Collins - b. ———— - m. 1st. Mary Grimm -
      m. 2nd.
    6. Anne - b. ———— - m. Josiah Oakes.
    7. James - b. —————

14. JAMES CUNNINGHAM (John) - b. ———— - d. ————
    - m. Nancy McMillan - b. ———— - d. ———— daughter of
    —————

        Children:
    1. Anne - b. ———— - d. ———— - m. —————
    2. Mary - b. ———— - d. ———— - m. John Eicher.
    3. Martha - b. ———— - d. ———— - m. William Eicher.

15. JOHN CUNNINGHAM (John) - b. Apr. 28, 1806 - d. Nov.
    10, 1875 - m. Elizabeth Marietta - b. Feb. 7, 1817 - d. Jan. 16,
    1898, daughter of George Marietta. Both are buried at Bethel
    Church, Paddytown, Somerset County, Penn.
        Children:
    1. Wesley - b. Aug. 28, 1843 - d. Apr. 30, 1887 - m. Belle
    Scharff.
    2. Fletcher - b. Feb. 7, 1845 - d. Nov. 23, 1884 - m. —————
    3. Emma - b. 1847 - d. 1915 - m. Frank Rager (no children).
    4. Brooklyn - b. 1849 - d. 1919 - m. Barbara Saylor.
    5. John - b. Apr. 17, 1851 - d. May 10, 1930 - m. 1st. Margaret
    Romesburg. - m. 2nd. Sarah Trimpey.

6. Emmett - b. Mar. 9, 1852 -d. Sept. 13, 1924 - m. Cora Mc-
   Clellan.
7. Coston - b. ――― 1854 - d. ――― 1929 - m. ―――――
8. Susan Melissa - b. Aug. 25, 1856, Turkeyfoot Township,
   Somerset Co., Penn. - d. March 8, 1922, buried at Brownsville, Penn. - m. Feb. 18, 1883, Turkeyfoot, Somerset County, Penn. DAVID WESLEY ENFIELD - b. Dec. 1, 1853
   - d. Oct. 2, 1914, buried at Brownsville, Penn., son of
   Emanuel Enfield. Children:
   i. Harry Orin Enfield - b. Jan. 22, 1885, Mt. Pleasant, Penn.
      - m. Anna Lillian Cox - b. Dec. 22, 1889, Brownsville,
      Penn., daughter of Margaret Thomas and Edward Cox.
      Children of Harry Orin Enfield:
      a. Grace Melissa Enfield - b. Jan. 29, 1909, Brownsville,
         Penn.
      b. Harry Orin Enfield, Jr. - b. Nov. 10, 1912, South
         Brownsville, Pa.
      c. Bernadine Elizabeth Enfield - b. July 31, 1923, South
         Brownsville, Pa.
   ii. Otto Wesley Enfield - b. Feb. 27, 1888, Tarr Station,
       Penn. - m. Mary Maude Hosler - b. Aug. 22, 1891 —
       Children:
       a. Raymond Otto Enfield - b. Jan. 30, 1911 -
       b. Viola Maude Enfield - b. Oct. 25, 1913 - m. Edward
          Kurtz.
       c. Nora Mae Enfield - b. Mar. 30, 1915 -
       d. Ruth Marie Enfield - b. Oct. 28, 1917 -
       e. Alice Melissa Enfield - b. Apr. 12, 1920 -
       f. David Wesley Enfield - b. Sept. 19, 1929 -
9. Mary E. - b. Aug. 1, 1861 - d. May 3, 1907 - single.
10. Belle - b. ――― 1863, Paddytown, Somerset County,
    Penn. - d. Dec. 3, 1931, Boynton, Pa. - m. July 4, 1881, Con-
    fluence, Penn. THOMAS GRAY - b. June 4, 1857, Butler,
    Penn. - d. Sept. 3, 1928, both are buried in Salisbury, Penn.
    Son of John Gray and Elizabeth McKennon. Children:
    i. John Coston Gray - b. Aug. 16, 1882, Connellsville, Pa.
       - m. Maude Starr.
    ii. Thomas Fletcher Gray - b. July 7, 1886, Connellsville,
        Penn. - m. Gertie Ross.
    iii. Eddy Raymond Gray - b. Nov. 8, 1889, Connellsville,
         Penn. - m. Ilga Sipe.
    iv. Harry Raymond Gray - b. May 1, 1891, Paddytown, Pa.
        - m. Mary Keller.

   v. Elmer Cunningham Gray - b. Nov. 27, 1892, Paddytown,
       Penn. - m. Hazel Kaughman.

  vi. Emma Belle Gray - b. Mar. 5, 1900, Paddytown, Penn. -
       m. Homer Richey.

17. ROBERT CUNNINGHAM (John) - b. Oct. 31, 1808 - d. June
    7, 1889 - m. 1st. Sarah Pinkerton - b. 1808 - d. June 9, 1880,
    daughter of Matthew Pinkerton, of Somerset Co., Penn. Both
    are buried near Rockville, and in Pleasant District, Preston
    County, W. Va. - m. 2nd. June 1, 1881, Nancy Lambert - b.
    Mar. 22, 1859, living 1933, daughter of Peter Lambert and
    Lucinda Cupp.

          Children by 1st marriage:

1. Rachel - b. Mar. 6, 1833 - d. Sept. 27, 1906 - m. ABRAHAM
   WILLIAMS - b. ————— - d. ——— son of —————
   Children:
     i. Mary Jane Williams - b. ——— - m. ———
    ii. Sarah Williams - b. ——— - m. ———
   iii. Belle Williams - b. ——— - m. ———
    iv. Alice Williams - b. ——— - m. ———
     v. Frank Williams - b. ——— - m. ———

2. Nancy - b. May 5, 1835 -d. Mar. 10, 1923 - m. John Mason
   (no Children).

3. Francis Marion - b. Dec. 21, 1837 - d. May 11, 1919 - m.
   Sarah Jane Skinner.

4. James Lawrence - b. Feb. 3, 1840 - d. Danville or Andersonville Prison.

5. Thaddeus Sobiski - b. Oct. 16, 1842 - d. Jan. 22, 1925 - m.
   Eliza Jane Liston.

6. Clarissa - b. ——— - d. Dec. 11, 1911 - m. Elijah Har-
   baugh.

7. Matthew - b. Oct. 31, 1845 - d. Oct. 12, 1887 - m. Margaret
   Bodkin.

8. Ross - b. Mar. 17, 1848 - living 1933 - m. Tabitha Skinner
   (no children).

9. Martha - b. Mar. 24, 1850 - d. Jan. 22, 1912 - m. REUBEN
   LEONARD - b. ——— - d. ——— son of —————
   Children:
     i. Bruce Leonard - b. ——— - d. ———
    ii. Clara Leonard - b. ——— - m. ——— Holt.
   iii. Hazel Leonard - b. ———
    iv. Harry Leonard - b. ———

10. Sarah - b. 1852 - d. 1862 - bur. in Indian Creek Cemetery, Fayette Co., Pa.

Children of Robert Cunningham by 2nd marriage:

11. Rosetta - b. Apr. 12, 1881 - m. ARTHUR WINFIELD WILHELM - b. Dec. 28, 1881, son of George W. Wilhelm and Catherine Maust. Children:

    i. Lloyd Allen Wilhelm-b. May 17, 1898, Rockville, W. Va.
    ii. Alta Nora Wilhelm - b. Sept. 28, 1904 - m. William H. Christopher.
    iii. Ida Blanche Wilhelm - b. Mar. 20, 1906, Rockville, W. Va.
    iv. Nettie Ruth Wilhelm - b. Dec. 2, 1907, Rockville, W. Va,
    v. Floyd Chester Wilhelm - b. Dec. 2, 1909, Rockville, W. Va.
    vi. Mary Avis Wilhelm - b. June 22, 1912 - m. Ralph Edgar Caton.
    vii. Inez Irene Wilhelm-b. Sept. 26, 1914, Rockville, W. Va.
    viii. Charles Bruce Wilhelm - b. Nov. 25, 1917, Rockville, W. Va.

12. Lucretia - b. May 3, 1882 - d. 1889, buried at Cunningham Farm, Rockville.

13. Eston - b. June 1, 1883 - d. Oct. 19, 1924 - single.

14. Kosciusko - b. Nov. 16, 1884 - d. 1889.

15. Robert Bruce - b. April 11, 1886 - m. Edith Essington.

16. Troy L. - b. Dec. 31, 1887 - m. Etta Gibson.

17. Emma F. - b. Nov. 11, 1889 - m. William H. Dunaway.

1-11. ESTON CUNNINGHAM (John) - b. 1813 - d. May 23, 1886 - m. Rachel McClintock - b. 1813 - d. Dec. 6, 1887, daughter of John McClintock (Alexander) and Jane Pinkerton.

    Children:

    1. Adeline - b. ———— - m. ———— Hostetler.

115. GEORGE CUNNINGHAM (Alexander - John) - b. ———— 1838 - d. Aug. 9, 1914 - m. ————

    Children:

    1. Bruce - b. ————
    2. John - b. ————
    3. James - b. ————
    4. Harvey - b. ————
    5. Edward - b. ————
    6. Albert - b. ————

7. Robert - b. ————
8. Minnie - b. ———— - m. Harrison France.
   Four others.

117. HARRISON CUNNINGHAM (Alexander - John) - b. ————
     - d. ———— - m. Allila Bear - b. ———— - d. ————
            Children:
     1. Ella - b. ————
     2. Alice - b. ———— - m. Emmet Collins.
     3. Harry - b. ————
     4. Robert - b. ————
     5. Bernard - b. ————

118. JAMES C. CUNNINGHAM (Alexander - John) - b. ————
     - d. ———— - Ran away from home at the age of fifteen and
     enlisted in the Civil War, after which he went to Indiana,
     where his sister, Catherine Yard lived, where he married and
     died.

121. THOMAS CUNNINGHAM (William - John) - b. ————
     - d. Sept. ———— 1912 - m. Harriett Buttermore - b. ————
     - d. Jan. 25, 1923.   Daughter of George Buttermore and Bar-
     bara Smith.
            Children:
     1. Charles Smith - b. Dec. 6, 1860 - d. April, 1914 - single.
     2. Eva Virginia - b. Oct. 29, 1862 - d. Jan. 10, 1894 - m. AMOS
        UMBEL - b. June 1, 1859, son of Michael Umbel and Maria
        Van Sickle.   Children:
          i. Minnie Umbel - b. May 15, 1884 - m. Bruce Friend.
          ii. Cora Umbel - b. Apr. 7, 1886 - m. Owen Evans.
          iii. Charles Umbel - b. May 23, 1888 - m. Jean McMaster.
          iv. Perry Umbel - b. Sept. 6, 1890 - m. Ruth Friend.
          v. Roy Umbel - b. Apr. 30, 1893-m. Margaret Humberston.
     3. Lilly Nevada - b. Mar. 29, 1865 - d. Sept. 13, 1931 - m. 1883,
        JOHN H. LEIGHTY - b. ———— son of ————————
        Children:
          i. Walter Leighty - b. 1885 -
          ii. Ralph Leighty - b. 1887 - d. June 28, 1932 - single.
     4. George Newcomber - b. Nov. 22, 1867 - m. Mary Norsetta
        Cunningham.
     5. Caroline Elizabeth - b. Mar. 17, 1870 - d. July 30, 1919 - m.
        WILLIAM H. GANIER - b. ———— son of ————————
        Children:
          i. Fern Ganier - b. Jan. 24, 1889 - m. John Cowan.

    ii. Marietta Ganier - b. Jan. 26, 1891 - d. Feb. 20, 1930 - m. Harold Clasper.

  6. Anna Laurie - b. Aug. 11, 1872 - d. Mar. 31, 1897 - m. June 30, 1896, William Waite.

  7. Daisy Ellen - b. Sept. 19, 1874 - single.

  8. Richard Thomas - b. Dec. 31, 1876 - m. Margaret Haines.

  9. Harry Buttermore - b. Aug. 22, 1878 - m. Virginia Tishul.

 10. Mary Blanche - b. Aug. 1, 1880 - d. May 2, 1895.

122. AUSTIN CUNNINGHAM (William - John) - b. ———— - d. ————— - m. 1st. Caroline Barnhart - b. ———— - d. ———— - m. 2nd. ———— Haines - b. ———— - d. ————
    Children by 1st marriage:

  1. Nora - b. ———— - m. ———— Cochran.

  2. Carrie - b. ———— - m. Cassuis Ritenour.

  3. Lee - b. ————
    Children by 2nd marriage:

  4. Ruth - b. ————

  5. Sylvia - b. ————

123. JOHN CUNNINGHAM (William - John) - b. ———— - d. ———— - m. Caroline Sechrist - b. ———— - d. ————
    Children:

  1. Abner - b. ————

  2. Charles - b. ————

  3. Louise - b. ———— - m. ———— Blosser.

  4. Wade - b. ————

124. GEORGE CUNNINGHAM (William - John) - b. ———— - d. ———— - m. ————
    Children:

  1. William - b. ———— - m. Harriet Moats.

  2. Isaac - b. ————

127. JAMES CUNNINGHAM (William - John) - b. ———— - d. ———— - m. ————
    Children:

  1. Flora - b. ———— - d. ———— - m. JOSEPH LYTLE - b. ———— - d. ———— son of ———— Children:

    i. Beulah Lytle - b. ———— - d. Oct. 10, 1919 - m. Chandler Maxwell.

    ii. Emma Jo Lytle - b. ———— - m. James Long.

      iii. Irene Lytle - b. ————— - m. James Grossman.

      iv. Julia Lytle - b. ————— - m. David Brown.

  2. Emily - b. ——— - m. ————— Sarver.

154. (See Page 36).

155. JOHN CUNNINGHAM (John - John) - b. April 17, 1851 - d. May 10, 1930 - m. 1st. 1872, Margaret Romesburg - b. May 27, 1851 - d. May 12, 1891, daughter of Jones Romesburg. m. 2nd. 1893, Sarah Trimpey - b. Sept. 7, 1866, daughter of Jno. Trimpey.

      Children by 1st marriage:

    1. Fletcher William - b. Oct. 14, 1873 - m. Gertrude Fleming.

    2. Thomas Russell - b. Sept. 13, 1876 - m. Stella Harlan.

    3. Clark - b. Apr. 14, 1880 - m. Ella Ansell.

    4. Homer - b. June 21, 1883 - m. Blake McWilliams.

    5. Ethel - b. July 13, 1878 - m. William Young.

    6. Bertha - b. Mar. 17, 1886 - single.

      Children by 2nd marriage:

    7. Ruth - b. ——— 1896 - m. ——— Huestin.

    8. Paul - b. Nov. 29, 1898 -

    9. Robert - b. Jan. 19, 1902 - m. Sadie Pettry.

156. EMMET CUNNINGHAM (John - John) - b. March 9, 1852, Upper Turkeyfoot Township, Somerset County, Penn. - d. Sept. 13, 1924, buried at Confluence, Pa. - m. May, 1874, at Ursina, Penn., Cora McClellan - b. March 5, 1858 - d. Feb. 18, 1918, buried at Confluence, Penn., daughter of Charles G. McClellan and Hester Switzer.

      Children:

    1. Frank - b. Aug. 2, 1876, Ursina, Pa. - m. Edith M. Show.

    2. John W. - b. April 15, 1878, Somerset Co., Pa. - m. Charlotte Livengood.

    3. Emma Hester - b. Feb. 7, 1880, Somerset Co., Pa. - m. W. D. Lingenfelter.

    4. Anna Belle - b. Aug. 7, 1882, Somerset Co., Pa. - m. J. B. Younkin.

    5. Charles M. - b. Sept. 5, 1884, Somerset Co., Pa. - m. Daily Wilson.

    6. Elizabeth Marie - b. Nov. 20, 1887 - d. Jan., 1907, buried at Paddytown, Pa.

173. FRANCIS MARION CUNNINGHAM (Robert - John) - b. Dec. 21, 1837, Somerset Co., Penn. - d. May 11, 1919, buried at Sugar Grove Cemetery near Ohio Pyle, Pa. - m. Aug. 26, 1861, Sarah Jane Skinner - b. Jan. 29, 1839, Dunbar Township, Fayette County, Penn. - d. Mar. 23, 1915, buried at Ohio Pyle, Pa., daughter of Sylvester Coburn Skinner (William) and Adaline Thorp (James - Rheuben - Job). - Served during Civil War with Co. H, 1st. West Virginia Cavalry, and received a medal of honor from Congress for distinguished bravery under fire at the battle of Sailors Creek, Virginia. He was also presented with medal by General George A. Custer for bravery. Was a member of General Custer's staff and was present at Appotomox Court House when General Lee surrendered to General Grant, April 9, 1865.

Children:

1. James Lawrence - b. April 21, 1866 - m. 1st. Annis Williams - d. Oct. 1, 1904 - m. 2nd. Mar. 8, 1912, Jennie Thomas.

2. Charles Buford - b. July 24, 1867 - m. Agnes Corriston.

3. Mary Norsetta - b. Sept. 1, 1871 - m. George Cunningham (see 1215).

4. Adaline - b. June 18, 1874 - m. Dec. 13, 1894, WILLIAM JOHNSON - b. Aug. 14, 1865, son of Andrew Johnson.

Children:

i. Ethel Johnson - b. July 21, 1895 - d. Sept. 30, 1903.

ii. Alexander Johnson - b. Oct. 2, 1897 - d. June 7, 1927 - m. June 30, 1921, Aileen Moore. Children:

a. Bruce Moore - b. Apr. 20, 1922.

b. George Moore - b. April 7, 1924.

iii. Henry Johnson - b. July 25, 1899 - m. Mabel Hager. Children:

a. William Hager Johnson - b. Mar. 3, 1927.

iv. George Johnson - b. Oct. 21, 1902 - m. Viola Stuck. Children:

a. Betty Johnson - b. ———

b. James Johnson - b. ———

c. Alcinda Johnson - b. ———

d. Barbara Johnson - b. ———

v. Frank Johnson - b. May 23, 1905 -

vi. Allen Theodore Johnson - b. Nov. 14, 1906 - d. Feb. 21, 1917.

vii. Infant unnamed deceased.

viii. William Johnson, Jr. - b. June 14, 1909 - m. Eileen
       Sargent.

ix. Infant b. Mar. 29, 1916, deceased.

5. Martha Alice - b. Nov. 18, 1876 - d. July 16, 1902 - m. Dec.
    14, 1899, HENRY POLLARD - b. ———— - son of ———
    One child died at age of four months.

6. Anna Belle - b. Aug. 11, 1879 - m. Oct. 2, 1899, JOHN
    BOYD - b. Mar. 25, 1876, son of Frank Boyd. Children:

    i. Alice Boyd - b. Aug. 9, 1901 - m. Jan. 6, 1929, Lynn
        Slocum.

    ii. Thomas Reed Boyd - b. June 4, 1904 - m. Aug. 12, 1927,
         Erma Lee.

    iii. Miriam Boyd - b. Aug. 30, 1910 -

    iv. John Connor Boyd - b. Nov. 5, 1913 -

    v. Samuel Boyd - b. July 15, 1915 -

175. THADDEUS SOBISKI CUNNINGHAM (Robert - John) -
      b. Oct. 16, 1842, Somerset County, Penn. - d. Jan. 22, 1925, bur-
      ied at Bruceton Mills, W. Va. - Enlisted Aug. 13, 1862, served
      with Co. H, 142nd Penn. Vol. Infantry, in battle of Fredericks-
      burg, Va., Dec. 13, 1862, wounded, losing his left arm. Dis-
      charged Mar. 6, 1863. School teacher for eighteen terms.
      Taught school at Hopewell, Grant District, Preston County,
      W. Va., in the log school house which was replaced in 1871 by
      a more modern building. - m. at Ohio Pyle, Penn., Dec., 1867,
      Eliza Jane Liston - b. Dec. 3, 1849, Fayette County, Penn. - d.
      Mar. 6, 1930, buried at Bruceton Mills, W. Va., daughter of
      Everhart Liston, 1822 - 1888 (John) and Thankful Thorp
      (James - Rheuben - Job) (see Thorpe Gen.).

         Children:

1. Katie E. - b. Feb. 2, 1869 - m. Thurman M. King (see King
    Gen.).

2. Sarah Belle - b. Apr. 11, 1870 - m. Jesse Wheeler (see
    Wheeler Gen.).

3. Emma C. - b. Jan. 12, 1873 - m. Lawrence Conner (see Con-
    ner Gen.).

4. Francis M. - b. Mar. 31, 1874 - m. Jessie McNair.

5. Edward E. - b. Sept. 17, 1876 - m. Effie Yeast.

6. Albert D. - b. Mar. 20, 1878 - m. Lulu Bowermaster.

7. Alfred Emmet - b. Dec. 15, 1882 - m. Caroline Lawrence.

17-15. ROBERT BRUCE CUNNINGHAM (Robert - John) - b. April 11, 1886 - m. at Flatwoods, Penn., Sept. 11, 1912, Edith Essington - b. Sept. 26, 1882, Perry Township, ——————— County, Penn., daughter of Daniel G. Essington (Shepler) and Frances Murphy (Thomas). Living at Connellsville, Pa.
Children:
1. Dorothy Frances - b. Jan. 17, 1915, Star Junction, Penn.

17-16. TROY L. CUNNINGHAM (Robert - John) - b. Dec. 31, 1887 - m Jan. 19, 1910, Etta Gibson - b. Oct. 7, 1872, daughter of Nelson Gibson (Levi) and Virginia Falkenstine (David). Living at Hudson, Preston County, W. Va.
Children:
1. Gladys Beryl - b. Apr. 12, 1911 - d. May 4, 1911 - buried at Cress Cemetery.
2. Valetta - b. Nov. 10, 1912 -

1214. GEORGE NEWCOMBER CUNNINGHAM (Thomas - William - John) - b. Nov. 22, 1867, Connellsville, Penn. - m. June 8, 1894, at Connellsville, Penn., Mary Norsetta Cunningham - b. Sept. 1, 1871, daughter of Francis Marion Cunningham (Robert - John) and Sarah Jane Skinner (Sylvester - William).
Children:
1. Verna Blanche - b. Mar. 13, 1895, Mt. Pleasant, Pa. - m. Fred Diederichs.
2. Mary Frances - b. Feb. 24, 1896, Connellsville, Pa. - d. Aug. 18, 1896.
3. George Custer - b. Mar. 2, 1897, Connellsville, Pa.
4. Donald Lee - b. Mar. 28, 1898 - m. Harriet Meicrantz.
5. Fred Willard - b. Dec. 12, 1899, Connellsville, Pa.
6. Evelyn - b. April 1, 1901, Connellsville, Pa.
7. Washington - b. Feb. 22, 1903 - d. July 19, 1903, buried at Connellsville, Pa.
8. Theodore Sylvester - b. April 28, 1904 - m. Marie Brocking.
9. Christina - b. Nov. 29, 1905, Connellsville, Penn.
10. Bertha - b. Aug. 24, 1907, Connellsville, Penn.

1561. (See Page 36).

1732. CHARLES BUFORD CUNNINGHAM (Francis M. - Robert - John) - b. July 24, 1867, - m. Sept. 14, 1895, Agnes Corriston - b. July 6, 1868 - d. Aug. 24, 1927, buried near Farmington, Penn., daughter of High Corriston.
Children:
1. Francis Marion - b. Nov. 24, 1896 -
2. Olive Elizabeth - b. Mar. 28, 1898 - m. 1918, JOHN WEAVER. Children:

    i. Helen Weaver - b. Oct. 30, 1918 -
    ii. Charles Weaver - b. June 17, 1920 -
    iii. Elizabeth Weaver - b. Oct. 21, 1922 -
3. Ross - b. Oct. 6, 1899 - m. Helen Rush.
4. Walter Charles - b. May 28, 1901 - m. Elma Rholfe. Children:
    i. Walter - b. July 5, 1931.
5. Flora Belle - b. Mar. 10, 1903 - m. Sept. 4, 1919, JOHN EMMERT, son of Phillip Emmert. Children:
    i. Phillip Emmert - b. ———— 1924 - d. May, 1932.
    ii. John Junior Emmert - b. Aug. 3, 1927.
6. Thomas Buford - b. May 13, 1905 -

1754. FRANCIS M. CUNNINGHAM (Thaddeus - Robert - John) - b. Mar. 31, 1874 - m. at Bruceton Mills, W. Va., May 23, 1897, Jessie McNair - b. May 20, 1873, Bruceton Mills, W. Va., daughter of Andrew S. McNair, 1836 - 1917, and Sophia E. Michael, 1836 - 1927 (Philip).

Children:
1. Bernice Merle - b. Oct. 12, 1899 - d. Aug. 4, 1901, buried at Bruceton Mills.
2. Frank Ward - b. Feb. 25, 1905 - m. Bernice Spiker.
3. Edith Emily - b. Dec. 22, 1912 - d. Aug. 20, 1921, buried at Bruceton Mills.
4. Harold Andrew - b. Dec. 27, 1920 -

1755. EDWARD E. CUNNINGHAM (Thaddeus - Robert - John) - b. Sept. 17, 1876, Bruceton Mills, W. Va. - Enlisted at Connellsville, Penn., Sept. 12, 1899, served with Co. C, 41st. Inft., U. S. A. Left New York Nov. 20, 1899, on U. S. S. Logan, on duty Luzon Island near Manilla, P. I., returned to San Francisco on U. S. S. Buford and discharged July 3, 1901. - m. at Bruceton Mills, W. Va., Aug. 6, 1899, Effie Yeast - b. Feb. 6, 1883, Bruceton Mills, W. Va., daughter of William Alexander Yeast (Adam) and Catherine Jane Ross (Henry).

Children:
1. Edward Daryl - b. April 27, 1900 - m. Marie Collins.
2. Glena Katherine - b. Dec. 29, 1902, Bruceton Mills, W. Va. - - m. Nov. 9, 1918, at Uniontown, Penn., CHARLES H. LISTON - b. Feb. 4, 1889, at Rockville, W. Va., son of Amaziah Liston and Amanda Goodwin (Sylvanus) - Musician in U. S. Navy, Nov. 19, 1907 to July 14, 1922, with the following ships and stations: U. S. S. Franklin, Nov. 20, 1907, to June 12, 1908; U. S. S. Idaho, June, 1908, to Nov.

11, 1911; Naval Training Station, Great Lakes, Ill., U. S. S. Niagara and U. S. S. Wolverine, Nov., 1911, to Sept. 1913; U. S. S. Wyoming, 1913 to April, 1914; U. S. S. Arkansas, April, 1914, to May, 1914; U. S. S. Wyoming, May, 1914, to Oct., 1914; U. S. S. New York, Oct., 1914, to Jan., 1915; U. S. S. Wyoming, Jan., 1915, to Nov., 1915; U. S. S. Lancaster, Nov., 1915, to June, 1916; U. S. S. Pennsylvania and U. S. S. Kentucky during World War, attached to Allied Fleet, saw active service in English, French and Italian waters, also Mexican, Hatiian, Nicaraguan waters during various uprisings. Transferred to Naval Reserve July 14, 1922. Children:

   i. Phyllis Liston - b. June 13, 1920, Uniontown, Penn.
   ii. James Stanley Liston - b. May 23, 1923, Bruceton Mills, W. Va.

1756. ALBERT D. CUNNINGHAM (Thaddeus - Robert - John) - b. Mar. 20, 1876, Bruceton Mills, W. Va. - Enlisted at Fairmont, W. Va., June 18, 1898, served with Company F, First W. Va. Infantry, during Spanish American war, discharged at Columbus, Ga., Feb. 4, 1899 - m. at Bruceton Mills, W. Va., Oct. 23, 1901, Lulu Bowermaster - b. March 31, 1885, Rockville, W. Va.

   Children:

1. Mabel - b. Nov. 8, 1902, Bruceton Mills, W. Va. - m. Mar. 19, 1921, BENJAMIN FRANKLIN MANNING - b. April 26, 1902, son of Benjamin F. Manning (Benj. - Benj. - Benj.) and Clara Cover, of Smithfield, Pa. Children:
   i. Benjamin Franklin Manning VI. - b. Feb. 26, 1922, Uniontown, Penn.
2. Margaret - b. Feb. 11, 1908, Kingwood, W. Va.
3. Jean - b. Jan. 13, 1913, Kingwood, W. Va.
4. Thomas S. - b. July 22, 1916, Oliphant, Penn.

1757. ALFRED EMMET CUNNINGHAM (Thaddeus - Robert - John) - b. Dec. 15, 1882, Bruceton Mills, W. Va. - m. Caroline Lawrence.

   Children:

1. Elizabeth Francis - b. July 5, 1917, Charleston, W. Va.
2. James Phillip - b. Feb. 26, 1921, Charleston, W. Va.
3. Patricia Jean - b. Nov. 23, 1924, Charleston, W. Va.
4. Phillis Ann - b. July 16, 1929, Charleston, W. Va.

17551. EDWARD DARYL CUNNINGHAM (Edward E. - Thaddeus - Robert - John) - b. April 27, 1900, Bruceton Mills, W.

Va. - Enlisted May 24, 1918, at Baltimore, Md.. U. S. Naval Air Service, served at St. Helena Training Station, Norfolk, Va.; on the U. S. S. Neptune to Cuba; U. S. S. Supply and U. S. S. Columbia, making eight trips on these two ships, the last being a Trans-Atlantic in which he assisted in the rescue of the NC-4 off the Azores. Lieut. Com. Bellinger, his former commander, being one of the survivors of the NC-4. Discharged Aug. 22, 1921, at Hampton Roads, Va. Member of the Veterans of Foreign Wars, serving as chaplain in 1929, and Commander of De La Loma Post No. 15 in 1930 and again as chaplain in 1931. Has been recommended for distinguished service citation for services performed. - m. at Uniontown, Penn., Aug. 19, 1920, Marie Collins - b. July 6, 1902, daughter of Lucian E. Collins and Lilly Jane Thomas, of Markleysburg, Pa.

Children:

1. Alberta S. - b. May 27, 1921, Brandonville, W. Va .

17542. FRANK WARD CUNNINGHAM (Francis M. - Thaddeus - Robert - John) - b. Feb. 25, 1905, Bruceton Mills, W. Va. - m. at Oakland, Md., Nov. 22, 1927, Bernice Loretta Spiker - - b. June 25, 1909, at Brandonville, W. Va., daughter of Bernard Spiker (John - Henry) and Laura Metheny (William H. - Isaiah - Nathan - James) (see Metheny Gen.).

Children:

1. Laura Jean - b. June 11, 1928, Bruceton Mills, W. Va.
2. Darwin Franklin - b. Mar. 13, 1931, Bruceton Mills, W. Va.

154. BROOKLYN CUNNINGHAM (John - John) - b. June 6, 1849, Markletown, Penn. - d. Feb. 22, 1919, Dawson, Penn., buried at Dickerson Run - m. 1903, at Mountain Lake Park, Md., Barbara Saylor - b. Sept. 21, 1871, Mill Run, Penn., daughter of Jacob F. Saylor and Martha J. Saylor. Lived at Dawson, Penn .

Children:

1. Charles - b. April 8, 1908, Dawson, Penn.
2. Elizabeth - b. Nov. 18, 1910, Dawson, Penn.

1561. FRANK CUNNINGHAM (Emmet - John - John) - b. Aug. 2, 1876, Ursina, Penn. - m. at Pittsburgh, Penn., Feb. 26, 1920, Edith M. Show - b. May 13, 1888, Confluence, Penn., daughter of Luther Show and Druzella Critchfield.

Children:

1. George S. - b. Nov. 28, 1924, Confluence, Penn.
2. Jane D. - b. Dec. 20, 1920, Confluence, Penn.

JAMES KING
OF LAUREL RUN, (NOW) GRANT DISTRICT, PRESTON COUNTY, WEST VIRGINIA

1. JAMES KING - b. June 5, 1777 - d. April 29, 1864, buried on the "Tiny" (Valentine) King farm, now owned by Albert Metheny near Laurel Run Church. Probably married twice, 1st, according to the Preston County History (Cole and Morton) Elizabeth Hempstead, and 2nd, according to grave stone record, Emma Short - b. 1779 - d. May 8, 1843, buried near the grave of James King. James King was one of five King brothers who was enroute westward from Oldtown or Winchester, Virginia, and it is claimed by some that these Kings were from Staunton, Va. James, John and Valentine settled along Laurel Run, while Thomas and Isaac seem to have continued westward, as very little record can be found of the latter two.

Children of James King:
1. Anne - m. Bayles Shaw, and died near Mannington, W. Va.
2. Thomas - b. Dec. 23, 1804 - d. Feb. 25, 1878 - m. Jane Brandon.
3. Martha - b. April 30, 1807 - d. Sept. 20, 1882, paralysis, buried at Bruceton Mills, W. Va. - m. May 15, 1827, HENRY SMITH - b. Dec. 7, 1805 - d. July 29, 1862, accidentally killed, buried at Bruceton Mills, W. Va., son of Jacob Smith - b. Mar. 11, 1764 - d. Mar. 30, 1860, and Deborah Wellington - b. Aug. 11, 1782 - d. June 12, 1860. Jacob Smith came from Somerset County, Penn., in 1819, and purchased 900 acres of land two miles north of Bruceton Mills, W. Va. Children of Henry and Martha King Smith:
   i. Julia Ann Smith - b. Oct. 8, 1828 - d. Feb. 2, 1904, buried at Shawnee, Kansas - m. Sept. 24, 1856, Thomas Douglas - d. Jan. 4, 1895, buried at Shawnee, Kansas. Had six children probably living at Shawnee, Kansas.
   ii. Lucian Henry Smith - b. Aug. 4, 1830 - d. July 5, 1905, buried at Bruceton Mills, W. Va. Never married.
   iii. Ashbel Green Smith - b. Sept. 15, 1834 - d. Mar. 12, 1898 m. Oct. 31, 1864, Anna Maria Rankin - d. June 11, 1886, buried at Bruceton Mills, W. Va. Two children, Harry, buried at Clarksburg, W. Va., and Gertrude, married Duncan living in Clarksburg, W. Va.
   iv. Martha Ann Smith - b. Dec. 12, 1836 - d. Sept. 20, 1882, buried at Bruceton Mills, W. Va. - m. May 11, 1858, Dr.

Jesse Beerbower - d. Dec. 1865, buried at Bruceton
Mills, W. Va. One child, Zoie - b. May 12, 1860 - d.
Dec. 31, 1879, buried at Bruceton Mills, W. Va.

v. Henry Clay Smith - b. Dec. 14, 1838 - d. May 3, 1863,
smallpox, buried at Paro Paro Island near Millikens
Bend, Louisiana, served during Civil War with Co. C,
12th Reg., Iowa Vol. Inft. Never married.

vi. Emma Ann Smith - b. Mar. 12, 1841 - d. Mar. 14, 1922,
buried at Bruceton Mills, W. Va. Never married.

vii. Persis Annie Smith - b. Nov. 23, 1843 - d. Jan. 26, 1909,
buried at Bruceton Mills, W. Va. Never married.

viii. Norval Pieston Smith - b. May 10, 1846 - d. Oct. 9,
1904, buried at Dawson, Fayette County, Penn. - m.
Aug. 4, 1880, Annie Houston Cochran. Children:

  a. James Henry Smith - b. ————
  b. Clara Smith - b. ———— - m. Paul McKeel.
  c. Lucian P. Smith-lost on the Titanic, April 12, 1912.

ix. William Winfield Smith - b. Oct. 29, 1848 - d. Sept. 7,
1911, buried at Bruceton Mills, W. Va. Never married.

4. Elizabeth - b. Mar 12, 1809 - d. Feb. 4, 1897, buried near Newburg, Preston County, W. Va. - m. WILLIAM HARRING-
TON - b. July 20, 1805 - d. Dec. 11, 1877, buried at Newburg, W. Va. Children:

i. James Harrington - b. July 31, 1831 - d. Jan. 14, 1911 - m.
about 1852, Sarah Ann Snider - b. Nov. 11, 1829 - d. July
27, 1906.

ii. Margaret Harrington - b. Mar. 29, 1834 - d. Sept. 24, 1894
- m. Dec. 24, 1865, James Anthony Smith - b. Jan. 11,
1834 - d. Jan. 24, 1887.

iii. William John Harrington - b. Feb. 22, 1836 - d. Dec. 18,
1912 - m. Sophia Simpson - b. Sept. 22, 1838 - d. April
6, 1915.

iv. Josephus Harrington - b. Dec. 23, 1837 - d. Sept. 3, 1918
- m. Nancy Jane Robins - b. Dec. 15, 1836 - d. Aug. 4,
1908. Children:

  a. William Harrington - b. ————
  b. Effie Harrington - b. ———— - m. ———— Bowman.

v. Thomas Harrington - b. April 22, 1840 - d. Aug. 26, 1914
- m. Aug. 22, 1862, Missouri E. Zinn - b. Aug. ——, 1844
- d. Aug. 28, 1919.

vi. Francis Harrington - b. Aug. 15, 1842 - d. Dec. 15, 1924
- m. 1st. Jan. 1, 1871, Sarah Wilkins - b. Sept. 9, 1840 -

- d. May 13, 1880 - m. 2nd, Sept. 21, 1884, Virginia
Howell - d. Aug. 15, 1894.

vii. Minerva Harrington - b. April 7, 1844 - d. Nov. 24, 1854.

viii. Curtis Harrington - b. Dec. 23, 1846 - d. Dec. 4, 1850.

ix. Naomi Harrington - b. May 24, ——— - d. Sept. 4, ———

5. William - b. ———— - went to Missouri.

6. Sophia - b. ———— - m. William Douglas - died in Jackson County, Ia.

7. Eliza - b. April 24, 1816 - d. Sept. 29, 1881, buried in Jenkins Cemetery near Mt. Nebo Church, Pleasant District, Preston County, W. Va. - m. GRAHAM JENKINS - b. Jan. 29, 1811 - d. Dec. 13, 1869, buried in Jenkins Cemetery, son of Jonathan Jenkins, 1771 - 1859 (John 1751 - 1834) and Esther Graham. Children:

i. Hester A. Jenkins - b. Sept. 1, 1839 - d. July 7, 1880 - m. William M. Wolf (see Wolf Genealogy).

ii. William M. Jenkins - b. Jan. 10, 1841 - d. Feb. 28, 1903 - m. Elizabeth Gibson - b. Oct. 12, 1847 - d. Dec. 10, 1920 both buried at Kingwood, W. Va.

iii. Mary Jenkins - b. ———— - d. ———— - m. ————
Robinson.

iv. James K. Jenkins - b. Feb. 5, 1846 - d. Oct. 16, 1853, buried in Jenkins Cemetery, near Mt. Nebo Church, Pleasant Dist., Preston Co., W. Va.

v. Sanford C. H. Jenkins - b. Dec. 12, 1847 - d. June 4, 1875.

vi. Isaac Jenkins - b. ———— - d. ———— buried at Ursina, Penn. - m. Persis I. King - b. Feb. 22, 1841 - d. Sept. 24, 1866, buried in Jenkins Cemetery. Daughter of Thomas King. Children:

a. Rosa Jenkins - b. ———— - m. Thaddeus Allison.

vii. Julia Jenkins - b. Jan. 29, 1853 - d. June 6, 1860.

8. Margaret - b. July 20, 1818 - d. Jan. 29, 1911 - m. HENRY CHIDESTER - b. April 19, 1817 - d. Dec. 23, 1897. Children:

i. Ashbel S. Chidester - b. 1861 - d. 1925 - m. ————

ii. Wesley Chidester - b. ———— - m. Lizzie Gibson.

iii. James Chidester - b. ———— - m. Mollie Hardesty.

iv. Mary Chidester - b. ————

9. Alpheus - b. Jan. 9, 1822 - d. Sept. 23, 1915 - m. Margaret Jenkins.

12. THOMAS KING (James) - b. Dec. 23, 1804 - d. Feb. 25, 1878, buried at Pisgah, W. Va. - m. Jane Brandon - b. Aug. 11, 1806 - d. Feb. 19, 1890, buried at Pisgah, W. Va., daughter of William

Brandon, 1781 - 1860 (Alexander) and Mary Gribble 1784 - 1870 (John). Lived near Laurel Run in Grant District, Preston County, W. Va.

Children:

1. Albert F. - b. June 12, 1825 - d. Prison - m. Hester A. Jenkins.
2. Serenia - b. July 13, 1828 - d. 1914, buried in Mt. Zion Cemetery, Masontown, W. Va. - m. Oct. 12, 1847, AMI JENKINS - b. Sept. 8, 1825 - d. 1865. Children:
   i. Sophrona Jenkins - b. Sept. 8, 1849 - d. 1853 - buried in Masontown, W. Va.
   ii. Mary M. Jenkins - b. 1851 - d. 1920 - m. Alf. Shaffer.
   iii. Lucinda Jane Jenkins - bur. in Reedsville, W. Va. - m. Geo. W. Ashburn.
   iv. George O. Jenkins - b. 1858 - d. 1929 - m. Frances Greathouse.
   v. Malissa C. Jenkins - b. 1858 - d. May 30, 1932 - m. G. Israel Taylor.
   vi. Lowry M. Jenkins - b. 1862 - m. Sarah Delena Taylor.
   vii. Ira J. Jenkins - b. 1864 - buried in California.
   viii. Ami K. Jenkins - b. 1866 - m. Della Greathouse.
3. William J. - b. Oct. 20, 1832 - d. in Prison - m. Elizabeth H. Street.
4. George - b. Oct. 4, 1837 - d. Sept. 12, 1915 - m. Frances A. Christopher.
5. Persis I. - b. Feb. 22, 1841 - d. Sept. 24, 1866, buried in Jenkins Cemetery near Mt. Nebo Church, Pleasant District, Preston County, W. Va. - m. Isaac Jenkins - went to Ursina, Penn. Buried there.
6. Eugenus - b. May 27, 1843 - d. May 6, 1933 - m. 1st., Sept. 29, 1867, Mary Smith - b. Feb. 17, 1839 - d. Aug. 29, 1898, buried at Pisgah, W. Va., daughter of Josiah Smith, 1811 - 1899 (Jacob 1764 - 1860) and Jane McLean - m. 2nd, Mar. 14, 1901, at Bruceton Mills, W. Va., Ida Gribble Groves - b. Dec. 18, 1865, daughter of Harrison Gribble (Archibald) and Mary Faucett. Enlisted during Civil War with Co. I, 17th W. Va. Inft. - No children.
7. Mary C. - b. Aug. 19, 1847 - d. Mar. 26, 1906 - m. Irvin Christopher.
8. Thomas Hudson - b. Oct. 27, 1850 - d. June 28, 1927 - m. Catherine E. Haines.

19. ALPHEUS KING (James) - b. Jan. 9, 1822, near Laurel Run - d. Sept. 23, 1915 - buried at Pisgah, W. Va. - m. Margaret

Jenkins - b. Mar. 20, 1818 - d. May 5, 1902, buried at Pisgah, W. Va., daughter of Evan Jenkins, 1789 - 1877 (Thomas) and Hannah Graham 1792 - 1866 (David).

Children:

1. James B. - b. Apr. 16, 1843 - d. Mar. 30, 1930 - m. Cerilda Liston.
2. Hannah - b. July 26, 1845 - d. Nov. 20, 1919 - m. HENRY EVERLY - b. July 4, 1840 - d. May 15, 1886, son of Lewis Everly and Eva Zweyer (Adam 1772 - 1833) both are buried at Pisgah, W. Va. Children:
   i. James S. Everly - b. Feb. 22, 1867 - d. Jan. 17, 1930 - m. Mary Ann McNair.
   ii. Charles C. Everly - b. Sept. 24, 1870 - m. Cora Galloway.
   iii. Emma Olive Everly - b. Apr. 15, 1871 - d. Mar. 2, 1876.
   iv. H. Benton Everly - b. ———— - m. Elizabeth ————
   v. Leota Everly - b. ———— - m. Harry King.
3. Emma - b. Nov. 28, 1847 - living in 1933 - m. William Metheny.
4. Marshall - b. Nov. 1, 1849 - d. May 22, 1919, buried at Pisgah, W. Va. Single.
5. Martha - b. Sept. 25, 1852 - d. Mar. 21, 1931 - m. John A. Wolf.
6. Phoebe - b. May 16, 1856 - d. Dec. 10, 1896 - m. James Harvy Walls.
7. Adelia - b. Mar. 17, 1859 - m. Thomas Ryan (see Ryan Genealogy).
8. Dora Alice - b. Aug. 30, 1861 - d. Apr. 16, 1915 - m. Daniel Ryan.

121. ALBERT F. KING (Thomas - James) - b. June 12, 1825 - d. in prison during Civil War, probably Andersonville or Libby Prison. Served with Co. H 3rd Regt., Potomac Home Brigade, Maryland Inft. - m. 1846, Hester A. Jenkins - b. April 18, 1823 - d. May 18, 1920, buried at Pisgah, W. Va., daughter of Evan Jenkins, 1789 - 1877 (Thomas) and Hannah Graham 1792 - 1866 (David). Lived near Laurel Run, Grant Dist., Preston Co., W. Va.

Children:

1. Alsyneus Judson - b. Nov. 29, 1847 - d. Feb. 27, 1922 - m. Annetta Clover.
2. Mary Armena (twin) - b. Nov. 29, 1847 - d. Apr. 11, 1905 - m. Silas M. Metheny.
3. Thomas Winfield - b. Nov. 3, 1849 - m. Mary E. Haines.

4. Jehu - b. Dec. 19, 1851 - d. June 6, 1928 - m. Mary A. Collins.
5. Evan - b. Nov. 12, 1855 - d. May 4, 1923 - m. Olive Oneda Walls.
6. Hannah - b. Sept. 24, 1859 - m. in 1884, BENJAMIN HUGINS - b. April 16, 1856, in Memphis, Missouri, son of William Huggins, a Union Soldier of the Civil War and Elizabeth Michael Huggins, who moved with the family to Preston County, W. Va. Children of Hannah and Benjamin Huggins:

    i. Jessie Bernice Huggins - b. April 22, 1882, Rockville, W. Va. - m. Sept. 1, 1909, Earl Fairfax Martin.
    ii. Gilbert Earl Huggins - b. April 18, 1884, Rockville, W. Va. - m. Jane Crawford, of Pittsburgh, Penn.
    iii. Mary Florence Huggins - b. July 27, 1886, Rockville, W. Va. - m. Rupert E. Frailey of Terra Alta, W. Va.
    iv. William Harry Huggins - b. Jan. 29, 1889, Rockville, W. Va. - d. Feb. 9, 1915.
    v. Charles Roscoe Huggins - b. Aug. 13, 1893, Brandonville, W. Va. - m. Margaret Temple, of Baltimore, Md.
    vi. Lloyd K. Huggins - b. Feb. 27, 1896, Bruceton Mills, W. Va. - d. April 9, 1927 - m. Mae Kelley, of Terra Alta, W. Va.
    vii. Mabel Pauline Huggins - b. June 3, 1901, Bruceton Mills, W. Va. - m. Thomas Nolan.
7. Sarah E. - b. Oct. 24, 1861 - d. Dec. 25, 1884, buried at Pisgah, W. Va. - m. Marshall Harned - b. Feb. 18, 1852, son of William Harned (Edward) - No Children.

123. WILLIAM J. KING (Thomas - James) - b. Oct. 20, 1832 - d. in Prison (Libby or Andersonville) Enlisted with Co. H 3rd Regt., Potomac Home Brigade, Maryland Inft. (called West Virginia Snake Hunters) Oct. 5, 1861. Mustered out Oct. 2, 1864 - taken prisoner. - m. June 13, 1854, Elizabeth H. Street - b. Dec. 14, 1833 - d. July 20, 1917, buried at Pisgah, W. Va. - daughter of George Washington Street (Jackson) - b. Nov. 3, 1806 - d. June 11, 1898, and Ethelinda Kelley - b. Sept. 22, 1809 - d. Dec. 21, 1893 (William - John). Lived on Laurel Run.

    Children:
1. Isabelle - b. Feb. 18, 1853 - d. Mar. 21, 1927 - m. Jehu Christopher.
2. E. Preston - b. Apr. 14, 1855 - m. Sarah Jane Everly.
3. Marcellus Hosea - b. Nov. 7, 1856 - d. Sept. 2, 1932 - m. Julia A. Ryan.

4. Zar K. - b. Oct. 15, 1858 - m. 1st. Lizzie Cale. 2nd, Grace First.

5. Ethelinda - b. Apr. 30, 1861 - d. Mar. 18, 1862, buried near Laurel Run.

6. Thurman Malvern - b. Mar. 20, 1863 - d. July 29, 1930 - m. Katie Cunningham.

124. GEORGE H. KING (Thomas - James) - b. Oct. 4, 1837 - d. Sept. 12, 1915, buried at Pisgah, W. Va. - m. Feb. 28, 1862, Frances A. Christopher - b. Sept. 2, 1836 - d. June 1, 1907 - buried at Pisgah, W. Va., daughter of John Christopher, 1814 - 1891 and Mary Lawson. - Lived near Pisgah. Children:

1. Lowry C. - b. Jan. 20, 1863 - d. Jan. 10, 1876, buried at Pisgah, W. Va.

2. Isaloma E. - b. Oct. 1, 1864 - m. Oct. 29, 1885, at Pisgah, W. Va., HERMAN DARBY - b. Jan. 12, 1863, Bruceton Mills, W. Va., son of Samuel T. Darby - b. Sept. 6, 1827 - d. May 24, 1907 (John - Samuel who enlisted in the Revolution June 1, 1776, was in the battles of Long Island, Aug. 27, 1776; White Plains, Oct. 28, 1776; Connecticut, June 7, 1780; and Springfield, June 23, 1780) and Susannah Ringer - b. May 15, 1832 - d. Dec. 14, 1902 (Phillip) - lived near Bruceton Mills, W. Va. Children:

   i. Anna May Darby - b. Mar. 17, 1887 - m. Homer Gibson.
   ii. Guy Allen Darby - b. Nov. 17, 1888 - m. Norma Bryte.
   iii. Nellie Blanche Darby - b. Aug. 5, 1890 - m. Clyde Forman.
   iv. Lee Roy Darby - b. Dec. 29, 1891 - m. Mae Thomas.
   v. Junior King Darby - b. June 1, 1897-m. Lydia Galloway.
   vi. Cora Maude Darby - b. Nov. 1, 1904 - m. Gilbert Walls (see Walls Gene.).

3. Ulyssus - b. Jan. 29, 1867 - d. Jan. 22, 1878, buried at Pisgah, W. Va.

4. Nora J. - b. Feb. 3, 1869 - d. Feb. 12, 1872 - buried at Pisgah, W. Va.

5. Ida C. - b. Apr. 18, 1872 - d. Jan. 28, 1878, buried at Pisgah, W. Va.

6. Marshall - b. Nov. 24, 1874 - d. Jan. 11, 1875, buried at Pisgah, W. Va.

7. Lillian B. - b. Dec. 17, 1875 - m. Dec. 30, 1900, BRUCE H. GIBSON - b. June 29, 1879, Rockville, W. Va., son of Jonathan Gibson (Levi - James - Thomas) and Mary Smith (John) - Lived near Pisgah, W. Va. Children:

   i. Mabel F. - b. May 23, 1902 - m. Gervis Benson.

    ii. Dwight K. - b. April 23, 1903 - m. Mae Metheny (see Metheny Gen.).

    iii. George H. - b. July 7, 1915 -

128. THOMAS HUDSON KING (Thomas - James) - b. Oct. 27, 1850 - d. June 28, 1927 - buried at Pisgah, W. Va. - m. April 10, 1870, at Bruceton Mills, W. Va., Catherine E. Haines - b. Mar. 15, 1851, living in 1933, daughter of Henry Haines - b. Sept. 13, 1823 - d. Sept. 12, 1902 (John 1784 - 1861) and Nancy Ann Garner - b. Sept. 18, 1827 - d. Nov. 20, 1888, buried near Uniontown, Penn. - Lived in Connellsville, Penn. Children:

    1. Henrietta - b. Jan. 17, 1871, at Pisgah, W. Va. - m. Feb. 22, 1892, at Connellsville, Penn., DANIEL C. SPRINGER - b. Apr. 28, 1871, at Belle Vernon, Penn., son of Monoah Springer - b. Aug. 18, 1844 (Daniel - b. 1810 - Joseph - b. 1775 - Daniel - Michael - Carl - b. 1658 - Christopher - b. 1592 - d. 1669) and Mary McWilliams (William) - Children:

        i. Gwendolin Springer - b. June 5, 1893, Connellsville, Penn. - m. at Pittsburgh, Penn., Feb. 16, 1921, Lloyd S. McClelland.

        ii. Ethel Springer - b. July 26, 1895, Connellsville, Penn. - m. at Cumberland, Md., Nov. 24, 1914, Louis R. Metcalfe. Children:

          a. Marietta Louisa Metcalfe - b. May 29, 1916, Connellsville, Penn.

          b. Robert Lloyd Metcalfe - b. Aug. 2, 1919, Connellsville, Penn.

        iii. Daniel M. Springer - b. April 5, 1900, Connellsville, Penn. Enlisted for service during World War at Uniontown. Penn., Dec. 27, 1917, stationed at Fort Thomas, New Port, Ky., Dec. 28, 1917; Camp Taylor, Louisville, Ky., Jan. 10, 1918; Kelly Field, San Antonio, Tex., Jan. 14, 1918; 14th Balloon Co., Fort Omaha, Omaha, Neb., Mar. 7, 1918; Camp Morris, Newport News, Va., July 4, 1918; Over-seas service until the signing of the Armistice; Coblentz in the army of Occupation until Aug. 4, 1919; discharged at New York, N. Y., Aug. 12, 1919.

        iv. Katherine Springer - b. Dec. 3, 1897, Connellsville, Penn. - m. June 16, 1920, at Greensburg, Penn., Marion A. Harris.

        v. Clara Walton Springer - b. July 23, 1902 - m. William Menzie.

    2. Clara Alice - b. Feb. 20, 1878, Pisgah, W. Va. - m. at Connellsville, Penn. HERBERT E. WALTON -b.Apr. 8, 1872

- d. May 29, 1925, buried at Connellsville, Penn., son of Joseph Walton and Catherine Elizabeth Martin. Children:
  i. Herbert Walton, Jr. - b. Sept. 11, 1897 - died in infancy.
3. Nancy Jane - b. Oct. 7, 1879 - d. Oct. 12, 1891.
4. Rufus Homer - b. June 8, 1873 - m. Phoebe Rowan.
5. Chester Lloyd - b. June 19, 1876 - m. Sarah King.
6. Arthur Blaine - b. Feb. 20, 1884 - m. Retta Bierer.

191. JAMES B. KING (Alpheus - James) - b. April 16, 1843 - d. Mar. 30, 1930, buried at Pisgah, W. Va. - m. Aug. 24, 1871, near Rockville, W. Va., Cerilda Liston - b. Jan. 3, 1847, living in 1933, daughter of Abraham Liston (John) and Elizabeth Smith 1817 - 1897 (Jonathan) - lived near Laurel Run church, Grant District, Preston County, W. Va. Children:
1. Maggie E. - b. Feb. 23, 1873, Volcano, W. Va. - d. Feb. 19, 1923, buried at Pisgah, W. Va. - m. October, 1899, at Brandonville, W. Va., LAWRENCE W. KELLEY - b. Nov. 12, 1877, son of Wesley Kelley. Children:
  i. Earnest Kelley - b. Nov. 29, 1901, Pisgah, W. Va. - m. Berthal Frye.
  ii. Gladys Kelley - b. Feb. 15, 1907, Bruceton Mills, W. Va. - m. James Frye.
2. Anna Grace - b. July 11, 1876, Laurel Run - m. Sept. 2, 1897, Laurel Run, THADDEUS S. BENSON - b. Aug. 23, 1875, Bruceton Mills, W. Va., son of Henry Clay Benson (Joseph-James - William from Winchester, Va. 1773) and Mary Martha Brown (Jacob) - Children:
  i. Darrel King Benson - b. April 14, 1898.
  ii. Gervis Benson - b. Nov. 22, 1899 - m. Mabel Gibson.
  iii. Loye Benson - b. Mar. 19, 1904 - m. Lloyd Royce.
  iv. Inez Benson - b. July 18, 1906-m. Arliegh Cunningham.
  v. Marlin Benson - b. Sept. 14, 1909 - m. Beatrice Gribble.
3. Maude - b. Jan. 3, 1884 - m. J. Ormond Walls (see Walls Genealogy).

1211. ALSYNEUS JUDSON KING (Albert F.-Thomas-James) - b. Nov. 29, 1847, Laurel Run, W. Va. - educated at Georges Creek Academy; Reid Institute; Mon. College; Crozier Seminary; - Baptist minister - d. Feb. 27, 1922, buried at Pittsburgh, Penn. - m. at Clarion, Penn., July 4, 1872, Annetta Clover - b. Dec. 25, ———, Clarion, Penn. - d. Feb. 5, 1917, buried at Pittsburgh, Penn., daughter of Judge Peter Clover, of Clarion, Penn. Children:
1. Helen Mary - b. Nov. 15, 1877, Monogahelia City, Pa. - m. at Pittsburgh, Penn., April 19, 1900, JOHN A. BROWN - b. Aug. 6, 1875, in Wales, son of Charles Brown and Mar-

garet Wellington. Children:
   i. Earl Brown - b. Mar. 10, 1902, Pittsburgh, Penn.
   ii. Mildred Brown (twin) - b. Mar. 10, 1902, Pittsburg, Penn.
   iii. Charles King Brown - b. Jan. 5, 1918, Pittsburgh, Penn.
  2. Violet Hester - b. April 14, 1881, Chester, Penn. - m. at
    Pittsburgh, Penn.; Dec. 28, 1907, CHARLES E. PARR -
    son of Fred Parr and Lea Jordan.
  3. Franklin Clover - b. Feb. 12, 1884, Braddock, Penn - m.
    Edith Lowe.
  4. Gertrude Sophia - b. April 27, 1886, Clarion, Penn. - m.
    James Cassidy.
1213. THOMAS WINFIELD KING (Albert F.-Thomas-James)
   - b. Nov. 3, 1849, near Laurel Run, living in 1933 at Bruceton
   Mills, W. Va. - m. April 10, 1870, at Bruceton Mills, W. Va.,
   Mary F. Haines - b. Nov. 9, 1853, Bruceton Mills, W. Va. - d.
   July 24, 1926, buried at Pisgah, W. Va., daughter of Henry
   Haines (John 1784 - 1861) and Nancy Ann Garner.
   Children:
  1. Cora Blanche - b. Feb. 3, 1874 - m. at Bruceton Mills, W.
    Va., Dec. 8, 1892, CHARLES E. FEATHER - b. April 11,
    1861, Albright, W. Va. - d. Sept. 7, 1931, son of Abraham
    Feather (John 1794 - 1870 - Jacob 1759 - 1822) and Eliza-
    beth Boylan (James) - Children:
   i. Mae Feather - b. Nov. 10, 1893, Deer Park, Md.
   ii. Freda Feather - b. Nov. 9, 1894, Bruceton Mills, W. Va.
   iii. Mabel Feather - b. Jan. 29, 1896, Bruceton Mills, W. Va.
    - m. at Oakland, Md., Nov. 25, 1914, Charles Samuel
    Harris - b. 1893, Fairmont, W. Va., son of Eli Harris and
    Nora DeVault. Children:
    a. Samuel Charles Harris, Jr. - b. Dec. 18, 1916, Fair-
      mont, W. Va.
    b. Harold Elza Harris - b. July 7, 1918, Fairmont, W.
      Va.
    c. William Edgar Harris - b. Oct. 22, 1924, Fairmont,
      W Va.
   iv. Hazel Feather - b. Mar. 23, 1899, Mannington, W. Va. -
    m. at Cumberland, Md., July 23, 1920, Clyde J. Spiker.
  2. William O. - b. June 29, 1883, near Pisgah, W. Va. - d. July
    26, 1903, of cholera in the Philippine Islands, buried at San
    Francisco, Calif. Enlisted August, 1902, in Washington,
    D. C., as a musician, served during Spanish American War
    with Troop K 11, U. S. Cavalry, stationed at Vigan, Ilicao,
    Sur Luzan, P. I. - His diary shows he went off duty at five

in the afternoon, taken to a hospital at nine o'clock, and died at midnight.

1214. JEHU KING (Albert F. - Thomas - James) - b. Dec. 19, 1851, near Laurel Run - d. June 6, 1928, Point Marion, Penn. - buried at Pisgah, W. Va. - m. at Smithfield, Penn., Jan. 1, 1877, Mary A. Collins - b. July 21, 1855, Bruceton Mills, W. Va. - d. Mar. 7, 1927, Point Marion, Penn., buried at Pisgah, W. Va., daughter of Andrew Collins, 1811 - 1893 (James) and Olivia McClain, 1824 - 1909 (William) - lived near Laurel Run Church. Children:

1. Laura Olivia - b. Nov. 6, 1877, near Laurel Run Church, Grant District, Preston County, W. Va. - m. at Bruceton Mills, W. Va., Sept. 15, 1910, GEORGE STEWART - b. Feb. 4, 1871, Stewartstown, W. Va., son of Albert G. Stewart and Susan McElroy. Children:
   i. Virginia Pearl Stewart - b. Mar. 31, 1914, Point Marion, Penn.
2. Charles J. - b. May 31, 1879 - m. Eva Warman.
3. Pearl - b. Feb. 19, 1889, near Laurel Run Church, Grant District, Preston County, W. Va. - m. at Centreton, N. J., April 25, 1923, FRANK McKISHEN - b. Dec. 16, 1876, Bridgeton, N. J., son of John McKishen and Sarah Lacy. Children:
   i. Calvin McKishen - b. Mar. 4, 1924, Elmer, Salem County, N. J.
   ii. Herbert McKishen - b. Oct. 31, 1925, Elmer, Salem County, N. J.
   iii. Leroy McKishen - b. Feb. 2, 1930, Elmer, Salem County, N. J.

1215. EVAN KING (Albert F. - Thomas - James) - b. Nov. 11, 1855, near Pisgah, W. Va. - d. May 4, 1923, buried at Pisgah, W. Va. - m. at Pisgah, W. Va., Nov. 11, 1880, Olive Oneda Walls - b. April 18, 1862 - d. Dec. 10, 1931, buried at Pisgah, W. Va. (see Walls Genealogy) - lived near Pisgah,. W. Va. Children:

1. Mamie Belle - b. April 8, 1884, Pisgah, W. Va. - m. at Pisgah, W. Va., Oct. 2, 1902, JAMES GALLOWAY - b. Oct. 2, 1879, Bruceton Mills, W. Va., son of John Galloway and Lydia Laub. Children:
   i. Olive Galloway - b. June 29, 1903, Pisgah, W. Va. - m. Pratt Graham.
   ii. Charles Galloway - b. Dec. 26, 1904, Monessen, Pa. - m. Lucinda Christopher (see Christopher Genealogy).
   iii. Leahnoire Galloway - b. Mar. 7, 1906, Monessen, Pa. - m. Earl McNair.

    iv. Howard Galloway - b. Aug. 21, 1910, Pisgah, W. Va.

    v. Stanford Galloway - b. July 12, 1912, Pisgah, W. Va.

    vi. Dorothy Galloway - b. May 8, 1915, Pisgah, W. Va.

    vii. Julia Galloway - b. Oct. 29, 1917 - d. Nov. 19, 1917, buried at Pisgah, W. Va.

    viii. Lulu Galloway - b. Aug. 3, 1919 - d. Dec. 20, 1922, buried at Pisgah, W. Va.

    ix. Hilda Galloway-b. June 1, 1921, Bruceton Mills, W. Va.

    x. Verl Galloway - b. May 7, 1926, Bruceton Mills, W. Va.

2. Emmett Roy - b. July 11, 1886 - m. Naomi Blanche Lilly.

3. Paul DeWitt - b. Jan. 12, 1895 - m. Versie I. Welch.

4. Edna Belinda - b. Dec. 24, 1898, Pisgah, W. Va. - m. June 27, 1915, CURTIS FEATHER.

5. Edith Hester (twin) - b. Dec. 24, 1898, Pisgah, W. Va. - m. Sept. 13, 1915, ARLEY FORMAN, son of Rufus Forman.

1232. E. PRESTON KING (William J. - Thomas - James) - b. April 14, 1855, Laurel Run, Grant District, Preston County, W. Va. - m. at Harmony Grove, Dec. 21, 1878, Sarah Jane Everly - b. Dec. 31, 1855, at Harmony Grove, Pleasant District, Preston County, W. Va. - d. May 25, 1917, buried at Aurora, Preston County, W. Va., daughter of Lewis Everly, 1811 - 1893 (Henry 1785 - 1855) and Eva Zweyer, 1815 - 1886 (Adam 1772 - 1833) - Lived at Laurel Run, and Aurora, W. Va.

Children:

1. Edith Eva - b. Feb. 20, 1880, Laurel Run, Grant District, Preston County, W. Va. - d. Aug. 11, 1926, buried at Jenners, Somerset County, Penn. - m. April 12, 1917, Stoyestown, Penn., MARSHALL GRIFFITH - b. July 11, 1880, Jenners, Penn. - d. May 10, 1930, buried at Jenners, Penn., son of Jesse Griffith and Levina Cover. - Children:

    i. Harry King Griffith - b. Feb. 13, 1918, Jenners, Penn.

    ii. Twin—Mary Elizabeth Griffith - b. Feb. 13, 1918, Jenners, Penn.

    iii. Thelma Leota Griffith - b. Aug. 22, 1919, Jenners, Penn.

2. Alva Curtis - b. Nov. 16, 1882 - m. Ethel Washburn.

3. Elizabeth Ethel - b. Feb. 24, 1884, Laurel Run, Grant District, Preston County, W. Va. - d. Mar. 24, 1914, buried at Aurora, W. Va.

4. Harry Olen - b. Jan. 21, 1889, Aurora, W. Va. - d. Nov. 19, 1919, buried at Aurora, W. Va. Killed in an accident near Richwood, W. Va. - Enlisted in U. S. Navy, Dec. 3, 1917, served at Receiving Ship at New York; on U. S. S. Nevada; U. S. S. Arkansas, which was the flag ship of Commander Battleship Force Two, U. S. Atlantic Fleet, from

Nov. 13, 1917, to June 25, 1918, when she sailed for European waters and joined the Sixth Battle Squadron of the Grand Fleet, serving as a unit in this Squadron from July 25, 1918, until Dec. 1, 1918. The Sixth Battle Squadron of the British Grand Fleet was composed entirely of United States ships under the command of Rear Admiral Hugh Rodman, U. S. N. On Nov. 21, 1918, the U. S. S. Arkansas was a unit of the Grand Fleet which received the surrender of the German Fleet in the Firth of Forth. The surrendered German Fleet consisted of five battle cruisers, nine battleships, eight light cruisers, and fifty destroyers, all of the most modern construction and type. In accordance with General Order 422 of Sept. 25, 1918, Harry O. King was authorized to wear one Service Chevron. Discharged at Hampton Roads, Va., Receiving ship, July 31, 1919.

5. Roxa L. - b. July 14, 1891, Aurora, W. Va. -

6. Lona Faye - b. Apr. 22, 1895 - d. July 28, 1914, buried at Aurora, W. Va.

7. Mary Louise - b. Sept. 19, 1897 - m. at Morgantown, W. Va., April 24, 1923, GAY WHITESELL - b. Aug. 10, 1896, Grafton, W. Va., son of Jonathan Whitesell and Mary Springer. - Children:
   i. Mary Jane Whitesell - b. Oct. 24, 1924, Lowell, Maine.
   ii. Hazel Elizabeth Whitesell - b. Sept. 1, 1928, Kingwood, W. Va.
   iii. Noreen Gay Whitesell - b. Dec. 12, 1932, Kingwood, W. Va.

1233. MARCELLUS HOSEA KING (William J. - Thomas - James) - b. Nov. 7, 1856 - d. Sept. 2, 1932, buried at Pisgah, W. Va. - m. Sept. 16, 1876, in Fayette County, Penn., Julia Ann Ryan - b. Sept. 2, 1859, Pisgah, W. Va., daughter of Edward D. Ryan and Elizabeth Wolf - Lived near Laurel Run Church, Grant District, Preston County, W. Va.
   Children:
1. Elizabeth Gertrude - b. Sept. 30, 1877, Pisgah, W. Va. - m. at Oakland, Md., April 18, 1892, WILLIAM RUSSELL GRIBBLE - b. Dec. 29, 1871, Pisgah, W. Va., son of Jefferson Thompson Gribble (Archibald) and Frances Ann Michael (William). - Children:
   i. Troy Estille Gribble - b. April 20, 1894, Pisgah, W. Va. - d. Oct. 14, 1927 - served during World War with 501 Refrigeration Plant C o., U. S. Army - m. Gertrude Shakelford.
   ii. Harold Gribble - b. Mar. 13, 1905 -

iii.　Herbert Gribble - b. Nov. 10, 1908 -

iv.　Olivia Claire - b. Sept. 8, 1919 -

2.　Freeman Edison - b. Mar. 23, 1900 + m. Althea Coral Piper.

1234.　ZAR KELLEY KING (William J. - Thomas - James) - b. Oct. 15, 1858 - m. 1st., Aug. 25, 1890, at Oakland, Md., Lizzie Cale - b. Dec. 4. 1869, Pisgah, W. Va. - d. July 31, 1906, buried at Pisgah, W. Va., daughter of Jesse Cale (Jacob and Sarah Everly Cale) and Martha Liston (Abraham) - lived at Pisgah, W. Va., except during the years 1884 to 1889, in Illinois, Colorado and Nebraska. - m. 2nd., Oct. 17, 1917, at Morgantown, W. Va., Grace First Everly - b. Aug. 15, 1861, Harrisburg, Penn., daughter of George First and Eleanor Curry (John).

Children by 1st. marriage:

1.　Hattie Avis - b. Sept. 20, 1893 - m. Ralph Ryan (see Ryan Genealogy).

1236.　THURMAN MALVERN KING (William J. - Thomas - James) - b. Mar. 20, 1863, near Laurel Run Church, Grant District, Preston County, W. Va. - d. July 29, 1930, buried at Bruceton Mills, W. Va. - m. at Bruceton Mills, W. Va., Oct. 18, 1891, Katie Cunningham - b. Feb. 2, 1869, Ohio Pyle, Penn., daughter of Thaddeus S. Cunningham and Eliza Jane Liston (see Cunningham Genealogy) - lived near Hopewell Church, Grant District, Preston County, W. Va., except between the years 1887 and 1889 in Nebraska and Colorado.

Children:

1.　Edward Thorp - b. Sept. 25, 1895 - m. Viola Reed.

2.　Hazel McKinley - b. June 23, 1897 - m. 1st. at Bruceton Mills, W. Va., May 5, 1918, JAMES SUMNER ELLIOTT - b. Mar. 11, 1894, Davis, W. Va. - d. Oct. 30, 1918, Camp Mead, Md., buried at Terra Alta, W. Va., served during World War with Co. 8, 154 Depot Brigade, July 25, 1918, to Oct. 30, 1918, son of Edward P. Elliott and Electa Forman - m. 2nd at Morgantown, W. Va., Aug. 14, 1930, ZADOK WHITESELL - b. Aug. 14, 1894, Johnstown, Pa., son of Jonathan Whitesell and Mary Springer. - Children by 1st. marriage:

i.　Edward Sumner Elliott - b. Feb. 8, 1919, Bruceton Mills, W. Va.

3.　William Scott - b. Aug. 10, 1899 - m. Edna Mosser.

4.　Lyda Helen - b. Jan. 19, 1907 - m. at Bruceton Mills, W. Va., Oct. 2, 1926, THOMAS RICHARD FIELD - b. Jan. 16, 1904, Kingwood, W. Va., son of Samuel Field (Richard) and Mae Cool (Thomas) - residence, Kingwood, W. Va. - Children:

i. Donald King Field - b. July 31, 1927, Kingwood, W. Va.

ii. Robert Dale Field - b. Feb. 26, 1930, Kingwood, W. Va.

iii. Joseph Richard Field - b. Oct. 29, 1931, Terra Alta, W. Va.

1284. RUFUS HOMER KING (Thomas H. - Thomas - James) - b. June 8, 1873, Preston County, W. Va. - m. at Uniontown, Penn., June 14, 1898, Phoebe Rowan - b. Aug. 1, 1873, Connelsville, Penn., daughter of Joseph Rowan and Caroline Buttermore - living in Uniontown, Penn.

1285. CHESTER LLOYD KING (Thomas H. - Thomas - James) - b. June 19, 1876, near Bruceton Mills, W. Va. - m. Aug. 10, 1897, at Connellsville, Penn., Sarah Jane King - b. Oct. 18, 1876, Broadford, Penn. - d. Dec. 1, 1932, buried at Scottdale, Penn., daughter of Martin Vincent King (Martin) and Mary Anne Connelly (James) from County Galway, Ireland. - Residence, 416 Emerson Place, Youngstown, Ohio. Children:

1. Leonard - b. July 31, 1898 - d. Aug. 7, 1898, buried at Connellsville, Pa.

2. Chester L. - b. Aug. 31, 1899 - m. Lillian Pearl Eberhardt.

3. Nora - b. Nov. 14, 1900, Belle Vernon, Penn. - m. Joseph Drivas.

4. Martin - b. Mar. 12, 1902, Connellsville, Pa. - m. Violet Kramer.

5. Thomas H. - b. Jan. 12, 1904, Donora, Penn. -

6. Mary Katherine - b. July 27, 1906, Donora, Pa. - m. George Bosley.

7. Evaline - b. Dec. 20, 1912, Evarson, Penn. - m. Thomas Williams.

8. Arthur - b. Mar. 29, 1910, Evarson, Penn. -

9. Herbert - b. Feb. 28, 1914, Donora, Penn. -

10. John R. - b. Aug. 13, 1917, Donora, Penn. -

11. Claribell - b. June 25, 1908 - d. June 30, 1908, buried at Donora, Penn.

12. Helen - b. May 29, 1915 - d. May 29, 1915, buried at Donora, Penn.

1286. ARTHUR BLAINE KING (Thomas H. - Thomas - James) - b. Feb. 20, 1884 - m. Retta Bierer - b. ——————, daughter of ——————

Children:

1. Charles Arthur - b. —————— - m. Sarah Province.

2. Pearl - b. —————— - m. Lawrence Walters.

3. Clara May - b —————— - m. William Mason.

4. Harold Densel - b. ——————

5. Gwendolin - b. ——————

6. Robert - b. ─────────
7. William - b. ─────────
8. Catherine Lucretia - b. ─────────
9. Jennett Elaine - b. ─────────
10. Dorothy Jane - b. ─────────

12113. FRANKLIN CLOVER KING (Alsyneus J. - Albert F. — Thomas - James) - b. Feb. 12, 1884, Braddock, Penn.-Attorney - Educated at Illinois College of Law. - m. at Pittsburgh, Penn., April 19, 1911, Edith Cameron Lowe - b. ───────── daughter of ─────────
 Children:
 1. Franklin Albert - b. ─────────

12142. CHARLES J. KING (Jehu - Albert F. - Thomas - James) - b. May 31, 1879, Bruceton Mills, W. Va. - m. Aug. 29, 1903, at Bruceton Mills, W. Va., Eva Warman - b. Jan. 30, 1885, Monongalia County, W. Va., daughter of Lowry J. Warman and Hattie E. Glover. Residence near Bruceton Mills, W. Va.
 Children:
 1. Harold E. - b. April 1, 1909, Bruceton Mills, W. Va.

12152. EMMET ROY KING (Evan - Albert F. - Thomas - James) - b. July 11, 1886, Pisgah, W. Va. - m. Dec. 25, 1910, Naomi Blanche Lilly - b. Mar. 21, 1890, Grafton, W. Va., daughter of George Rosencrantz Lilly - b. Aug. 20, 1861 (Richard Lilly and Maria Altman) and Rose Williams - b. Dec. 14, 1866, Buchannon, W. Va. (Jerome Williams, 1830 - 1904 and Martha Ann Hyne b. Upshur County, W. Va.) - Residence, Reading, Penn.
 Children:
 1. Paul Emmet - b. June 27, 1911, Grafton, W. Va.
 2. Rosalie Olive - b. June 18, 1914, Wheeling, W. Va.
 3. Betty Jean - b. July 10, 1917, Grafton, W. Va.

12153. PAUL DeWITT KING (Evan - Albert F. - Thomas - James) - b. Jan. 12, 1895, Pisgah, W. Va. - m. at Albright, W. Va., June 2, 1923, Versie I. Welch - b. Dec. 3, 1895, Albright, W. Va., daughter of Joseph Welch and Virginia Gribble (John) - Residence near Pisgah, W. Va.
 Children:
 1. Clayton Edwin - b. Aug. 30, 1925, Pisgah, W. Va.

12322. ALVA CURTIS KING (E. Preston - William J. - Thomas - James) - b. Nov. 16, 1882, near Laurel Run Church, Grant District, Preston County, W. Va. - m. at Shinnston, W. Va., April 1909, Ethel Washburn - b. Jan. 9, 1892, Oberlin, Ohio, daughter of Joseph Carl Washburn and Ella Jane Wells - b. April 8, 1867 (William Wells - b. Feb. 22, 1830, and Mary Jane Quinby

- b. Mar. 19, 1833) - Residence, Lawndale, Calif.
Children:

1. Pearl Yvonne - b. Feb. 21, 1910, Shinnston, W. Va. - m. RICHARD BLYMILLER - b. ——————— - son of —— ——————— - Children:
   i. Carl Richard William Blymiller - b. Jan. 30, 1931, Lawndale, Calif.
2. Vernon - b. April 6, 1912, Aurora, W. Va.
3. Ruth Virginia - b. July 25, 1915, Clarksburg, W. Va.
4. Lloyd - b. Feb. 5, 1922, Leyden, Colorado.

12332. FREEMAN EDISON KING (M. Hosea - William J. - Thomas - James) - b. Mar. 23, 1900, Pisgah, W. Va. - m. at Oakland, Md., Oct. 1, 1917, Althea Coral Piper - b. Sept. 24, 1901, Pisgah, W. Va., daughter of William Roy Piper (William) and Jennette Walls (Richard - George - Charles - James) - Residence, 833 Charles Avenue, Morgantown, W. Va.
Children:
1. William Clyde - b. June 2, 1919.

12361. EDWARD THORP KING (Thurman M. - William J. - Thomas - James) - b. Sept. 25, 1895, near Hopewell Church, Grant District, Preston County, W. Va. - Enlisted in U. S. Navy at Denver, Colo., Sept. 28, 1917, and served at the following stations and ships: Navy Yard, Mare Island, San Francisco, Calif.; Receiving Ship, Puget Sound Navy Yard, Bremerton, Washington; U. S. S. West Apaum to Chile, S. A.; Receiving Ship, Navy Yard, Charleston, S. C.; Naval Station, Virgin Islands; U. S. Navy Radio Station, San Juan, and Cayey, Porto Rico; Receiving Ship, Bay Ridge Station, Brooklyn, N. Y., and discharged at Denver, Colo., Sept. 5, 1919. - m. at Boone, Iowa. Sept. 15, 1919, Viola Murree Reed - b. Oct. 24, 1894, Ayrshire, Palo Alto County, Iowa, daughter of James Edward Reed (Isaac - Jacob) and Lulu Belle Wheeler (Martin - Greene, 1820 - 1877). - Author of this work.

12363. WILLIAM SCOTT KING (Thurman M. - William J. - Thomas - James) - b. Aug. 10, 1899, near Hopewell Church, Grant District, Preston County, W. Va. - m. at Kingwood, W. Va., Oct. 15, 1922, Edna Mosser - b. June 22, 1895, Rockville, W. Va., daughter of William Mosser, 1842 - 1924 (Jacob 1810 - 1883 - Christian) and Jennie Huggins, 1860 - 1924. - Residence near Bruceton Mills, W. Va.
Children:
1. William Thurman - b. June 24, 1925, Bruceton Mills, W. Va.
2. Mary Virginia - b. June 4, 1927, Bruceton Mills, W. Va.
3. Mabel Fern - b. June 19, 1928, Bruceton Mills, W. Va.

4. Hazel Helen - b. Dec. 15, 1930, Bruceton Mills, W. Va.
5. Naomi Ruth - b. Feb. 22, 1932, Bruceton Mills, W. Va.

12852. CHESTER L. KING, JR. (Chester L. - Thomas H. - Thomas - James) - b. Aug. 31, 1899 - m. at New Salem, Penn., Oct. 1, 1925, Lillian Pearl Eberhardt. Children:
1. Jack Melvin - b. Dec. 1, 1928, Youngstown, Ohio.
2. Donald Francis -b. May 24, 1930, Struthers, Ohio.

THE KING FAMILY IN GRANT DISTRICT

2. THOMAS KING - One of the family of five brothers who supposedly came from Winchester, Virginia. No other record is found of this man, and he, in all probability, went on westward and did not remain at Laurel Run with his brothers, James, John and Valentine.

3. ISAAC KING - Did not remain for any length of time in Grant District, but no doubt went farther west in the early days of westward immigration. There is no record in Preston County of any of his family. His name appears in the Preston County History (Morton and Cole) as having married Elizabeth McCollum, daughter of Daniel, 1754 - 1842 (James 1725 - 1800). The name, I. D. King, appears in the Church records of the Hazel Run Baptist Church, when on Nov. 15, 1856, I. D. King was invited to preach the Church dedication sermon on Nov. 30, 1856. It is claimed by some that these early Kings were all ministers.

4. JOHN KING* - b. 1784 - d. Aug. 30, 1848, buried on the Jehu King farm near Laurel Run Church, Grant District, Preston County, W. Va. - Built and operated a saw and grist mill which was run by water power. The foundation of this old mill is located near the now abandoned Laurel Run school house near the present Laurel Run Church. - Very little information can be found of his family. He seems to have married Elizabeth Show or Betty Messenger, of Wood Grove Furnace. Lived near his mill and probably on the "Jimmie King" place near Laurel Run Church.
     Children:
7. Jane - m. Benjamin Michael.
2. Ann - m. George Michael.
3. Margaret - m. Thomas Douglas.

*NOTE—

> The writer can not vouch for the correctness of this family record as many conflicting reports were received regarding the families of John and Valentine King.

VALENTINE KING

AND SOME OF HIS DESCENDANTS

5. VALENTINE KING, one of the five King brothers, who came from near Winchester, Virginia, and settled at Laurel Run, in Grant District, Preston County, West Virginia. In 1788 he purchased 185 acres of land from George McDonald for three hundred and seventy dollars, with improvements. This farm was known as the "Tiny" King farm, and in later years owned by Jehu King. An abandoned cemetery on this farm contains the graves of many of the pioneers of the early Laurel Run settlement. One marker contains the letters "V. K.", probably the grave of Valentine King. His wife was Ruth Fleming- b. Mar. 6, 1796, daughter of John Fleming (Archibald). She died about 1882. A letter written August 19, 1890, by Francis A. Fleming, of Arcana, Grant County, Indiana, quotes "* * * Ruth Fleming married Voluntine King, had two children, William and Issac, and died at the age of 86 or 87." * * *

Children of Valentine King:

1. Eliza - b. July 14, 1817 - d. Feb. 16, 1903, buried at Mt. Nebo Church, Pleasant District, Preston County, W. Va. - m. JOHN JENKINS - b. Aug. 24, 1815 - d. April 7, 1894, son of Evan Jenkins and Hannah Graham. Children:

   i. Martha Jenkins - b. Aug. 28, 1841 - m. 1st., Isaac N. Forman - d. May 14, 1876 - m. 2nd., Randolph Protzman - b. April 16, 1848 - d. June 24, 1903, buried on Graham farm west of Valley Point, Preston County, W. Va.

   ii. Emma Jenkins - b. May 5, 1843 - d. May 4, 1845.

   iii. Cyrus Jenkins - b. Jan. 11, 1845 - d. Jan. 16, 1922 - m. Lydia Adams.

   iv. Carrie Jenkins - b. Dec. 26, 1846 - d. Jan. 30, 1928 - m. Butler Prince.

   v. William Jenkins - b. Dec. 23, 1848 - d. Jan. 6, 1928 - m. Zania Michael.

   vi. Margaret J. Jenkins - b. May 17, 1851 - d. Mar. 17, 1926 -m. J. M. Light.

   vii. Hannah A. Jenkins - b. Aug. 24, 1854 - d. Sept. 15, 1872.

   viii. James Clayton Jenkins - b. June 7, 1856 - m. Lou Allison.

   ix. George A. Jenkins - b. May 13, 1858 - m. Alice McKinney.

   x. John J. Jenkins - b. May 13, 1860 - m. 1st., Victoria Clark - d. Dec. 24, 1898 - m. 2nd., Flora Bucklew.

2. Isaac - b. 1818 - d. 1893.
3. James - m. Mary A. Forman and went to Kansas.
4. Jane - lived and died in Kansas.
5. Margaret - m. Rev. Phillip Brown - lived in Ohio.
6. William H. - b. June 13, 1827 - d. Aug. 17, 1892 - m. 1st., Mary A. Walls - m. 2nd, Elma McCollum.
7. Josephine - m. Alfred Spahr, lived in Montana. Their children were: Scott, John, Grace, Anna and Frank.

56. WILLIAM H. KING (Valentine) - b. June 13, 1827 - d. Aug. 17, 1892, buried at Albright, W. Va. - m. 1st., Jan. 8, 1856, Mary A. Walls - b. Jan. 14, 1832 - d. Apr. 25, 1872, buried at Albright, W. Va., daughter of Charles Walls (James) and Sarah Forman (Richard - Robert). - m. 2nd., Mar. 1, 1874, Elma McCollum - b. Mar. 2, 1848 - d. Aug. 24, 1893, buried at Albright, W. Va., daughter of Daniel B. McCollum (Daniel - James) and Ann Mosser.

Children by 1st marriage:

1. Ralph H. - b. Jan. 5, 1858, Mortons Mill (Clifton Mills) - d. Dec. 12, 1860, buried at Albright, W. Va.
2. Ella E. - b. Mar. 2, 1860, at Mortons Mill (Clifton Mills) Grant District, Preston County, W. Va. - m. June 1, 1881, at Albright, W. Va., JAMES A. LENHART - b. Mar. 15, 1860, Brandonville, W. Va., son of Aaron Lenhart, 1826 - 1900, and Catherine Metzler. Children:
   i. Nina Florence Lenhart - b. Mar. 7, 1889, Valley Point, W. Va. - m. Charles W. McNary.
   ii. Adria Mabel Lenhart - b. Dec. 7, 1891, Valley Point, W. Va. - m. David Oliver Sunderland.
   iii. Bernice King Lenhart - b. Feb. 16, 1895, Kingwood, W. Va. - m. John N. DeVoe.
   iv. Helen Josephine Lenhart - b. Mar. 2, 1896, Kingwood, W. Va. - m. French A. Yoke.
3. Georgiana - b. May 12, 1862, Albright, W. Va. - m. Joseph Graham.
4. Phil Sheridan - b. May 12, 1865, Albright, W. Va. - m. Sarah Etta Lenhart.
5. Flora Jane - b. Mar. 4, 1868 - m. April 10, 1888, THOMAS W. ELLIOTT - b. Aug. 3, 1861, at Herring, W. Va., son of Isaac Elliott (John) and Rachel Ervin (Jacob). Children:
   i. Hugh Elliott - b. Sept. 18, 1890, Albright, W. Va. - d. Feb. 29, 1916, buried at Kingwood, W. Va.
   ii. Max Elliott - b. Nov. 13, 1892, Davis, W. Va. - m. Tyrannus Maust.

iii. Frank Elliott - b. Mar. 14, 1894, Davis, W. Va. - m. Dina Durfesne.

iv. Hazel Elliott - b. June 12, 1896, Terra Alta, W. Va. - m. Earl Brand.

v. Charles Elliott - b. Mar. 17, 1900, Albright, W. Va. - single.

vi. Dallas Elliott - b. Feb. 24, 1903, Albright, W. Va. - m. Virginia Crane.

vii. Catherine Elliott - b. June 26, 1905, Albright, W. Va. - m. Dwight Foley.

viii. Dorothy Elliott - b. Jan. 24, 1907, Albright, W. Va. - single.

ix. Paul Elliott - b. Jan. 11, 1911, Albright, W. Va. - single. Children by 2nd marriage:

6. Leni Leoti - b. Jan. 12, 1875, Albright, W. Va. - m. Frank Spahr.

7. William B. - b. Dec. 13, 1883, Albright, W. Va. - went to Montana or Washington.

564. PHIL SHERIDAN KING (William H. - Valentine) - b. May 12, 1865, Albright, W. Va. - m. at Valley Point, W. Va., Sept. 2, 1870, Sarah Etta Lenhart - b. Aug. 23, 1869, near Clifton Mills, W. Va., daughter of Aaron Lenhart and Catherine Metzler.

Children:

1. Nina Maude - b. Apr. 14, 1892, Baird, W. Va. - m. FRANK HILEMAN - b. Jan. 27, 1892, son of David E. Hileman (William) and Ida Jane Hartman. Children:
i. Phylis Hileman - b. May 5, 1916 -
ii. Margaret Hileman - b. Mar. 26, 1918 -
iii. Mary Jane Hileman - b. May 3, 1921 -

2. Ralph E. - b. June 8, 1895, Davis, W. Va. - m. Callie Shaffer.

3. Bernice - b. Aug. 2, 1898, Davis, W. Va.-m. Earnest Zabeck.

4. Catherine - b. May 2, 1911, Rowlesburg, W. Va. -

5642. RALPH E. KING (Phil S. - William H. - Valentine) - b. June 8, 1895, Davis, W. Va. - m. at Oakland, Md., Nov. 9, 1916, Calla Ercil Shaffer - b. 1895, Dobbins, W. Va., daughter of T. W. Shaffer.

Children:

1. Ralph, Jr. - b. Jan. 2, 1919, Gary, Ind.

2. Robert Wayne - b. July 19, 1932, Gary, Ind.

JAMES METHENY

OF BEECH RUN HILL AND SOME OF HIS DESCENDANTS

1. JAMES METHENY and his wife, Mary, came to Beech Run Hill, Pleasant District, Preston County, W. Va., and purchased of Amos and Elizabeth Roberts 400 acres of land in 1798, for the sum of thirty pounds ($100). In later years this was known as the Henry C. Martin farm.

   Children:
   1. Nathan - b. Sept. 14, 1781 - d. Feb. 21, 1856 - m. Mary Everly.
   2. Mary - b. 1793 - d. 1887 - m. 1st., Peter Miller. 2nd., Jacob Martin.
   3. Susan - b. —————— - m. Isaac Martin. (of Daniel).
   4. Daniel - b. —————— - went west.
   5. William - b. —————— - went west.
   6. Moses - b. —————— - went west.
   7. Noah - b. —————— - went west.
   8. To 16 others.

11. NATHAN METHENY (James) - b. Sept. 14, 1781 - d. Feb. 21, 1856 - m. Mary Everly - b. Jan. 22, 1784 - d. Sept. 5, 1854, both are buried on Cheat Hill and lived near Rockville, Preston County, W. Va., about 1829, on land later known as the Silas M. Metheny farm.

    Children:
    1. Catherine - b. April 7, 1803 - d. Feb. 26, 1886, buried on the old Jesse Forman farm west of Valley Point, Preston County, W. Va. - m. STERLING GRAHAM (David - b. 1763) - b. Nov. 1, 1794 - d. Oct. 17, 1866, buried near his wife. Children:
       i. Margaret Graham - b. Jan. 17, 1845 - d. Sept. 7, 1845.
       ii. James S. Graham - b. April 4, 1858 - d. Sept. 10, 1862.
    2. Peter - b. Jan. 9, 1805 - d. Sept. 21, 1896 - m. Eva Cupp.
    3. Mary - b. Dec. 28, 1806 - d. —————— - m. John Smith.
    4. Leah - b. Feb. 29, 1809 - d. —————— - m. Fortner, went to Pennsylvania.
    5. James - b. June 7, 1811 - d. —————— - m. Christina Wolfe.
    6. Isaiah - b. Nov. 3, 1817 - d. Sept. 30, 1893 - m. Elizabeth Chidester.
    7. Asa - b. April 18, 1820 - d. July 21, 1883 - m. Nancy Smith.
    8. Huldah - b. Mar. 10, 1823 - d. —————— - m. Joseph Smith.

112. PETER METHENY (Nathan - James) - b. Jan. 9, 1805 - d. Sept. 21, 1896 - m. Eva Cupp - b. Dec. 16, 1809 - d. Oct. 18, 1888, both are buried in Beech Run Hill Cemetery, in Pleasant District, Preston County - daughter of John Cupp (Peter) and Sarah Wilhelm.

Children:

1. Sarah Jane - b. Oct. 8, 1833 - d. Aug. 11, 1851 - buried at Beech Run Hill.
2. Hosea - b. ———————— - d. ———————— - m. Rachel C. Elsey.
3. Amos - b. ———————— - d. ———————— - m. Margaret Groves.
4. Joel - b. ———————— - d. ———————— - m. Sarah Titchnell.
5. Perry - b. ———————— - d. ———————— - m. Servilla Liston - b. Oct. 20, 1838 - d. Oct. 2, 1901 - buried in Beech Run Hill Cemetery.
6. Ezra - b. Mar. 20, 1845 - d. Oct. 13, 1861, buried at Beech Run Hill.
7. Obadiah - b. ————, 1848 - d. ———————— - m. Nancy Otto, 1848 - 1923 - both are buried at Pisgah, Grant District, Preston County, W. Va.
8. Francis - b. ———————— - d. ———————— - m. 1st., Sarah Bower - 2nd., Margaret G. Titchnell Groves.

115. JAMES METHENY (Nathan - James) - b. June 7, 1811 - d. ———————— - m. Christina Wolfe - b. ———————— - d. ———— ———— - daughter of George Wolfe (Jacob - Jacob) and Elizabeth Teets.

Children:

1. Nathan - b. ———— - d. ———— - m. Catherine Vansickle.
2. George - b. ———— - d. ———— - m. Mary J. Wilhelm.
3. Mary - b. ———— - d. ———— - m. John Reckard.
4. Huldah - b. ———— - d. ———— - m. Noah Strawser.
5. Levi - b. ———— - d. ———— - m. Rosa Wilhelm.
6. Jacob - b. ———— - d. ———— - m. Charlotta Hardesty.
7. James - b. ———— - d. ———— - m. Frances Wilhelm.
8. Juliana - b. ———— - d. ———— - m. George W. Field.
9. Elizabeth - b. ———— - d. ———— - m. Jacob Wilhelm.
10. Rhoda - b. ———— - d. ———— - m. Samuel Vansickle.

116. ISAIAH METHENY (Nathan - James) - b. Nov. 3, 1817 - d. Sept. 30, 1893 - m. Elizabeth Chidester - b. April 8, 1820 - d. Jan. 29, 1891, both are buried near Mt. Nebo Church, in Pleasant District, Preston County, W. Va., daughter of ————

Children:

1. John - b. Nov. 18, 1837 - d. May 6, 1864, killed in the Seven Days Battle at Chancellorsville - m. Almira Alford.
2. Mary - b. April 26, 1840 - d. May 14, 1843, buried in Armstrong Cemetery near Bruceton Mills, W. Va.
3. Martha (twin to Mary) - b. April 26, 1840 - d. ————— buried in Iowa - m. Elisha Liston.
4. William H. - b. May 4, 1846 - d. Mar. 30, 1904 - m. Emma King.
5. Silas M. - b. April 21, 1848 - d. Sept. 5, 1927 - m. Mary Armena King.
6. George - b. Sept. 19, 1850 - d. ————————— - buried at Mt. Braddock, Penn. - m. Elizabeth Darnell.
7. Harriett - b. July 29, 1856 - m. 1st., Brooks Metheny - b. ————————— - d. ————— 1897, buried in Sugar Valley Cemetery, Pleasant District, Preston County, W. Va., son of Elijah Metheny and Christine Chidester - m. 2nd., Wilmer Collins - b. ————————— - d. ————————— - Children by 1st marriage:

    i. Pearl Metheny - b. ————————— - m. Bruce Goodwin.

    ii. Mary Metheny - b. Mar. 22, 1883 - m. Judson Goodwin (Amos - Daniel).

    iii. Marshall Metheny - b. ————————— - d. 1902, buried at Aurora, W. Va.

    Children by 2nd. marriage:

    iv. Mattie Collins - b. ————————— - m. 1st., Daniel Thomas - m. 2nd., Frank Bowman.

    v. Cora Collins - b. ————————— - m. Levi Zweyer.

1164. WILLIAM H. METHENY (Isaiah - Nathan - James) - b. May 4, 1846 - d. Mar. 30, 1904, buried at Pisgah, W. Va. - m. Jan. 13, 1867, Emma(King - b. Nov. 28, 1847, at Pisgah, W. Va., daughter of Alpheus King (James) and Margaret Jenkins (Evan - Thomas) - Lived near Laurel Run. Preston County, W. Va.

    Children:
1. Laura - b. May 5, 1871, Laurel Run - m. Sept. 30, 1892, BERNARD D. SPIKER (John - Henry) - b. Sept. 2, 1872, at Albright, W. Va. - Living at Bruceton Mills, W. Va. Children:

    i. Nellie Spiker - b. Sept. 3, 1895 -

    ii. Hazel Spiker - b. Sept. 30, 1897 -

    iii. Thelma Spiker - b. Oct. 30, 1904 - d. 1907.

    iv. Bernice Spiker - b. June 25, 1909 - m. Frank Ward Cunningham.

2. Darius Earl - b. Sept. 24, 1877 - m. Lulu Ethel DeWitt.

1165. SILAS M. METHENY (Isaiah - Nathan - James) - b. April 21, 1848, near Rockville, Preston County, W. Va. - d. Sept. 5, 1927, buried at Pisgah, W. Va. - m. Dec. 24, 1868, at Laurel Run, Mary Armena King - b. Nov. 29, 1847, at Laurel Run, W. Va. - d. April 11, 1905, daughter of Albert F. King (Thomas - James) and Hester S. Jenkins (Evan - Thomas) - Enlisted with Co. \K, 3rd. Regt., Potomac Home Brigade, Md. Inft., March 3rd, and mustered out at Baltimore, Md., in 1865 - m. 2nd., Nov. 25, 1908, Mary F. Spiker, daughter of Isaac Spiker. Children by 1st. marriage:

1. Albert Floyd - b. Mar. 3, 1870 - m. Cora Ann Michael.
2. Ida Belle - b. Sept. 15, 1871, Rockville, W. Va. - m. at Albright, W. Va., Oct. 27, 1892, WALTER CUPP - b. Nov. 23, 1871, Bruceton Mills, W. Va., son of Harry Cupp and Hannah Rodeheaver. Children:
   i. Mary Edna Cupp - b. July 30, 1892 - m. John Williams.
   ii. Verna Jeannette Cupp - b. Sept. 22, 1894-m. Clark Rude.
   iii. Dewey Clyde Cupp - b. Sept. 2, 1897 - m. Elsie Rexroad.
   iv. Vivian Merle Cupp - b. Aug. 20, 1902 - m. John Loudenslager.
   v. William Paul Cupp - b. Oct. 8, 1908 - m. Gladys Moore.
3. Anna - b. April 25, 1873 - d. Dec. 9, 1907, buried at Bruceton Mills, W. Va. - m. Nov., 1892, at ————————————————— - JAMES HARVEY BENSON - b. ——————————— - son of ——————————————— - Children:
   i. Otis Benson - b. Aug. 9, 1896 - d. Dec. 13, 1897.
   ii. Earl Benson - b. Nov. 4, 1895 - m. Lorena Scott.
   iii. Violet Benson - b. May 30, 1898 - m. Harry L. Thomas.
   iv. George Benson - b. July 27, 1901 - m. Ada Hilling.
   v. Hobart Benson - b. Aug. 28, 1903 - m. Irene Titchnell.
   vi. Burhl Benson - b. Nov. 15, 1907 - m. Chester L. Liller.
4. Walter - b. Oct. 1, 1875 - m. Oct. 24, 1900, at Albright, W. Va., Oca S. Forman - b. Dec. 21, 1877, daughter of Mathias and Alcinda Forman.
5. Hester Edith - b. Sept. 26, 1876, Rockville, W. Va. - m. Dec. 25, 1894, at Bruceton Mills, W. Va., AMOS M. WOLFE - b. Jan. 20, 1872, Friendsville, Md., son of William Wolfe (Daniel - George, 1752 - 1827). Children:
   i. Faye Wolfe - b. April 21, 1897 - m. P. W. Jenkins.
   ii. Olga Zephyr Wolfe - b. Dec. 11, 1898 - m. Troy Awman.
   iii. George Wallace Wolfe - b. Nov. 24, 1900 - d. June 13, 1903.
   iv. Charles Glen Wolfe - b. Dec. 25, 1903 -

     v. Norma Virginia Wolfe - b. Dec. 21, 1905 - d. Nov. 5, 1908.
     vi. Cecil Eugene Wolfe - b. July 19, 1920.
6. Bessie - b. Jan. 23, 1879, Rockville, W. Va. - m. Feb. 23, 1901, at Bruceton Mills, W. Va. - d. Nov. 19, 1931 - m. JOSHUA HITE GARNER - b. Feb. 5, 1874, son of Simon Henry Garner and Susan Snyder. Children:
     i. Alfred Joe Garner - b. Aug. 11, 1901, Rankin, Pa. - m; Audrey I. Kightlinger.
     ii. Raymond King Garner - b. Apr. 6, 1905, McKeesport, Penn. - m. Garnet Ruth Stewart.
     iii. Harold Waldo Garner - b. Sept. 10, 1922, McKeesport, Penn.
7. Sallie - b. Oct. 28, 1884 - d. Feb. 16, 1907 - m. CHARLES R. FORMAN - b. April 30, 1875, Kingwood, W. Va., son of John E. Forman (Robert).
8. Emmett Earl - b. May 18, 1889 - m. Jennie Nicholls.

11642. DARIUS EARL METHENY (William H. - Isaiah - Nathan - James) - b. Sept. 24, 1877, at Pisgah, W. Va. - m. Lulu Ethel DeWitt - b. Jan. 31, 1887, Terra Alta, W. Va., daughter of Baltus DeWitt and Ella Spindler (of Jonathan Spindler - b. Jan. 20, 1826 - d. Feb. 2, 1914, and Deborah Spindler - b. Jan. 28, 1828 - d. July 5, 1903. Residence, 823 East Jefferson Street, Butler, Penn.
     Children:
1. William Blake - b. June 1, 1910, Pisgah, W. Va.
2. Lillian Eileen - b. July 31, 1911, Pisgah, W. Va. - m. H. D. Whitmore.
3. Herbert DeWitt - b. Nov. 29, 1912, Pisgah, W. Va.
4. Willis King - b. May 10, 1914, Pisgah, W. Va.
5. Pauletta Pearl - b. May 28, 1916, Pisgah, W. Va.

11651. ALBERT FLOYD METHENY (Silas M. - Isaiah - Nathan - James) - b. Mar. 3, 1870, near Laurel Run Church, Grant District, Preston County, W. Va. - m. Mar. 30, 1892, at Bruceton Mills, W. Va., Cora Ann Michael - b. June 7, 1870, Bruceton Mills, W. Va., daughter of William Michael (John) and Rachel Forman (Robert). Residence, near Laurel Run Church.
     Children:
1. Ralph - b. Aug. 2, 1893, Bruceton Mills, W. Va. - d. Sept. 30, 1922, buried at Pisgah, W. Va. Served during World War with 15th Co., 20th Engineers, April 17, 1918, to Dec. 8, 1918; stationed at Camp Meade, Md.; Camp A. A. Humphries, Va.; and Camp Forest, Ga.

2. Mae - b. Mar. 12, 1895 - m. DWIGHT GIBSON - b. Apr. 23, 1903, at Pisgah, W. Va., son of Bruce Gibson (Jonathan - Levi - James - Thomas) and Lillian Blanche (King (George-Thomas - James). Children:
  i. Dallas Dale Gibson - b. Oct. 20, 1931.
3. Hugh - b. June 14, 1898 - m. Elizabeth Walls.
4. Guy - b. Sept. 14, 1900 - m. Inez Burnfield.
5. Ray - b. Dec. 23, 1904 - m. Adelia Michael.

11658. EMMETT EARL METHENY (Silas M. - Isaiah - Nathan-James) - b. May 18, 1889, at Bruceton Mills, W. Va. - m. Jan. 20, 1910, at McKeesport, Penn., Jennie Belle Nicholls - b. Feb. 12, 1888, at McKeesport, Penn., daughter of John H. Nicholls and Mary Frances Douglas. - Residence, 1403 Patterson Street, McKeesport, Penn.
  Children:
  1. Betty Le - b. Sept. 20, 1921, McKeesport, Penn.
  2. Ruth Louise - b. July 13, 1924, McKeesport, Penn.
  3. Robert Earl - b. Nov. 29, 1925, McKeesport, Penn.

116513. HUGH METHENY (Albert F. - Silas M. - Isaiah - Nathan - James) - b. June 14, 1898, near Laurel Run Church, Grant District, Preston County, W. Va. - m. Elizabeth Walls - b. Dec. 16, 1903, at Pisgah, W. Va., daughter of Homer Walls (Ami F. - Charles - James) and Disa Wolf (John A. - Augustine - Samuel). Residence, 917 Charles Avenue, Morgantown, W. Va.
  Children:
  1. Fredia Oneda - b. July 20, 1923, Pisgah, W. Va.
  2. Ronald Hugh - b. Nov. 17, 1926, Morgantown, W. Va.
  3. Twila Mae - b. Aug. 15, 1930, Morgantown, W. Va.

116514. GUY METHENY (Albert - Silas - Isaiah - Nathan - James) - b. Sept. 14, 1900 - m. Sept. 5, 1928, at Pontiac, Mich., Inez Burnfield - b. May 17, 1905, Washington, Penn., daughter of Perry Burnfield and Addie Hufford.
  Children:
  Ralph William and Richard Frank (twins) - b. June 12, 1929, at Detroit, Mich. - d. June 28, 1929, buried at Royal Oak, Mich.
  3. Kenneth Eugene - b. Sept. 27, 1930, at Detroit, Mich.
  4. Lola Lee - b. Aug. 31, 1932, at Detroit, Mich.

EDWARD D. RYAN
OF PISGAH, WEST VIRGINIA,
AND SOME OF HIS DESCENDANTS

1. EDWARD D. RYAN - b. Aug. 15, 1833, Dublin, Ireland - d. April 8, 1887, buried on his farm, four miles north of Pisgah, W. Va. Son of Daniel and Catherine Ryan, of Dublin, Ireland. Edward D. Ryan, the immigrant, came to America at the age of twelve years. Served as a private during the Civil War with Co. B, 14th W. Va. Inft. - m. Elizabeth Wolfe - b. Aug. 30, 1833, Cranesville, W. Va. - d. April 1, 1900, buried on the Ryan farm, four miles north of Pisgah, W. Va. Daughter of Augustine Wolfe (of Jacob) and Julia A. Everly (of Henry Everly). Children:

   1. Thomas - b. Mar. 10, 1858, at Pisgah, W. Va. - m. Adelia King.
   2. Julia Ann - b. Sept. 2, 1859, at Pisgah, W. Va. - m. Hosea King. (see King Genealogy).
   3. Daniel - b. May 22, 1861, at Pisgah, W. Va. - m. Dora Alice King.
   4. Ross - b. Mar. 23, 1863, at Pisgah, W. Va.-m. Rebecca Clark.
   5. Sanfred - b. May 23, 1866, at Pisgah, W. Va. - m. Ida May Maust.
   6. Effie Elizabeth - b. Oct. 18, 1875, at Pisgah, W. Va. - d. Dec. 31, 1922 - m. Ralph Christopher. (see Christopher Genealogy).

11. THOMAS RYAN (Edward D. - Daniel) - b. Mar. 10, 1858, at Pisgah, W. Va. - m. at Brandonville, W. Va., Aug. 17, 1878, Adelia King - b. Mar. 17, 1859, daughter of Alpheus King (James) and Margaret Jenkins (Evan - Thomas). Children:

   1. Leavie A. - b. Mar. 24, 1879 - m. WILLIAM E. SPEEL-MAN - b. June 17, 1875, son of John P. Speelman (b. Feb. 17, 1830 - d. Sept. 27, 1905) and Catherine Turney (b. Nov. 3, 1832 - d. Mar. 22, 1909). Children of Leavie and William E. Speelman:
      i. Pauline Speelman - b. July 4, 1898 - m. Albert Wheeler.
      ii. Diora R. Speelman - b. Aug. 30, 1902 - m. Alvin Arnold.
      iii. Carlus Earl Speelman - b. Jan. 24, 1909, Bruceton Mills, W. Va.
      iv. Jessie Elizabeth Speelman - b. Mar. 12, 1915, Bruceton Mills, W. Va.
   2. Charles G. - b. Jan. 17, 1881 - m. Daisy P. Christopher.

3. Mollie M. - b. May 23, 1883 - m. at Mountain Grove Church, Dec. 19, 1903, FREEMAN RAY HILEMAN - b. ——— - son of Wesley Hileman and Lulu Galloway. Children of Mollie and Freeman Hileman.

   i. Clyde Hileman - b. July 4, 1901 - m. Emma Harshbarger.
   ii. Gilbert Hileman - b. Mar. 6, 1905 - m. Mary Conn.
   iii. Edward Hileman - b. Apr. 12, 1906 - d. in 1906 - b. at Mountain Grove.
   iv. Merle Hileman - b. July 27, 1907 - m. Oral Grover.
   v. Troy Hileman - b. Mar. 11, 1909 - m. Jane Benson.
   vi. Erma Hileman - b. July 24, 1910 -
   vii. Marshall Hileman - b. Dec. 28, 1911 -
   viii. Wilma Hileman - b. Oct. 10, 1913 - m. Walter Teets.
   ix. Adelia Hileman - b. Oct. 19, 1915 -
   x. Jesse Hileman - b. Apr. 25, 1917 -
   xi. Dorothy Hileman - b. Aug. 30, 1920 -
   xii. Berwyn Hileman - b. Oct. 1, 1922 -
   xiii. Delmar Hileman - b. Feb. 3, 1925 -

4. Maggie E. - b. Aug. 19, 1885, at Pisgah, W. Va. - m. Oct. 27, 1900, at Kingwood, W. Va., CHARLES REMSEN MICHAEL - b. Feb. 1, 1880, son of Phillip Michael and Elva Walls. Children of Maggie and Charles Michael:

   i. Coral Blanche Michael - b. Mar. 10, 1902-d. Jan. 26, 1904.
   ii. Adelia Michael - b. June 28, 1903 - m. Ray Metheny.
   iii. Cecil Floyd Michael - b. Sept. 13, 1906 - m. Mildred Wolf.
   iv. Thomas Bunker Michael - b. Sept. 9, 1909 - m. Ruby Taylor.
   v. Julia Irene Michael - b. Oct. 17, 1915 -

5. Nellie F. - b. Feb. 12, 1887 - m. Mar. 25, 1908, at Uniontown, Penn., CHARLES RAY UPHOLD - b. Nov. 19, 1885, son of James Uphold and Elizabeth Guthrie. Children of Nellie and Charles Uphold:

   i. Beryl Uphold - b. Nov. 15, 1908 -
   ii. Helen Uphold - b. May 24, 1910 -
   iii. Donald Uphold - b. July 27, 1913 -
   iv. Dorothy Uphold - b. Oct. 7, 1915 -
   v. Ray Uphold - b. July 3, 1923 -

6. Eddie Harrison - b. Jan. 22, 1899 - m. Ethel Bailey.
7. Okey Marshall - b. Aug. 19, 1892 - m. Mary Weaver.
8. Jesse McKinley - b. July 7, 1894 - m. May Bryte.
9. Sadie Wilma - b. Aug. 4, 1896, Laurel Iron Works - m. Dec. 27, 1920, at Uniontown, Penn., OKEY FORMAN - b. Jan.

4, 1895, son of Jesse Forman (Samuel - b. 1843 - Jesse) and Shiloah Christopher (Jehu - John). Children of Sadie and Okey Forman:

   i. Berwyn Dale Forman - b. Jan. 30, 1921 - d. Jan. 4, 1926, buried in Park Cemetery, Uniontown, Pa.

   ii. Elinor Jean Forman - b. Sept. 9, 1924.

   iii. Robert Ray Forman - b. Jan. 29, 1930.

10. Alpheus Ray - b. Aug. 19, 1901 - m. Evaline Moyers.

13. DANIEL RYAN (Edward D. - Daniel) - b. May 22, 1861, at Pisgah, W. Va. - m. at Laurel Run, May 6, 1883, Dora Alice King - b. Aug. 30, 1861 - d. April 16, 1915, buried at Pisgah, W. Va., daughter of Alpheus King (James) and Margaret Jenkins (Evan - Thomas). (see King Genealogy).

   Children:

1. Harry - b. Sept. 27, 1884 - m. Emma Everly.
2. Emma - b. Aug. 19, 1888 - m. Thurman Christopher (see Christopher Genealogy).
3. Ralph - b. Sept. 7, 1890 - m. Avis King.
4. Grant - b. Jan. 1, 1894 - m. Ettie Brand.

14. ROSS F. RYAN (Edward D. - Daniel) - b. Mar. 23, 1863, at Pisgah, W. Va. - m. July 21, 1887, Rebecca Jane Clark, who was born April 14, 1871.

   Children:

1. Lou Ada - b. Aug. 26, 1888 - d. Jan. 22, 1895 - buried in Ryan Cemetery.
2. Roy Gilbert - b. Feb. 11, 1890 - m. Flora Gordy.
3. Elizabeth Florence - b. Feb. 7, 1892 - m. April 5, 1911, to NOBLE CARLYLE McCORMICK - b. —————— son of Noble McCormick. - Children:
   i. Virginia McCormick - b. Feb. 19, 1912.
   ii. William McCormick - b. Aug. 27, 1913.
4. Clara Belle - b. Oct. 11, 1893 - m. Oct. 13, 1910, GLEN STEWART - b. Oct. 15, 1882, —————— - son of Scott Stewart and Cora Arnett. Children:
   i. Louise Stewart - b. Mar. 18, 1918, at Steubenville, Ohio.
   ii. Glen Stewart, Jr.-b. Nov. 22, 1921, at Monongah, W. Va.
5. Lulu Gay - b. June 29, 1895 - m. WILLIAM ROSE - b. —————— - son of —————— - Children:
   i. Marline Rose - b. ——————
6. Hazel Blanche - b. Sept. 20, 1896.

7. Evelyn Marie - b. April 14, 1898 - m. WARREN GIR-ARDIN - b. ——————— - son of ——————— - Children:
   i. Marlyn Girardin - b. ———————
8. Beulah Gladys - b. Jan. 2, 1901 - m. June 13, 1923, to WIL-LIAM J. GREEN - b. ——————— - son of ——————— - Children:
   i. William Richard Green - b. July 1, 1925.
9. Donald Clark - b. Feb. 12, 1903 - d. Mar. 28, 1908, buried in Ryan Cemetery.

15. SANFRED RYAN (Edward D. - Daniel) - b. May 23, 1866, at Pisgah, W. Va. - m. Aug. 27, 1886, near Laurel Run Church, Ida May Maust - b. Dec. 31, 1869, at Pisgah, W. Va., daughter of William Maust.

   Children:

   1. Nora Pearl - b. Jan. 19, 1889, at Pisgah, W. Va. - m. June 25, 1913, at Morgantown, W. Va., JAMES MYERS - b. Oct. 1, 1891, son of Alpheus and Hannah Myers. Children of Nora and James Myers:

      i. Iona May Myers - b. Dec. 19, 1915.
      ii. Wanda Helen Myers - b. June 29, 1918.
      iii. James Marion Myers - b. May 30, 1921.
      iv. Omer Earl Myers - b. Oct. 15, 1923.
      v. Willard Delbert Myers - b. Oct. 10, 1925.
      vi. Donald Edgar Myers - b. Aug. 20, 1927.
      vii. Franklin Bendell Myers - b. Sept. 19, 1929.
      viii. Ida Elizabeth Myers - b. Sept. 17, 1931.

   2. Henry Franklin - b. Mar. 8, 1892 - m. Effie Everly.
   3. Dacie Viola - b. May 14, 1894 - m. Roy Wheeler (see Wheeler Genealogy).
   4. Hobart Sylvanus - b. Sept. 21, 1896 - m. Hazel Cupp.
   5. Minnie Coral - b. Oct. 15, 1898 - m. Mar. 20, 1920, HAR-OLD THOMAS - b. Apr. 4, 1899, son of Wayne Thomas and Rosie Hastings. Children of Minnie and Harold Thomas:

      i. Harold Sanfred Thomas - b. July 17, 1920, Allison, Penn.
      ii. Arthelia Vivian Thomas - b. Apr. 13, 1923, Allison, Pa.
      iii. Vertrude Leah Thomas - b. May 25, 1926, Brandonville, W. Va.

   6. William Edward - b. Mar. 1, 1901 - m. Rubie Ringer.
   7. Zettie Gertrude - b. June 23, 1904 - d. July 28, 1924 - m. at

Bruceton Mills, W. Va., MARSHALL METHENY. Children:

   i. James Sanfred Metheny - b. and d. Oct. 15, 1920, buried on Ryan farm.

   ii. Warden Ryan Metheny - b. Sept. 3, 1922.

8. Effie Ocie - b. Sept. 21, 1906, at Pisgah, W. Va. - m. at Brandonville, W. Va., Mar. 15, 1924, ORVAL GEORGE RUSH - b. May 25, 1901, son of Milton H. Rush. Children:

   i. Thresia Mildred Rush - b. Jan. 23, 1925 - d. Feb. 17, 1925. Buried at Pisgah, W. Va.

   ii. Retha Jean Rush - b. May 23, 1926, Friendsville, Md.

   iii. Vera Helen Rush - b. July 14, 1928, Friendsville, Md.

9. Julietta Elizabeth - b. Mar. 9, 1908 - m. at Oakland, Md., ELMER MOOMAW. Children:

   i. Ida Vaughn Moomaw - b. Aug. 4, 1928.

10. Willard Ward - b. Jan. 28, 1910 -

11. Playford Clayton - b. Feb. 29, 1912 -

112. CHARLES GARFIELD RYAN (Thomas - Edward D. - Daniel) - b. Jan. 17, 1881, at Pisgah, W. Va. - m. July 29, 1905, at "The Oaks" on Cheat River, Daisy Christopher - b. Nov. 6, 1877, at Pisgah, W. Va., daughter of Irvin E. Christopher (John) and Mary King (Thomas - James).
   Children:
1. Cecil Gail - b. May 27, 1916 -

116. EDDIE HARRISON RYAN (Thomas - Edward D. - Daniel) - b. Jan. 22, 1889, at Bruceton Mills, W. Va. - m. at Uniontown, Pa., Dec. 25, 1914, Ethel Bailey - b. Apr. 22, 1898, Uniontown, Penn., daughter of Edgar and Myrtle Bailey.
   Children:
1. Donald - b. May 27, 1916 -

2. Doris Jean - b. Aug. 24, 1921 - d. Feb. 12, 1922, buried in Park Cemetery, Uniontown, Penn.

117. OKEY MARSHALL RYAN (Thomas - Edward D. - Daniel) - b. Aug. 19, 1892, at Bruceton Mills, W. Va. - m. at Uniontown, Pa., July 29, 1914, Mary Weaver - b. July 11, 1893, at Scottdale, Penn., daughter of Harry and Elvira Weaver.
   Children:
1. Madalyn - b. Dec. 22, 1915 -

2. Harry - b. Dec. 6, 1917 -

3. Wilma Jean - b. Nov. 1, 1919 -

4. Okey, Jr. - b. Mar. 5, 1922 -
5. James - b. June 2, 1924 -
6. William - b. June 28, 1926 -
7. Patricia Elaine - b. Mar. 26, 1930 -

118. JESSE McKINLEY RYAN (Thomas - Edward D. - Daniel)
- b. July 7, 1894 - m. at Bruceton Mills, W. Va., Oct. 5, 1916,
Leota May Bryte - b. June 17, 1896, daughter of Alvy Nolen
Bryte (b. Sept. 20, 1864) (David) and Mary E. Forman (b. July
4, 1871).
  Children:
 1. Paul Arthur - b. Jan. 1, 1919 -
 2. Eleanor Irene - b. May 18, 1922 -
 3. Beatrice Jane - b. May 10, 1925 -

11-10. ALPHEUS RAY RYAN (Thomas - Edward D. - Daniel) -
b. Aug. 19, 1901 - m. Aug. 27, 1924, at Brandonville, W. Va.,
Evaline Leone Moyers - b. June 6, 1904, at Hazelton, W. Va.,
daughter of Samuel F. Moyers (George W. - Samuel) and Jennie Glover (Henry C. - Samuel).
  Children:
 1. Doris Jean - b. Feb. 25, 1925 -

131. HARRY RYAN (Daniel - Edward D. - Daniel) - b. Sept. 27,
1884 - m. Sept. 19, 1907, Emma Everly - b. Nov. 14, 1888,
daughter of Mintare Everly (John L. - b. 1837 - Lewis - b. 1811
- Henry - b. 1785) and Mary L. Speelman.
  Children:
 1. Mildred - b. Feb. 15, 1908 -
 2. Herbert - b. Sept. 24, 1909 -
 3. Quentin - b. July 20, 1912 -
 4. Gilbert - b. Oct. 28, 1914 -
 5. Elizabeth - b. March 10, 1917 -
 6. Mary - b. Jan. 11, 1931 -

133. RALPH RYAN (Daniel - Edward D. - Daniel) - b. Sept. 7,
1890, Pisgah, W. Va. - m. Mar. 31, 1914, at Bruceton Mills, W.
Va., Hattie Avis King - b. Sept. 20, 1893, at Parkersburg, W.
Va., daughter of Zar King (William J. - Thomas - James) and
Lizzie Cale (Jesse - Jacob).
  Children:
 1. Vada Alice - b. Mar. 23, 1916, at Pisgah, W. Va. - d. Jan. 5,
  1926, buried at Pisgah, W. Va.

2. Gladys Merle - b. Aug. 1, 1919 -
3. Ralph Gail - b. May 18, 1921 -

142. ROY GILBERT RYAN (Ross F. - Edward D. - Daniel) - b.
Feb. 11, 1890 - m. Sept. 7, 1914, Flora Gordy - b. Mar. 9, 1889,
daughter of ————————.

Children:
1. Louise - b. Nov. 20, 1918 -
2. Hazel - b. Aug. 24, 1919 -

152. HENRY FRANKLIN RYAN (Sanfred - Edward D. - Daniel) - b. Mar. 8, 1892 - m. Oct. 11, 1913, at Cumberland, Md.,
Effie Everly - b. Mar. 18, 1895, at Pisgah, W. Va., daughter of
James Spencer Everly (Henry - Lewis - Henry) and Mary Ann
McNair (Andrew S.).

Children:
1. Mary Ida - b. Dec. 24, 1914 - d. Dec. 3, 1932.
2. Eldrich Ray - b. Feb. 11, 1916 - d. Dec. 28, 1924, buried at
Pisgah, W. Va.
3. Ester Marie - b. Dec. 20, 1918 -
4. Wilma Lucille - b. Mar. 28, 1920 - d. May 18, 1930, buried at
Pisgah, W. Va.
5. Geraldine May - b. Nov. 28, 1921 -
6. Coraline Waneida - b. Apr. 15, 1923 -
7. James Sanfred - b. Apr. 15, 1925 -
8. Lynton Ray - b. Feb. 11, 1927 -
9. Effie Valgene - b. July 16, 1928 -
10. Emily Cathaleen - b. Apr. 22, 1930 -

154. HOBART SYLVANUS RYAN (Sanfred - Edward D. - Daniel) - b. Sept. 21, 1896, Pisgah, W. Va. Enlisted in Army Medical Department, Aug. 28, 1918, Private (3042518) Kingwood,
W. Va., and honorably discharged July 8, 1919, at Otisville, N.
Y. Served with U. S. A. Gen. Hospital No. 8 - m. at Morgantown, W. Va., Hazel Marie Cupp - b. June 29, 1899, near Elliottsville, Penn., daughter of Union Marshall Cupp and Nancy
Cupp.

Children:
1. Warren Sylvanus - b. Sept. 15, 1920, Pisgah, W. Va.
2. Minnis Bernice - b. Aug. 20, 1922, Pisgah, W. Va.
3. Clifford Lavard - b. April 5, 1924, Elliottsville, Pa.
4. Clayton Lavan - b. Jan. 25, 1927, Bruceton Mills, W. Va.

156. WILLIAM EDWARD RYAN (Sanfred - Edward D. - Daniel) - b. Mar. 1, 1901 - m. July 22, 1922, Rubie Ringer - b. June 17, 1905, daughter of Ezra Ringer (George) and Emma Rodeheaver.

Children:

1. Marjorie Lou - b. Nov. 30, 1925, at Allison, Pa.
2. Donald Edward - b. Dec. 10, 1927, at Brandonville, W. Va.
3. Elaine Ruth - b. Oct. 16, 1928, at Brandonville, W. Va.
4. Alberta Virginia - b. Aug. 14, 1931, at Brandonville, W. Va.

THE STREET FAMILY
IN PRESTON COUNTY, WEST VIRGINIA

1. JACKSON STREET - b. at Flintstone, Md., and with his family settled near Hazelton, Grant District, Preston County, W. Va., in 1815.
     Children:
     1. Son unknown.
     2. Melinda - m. John Burke.
     3. Harriet - m. ——————— Saunders.
     4. Sarah - m. Richard Glover, son of Amos Glover.
     5. George Washington - b. Nov. 3, 1806 - d. June 11, 1898 - m. Ethelinda Kelley.

15. GEORGE WASHINGTON STREET (Jackson) - b. Nov. 3, 1806, Flintstone, Md. - d. June 11, 1898, buried at Pisgah, W. Va. - m. Ethelinda Kelley - b. Sept. 22, 1809, at Brandonville, W. Va. - d. Dec. 21, 1893, buried at Pisgah, W. Va., daughter of William Kelley (John) and Hannah Brandon (Alexander).
     Children:
     1. William Jackson - b. Mar. 21, 1831 - d. Apr. 17, 1925 - m. Huldah Benson.
     2. Elizabeth H. - b. Dec. 14, 1833 - d. July 20, 1917 - m. William J. King (see King Genealogy).
     3. Berthenda K. - b. ——————— - d. July 5, 1862 - m. Jackson Gilmore.
     4. Mary Jane - b. ——————— - d. ——————— - buried at Austin, Preston County - m. Arthur Bailey.
     5. Edgar S. - Accidently killed Aug. 12, 1861. Served during Civil War with Co. H., 3rd W. Va., Inft.
     6. Emma K. - b. April 23, 1846 - living in 1933 - m. July 25, 1865, at Bruceton Mills, W. Va., WILLIAM CLARK MYERS - b. Dec. 3, 1841 - d. May 22, 1916, buried at Pisgah, W. Va. Children:
          i. Amelia Jane Myers - b. Dec. 22, 1865 - d. Apr. 15, 1925 - m. ——————— Turner.
          ii. Edgar Grant Myers - b. Oct. 1, 1867 - d. Dec. 11, 1896.
          iii. Rufus C. Myers - b. June 3, 1870 - d. Aug. 13, 1914.
          iv. Lauretta A. Myers - b. Oct. 12, 1872 - d. ———————
          v. Mary E. Myers - b. Dec. 12, 1874 - d. Oct. 7, 1929 - m. ——————— Murphy.
          vi. Harrison Elza Myers - b. Apr. 21, 1877 -

vii. Joseph C. Myers - b. Oct. 9, 1879 -

viii. James Washington Myers - b. Oct. 18, 1882 - d. Aug. 9, 1905.

ix. Hannah E. Maude Myers - b. Mar. 16, 1885 - d. Feb. 25, 1894.

x. Charles F. Myers - b. July 16, 1887 -

xi. Perry Russell Myers - b. Dec. 1, 1889 - d. 1922.

7. Harriet S. - b. Apr. 26, 1849 - d. Jan. 1, 1927 - m. Adam Wolfe (see Wolfe Genealogy).

151. WILLIAM JACKSON STREET (George W. - Jackson) - b. Mar. 21, 1831 - d. Apr. 17, 1925, buried at Rowlesburg, W. Va. - Served during Civil War with Co. C., 3rd W. Va. Cavalry, as a private - m. Aug. 23, 1855, Huldah Benson - b. Oct. 9, 1830, at Bruceton Mills, W. Va. - d. Aug. 17, 1908, buried at Rowlesburg, W. Va. - daughter of James Benson, 1794 - 1879 (William) and Melinda or Sarah Lewis, 1800 - 1877 (Henry).

Children:

1. Jesse C. - b. Feb. 20, 1859 - d. Aug. 11, 1880, buried at Terra Alta, W. Va.

2. Clara J. - b. Oct. 4, 1861 - m. E. T. Brown.

3. Sarah E. - b. Mar. 10, 1863 - m. Samuel Ayersman.

4. Blanche B. - b. Aug. 23, 1866 - m. JOSEPH N. HOOTON - b. —————— - d. —————— - son of ——————

Children:

i. Norwood D. Hooton - b. June 17, 1888 - m. Ruby Wiles.

ii. Margaret R. Hooton - b. Nov. 4, 1890 - d. Jan. 2, 1931, buried at Rowlesburg, W. Va. - m. W. J. Phillips.

iii. Nellie E. Hooton - b. Dec. 22, 1893-m. E. E. McMichael.

iv. Joseph C. Hooton - b. May 18, 1898 - m. Nellie Shaffer.

v. Benson C. Hooton - b. May 26, 1906-m. Naoma Gibbons.

5. Minnie May - b. Oct. 6, 1869 - d. Dec. 15, 1895, buried at Rowlesburg, W. Va.

6. Lizzie - b. Sept. 23, 1872 - d. Oct. 5, 1893, buried at Rowlesburg, W. Va.

SOME DESCENDANTS OF JOB THORP.

1. JOB THORP - b. about 1730 - d. about 1762, lived in Middlesex County, N. J., during the middle of the Eighteenth century. His wife, Sarah, was born April 7, 1733. More recent generations of this family added the letter "e" to the name, making it Thorpe, while the old Bible records spelled it Thorp.

   Children:
   1. Mary - b. April 30, 1752.
   2. Hannah - b. Oct. 12, 1753.
   3. Rheuben - b. Jan. 16, 1755 - d. Feb. 8, 1848 - m. Hannah Lobdell.
   4. Jennet - b. Mar. 21, 1757.
   5. Benjamin - b. Feb. 23, 1759.
   6. Eunes - b. June 19, 1761.

   After the death of Job Thorp his widow, Sarah, married WILLIAM SPENCER, who was born May 8, 1739. Children:
   i. Nathan Spencer - b. July 7, 1764.
   ii. Jacob Spencer - b. Feb. 4, 1766.
   iii. Sarah Spencer - b. Oct. 18, 1767.
   iv. William Spencer - b. Nov. 25, 1770.
   v. Elizabeth Spencer - b. July 13, 1772.
   vi. Morris Spencer - b. Oct. 26, 1773.

13. RHEUBEN THORPE (Job) - b. Jan. 16, 1755, Woodbridge Township, Middlesex County, N. J. - d. Feb. 8, 1848, buried on his farm near Ohio Pyle, Fayette County, Penn. - m. Aug. 23, 1778, Hannah Lobdell - b. Sept. 11, 1760 - d. Nov. 14, 1826, buried near Ohio Pyle, Penn. - This family came to Fayette County (Hist. of Fayette, by Ellis, 1882) in 1792, and purchased one hundred and fifty acres of land of the Askins tract, for one hundred pounds. Tradition has it that this family lived under an oak tree until they could construct a house. On this farm was an orchard of early bearing which was almost wholly destroyed by a storm in July, 1851. Some of the trees were taken up and carried a distance of half a mile and nearly everything in the line of the storm was destroyed. Rheuben Thorpe formerly had a public house and carried on a distillery in the days when the old Turkeyfoot road was one of the lines of travel from Somerset to Uniontown. Rheuben Thorpe served during the

Revolution between 1775 and 1780. The record of his services is found in the Adjutant General's Office, State of New Jersey; in Department of Interior, Bureau of Pensions; and in the Adjutant General's Office, War Department, Washington, D. C. (1378018). In the cemetery on the old Thorpe homestead near Ohio Pyle, Penn., is a large monument erected "to the memory of Rheuben Thorpe," by his descendants, and a bronze marker has been placed at his grave by the Monongahelia Chapter, Daughters of the American Revolution.

Children:

1. Hannah - b. May 23, 1779 - d. Oct. 10, 1851 - m. ————— Graham.
2. David - b. Mar. 9, 1781 - d. Feb. 2, 1828.
3. Mary - b. July 28, 1783 - d. —————.
4. John - b. July 4, 1785 - d. Feb. 10, 1839.
5. Rheuben - b. July 24, 1787 - d. —————.
6. Job - b. Mar. 6, 1790 - d. —————.
7. James - b. June 28, 1793 - d. July 30, 1881 - m. Huldah Rush.
8. Asa - b. Feb. 22, 1796 - d. —————.
9. William - b. Apr. 26, 1798 - d. Oct. 5, 1865 - m. Marion Mitchell.

137. JAMES THORPE (Rheuben - Job) - b. June 28, 1793 - d. July 30, 1881, buried near Ohio Pyle, Penn. - m. Mar. 16, 1815, Huldah Rush - b. Sept. 11, 1796 - d. July 28, 1878.

Children:

1. Thankful - b. Jan. 10, 1816, Ohio Pyle, Penn. - d. Dec. 18, 1901, buried at Mt. Nebo Church, Pleasant District, Preston County, W. Va. - Lived near Rockville, W. Va. - m. Mar. 8, 1846, at Ohio Pyle, Penn., EVERHART LISTON - b. Mar. 22, 1822 - d. May 9, 1888, buried at Mt. Nebo Church, near Rockville, W. Va., son of John Liston, 1777 - 1831, and Elizabeth Rubel. Children:

   i. Martha McCuen Liston - b. Jan. 16, 1847, Ohio Pyle, Pa. - d. Dec. 19, 1909, buried at Valley Point, W. Va. - m. Newton Graham.

   ii. Eliza Jane Liston - b. Dec. 3, 1849, Ohio Pyle, Penn. - d. Mar. 6, 1930, buried at Bruceton Mills, W. Va. - m. Thaddeus Cunningham (see Cunningham Genealogy).

   iii. John Marshall Liston - b. Aug. 4, 1852, Ohio Pyle, Penn. - d. Sept. 2, 1925, buried at Mt. Nebo, near Rockville, W. Va. - m. 1st., Rachel Cale; 2nd., Minnie Street.

   iv. Huldah Adaline Liston - b. Nov. 7, 1855, Ohio Pyle, Penn. - m. Evan J. Bowermaster, merchant, lived in

Kingwood, W. Va. Children:
   a. Marshall Conner Bowermaster - m. Marie McCabe.
   b. Blanche C. Bowermaster - m. Charles Edward Hawkins.
   c. Ira Benjamin - m. Nettie Mae Hawkins.
   d. Mary Bell Bowermaster - m. Arthur B. Spencer.
   e. John L. Bowermaster - m. Mary Robinson.
   v. George Arthur Liston - b. Sept. 29, 1858, Ohio Pyle, Penn. - m. Mitchel Nestor.
2. Adaline - b. June 4, 1820, Ohio Pyle, Penn. - d. Dec. 27, 1903, buried at Ohio Pyle, Penn. - m. Jan. 20, 1838, SYLVESTER SKINNER - b. Apr. 12, 1818 - d. Jan. 17, 1870, buried at Ohio Pyle, Pa., son of William Skinner. Sylvester Skinner was one of a family of twenty-one children, of whom all the boys were Baptist ministers. - Children of Adaline and Sylvester Skinner:
   i. Sarah Jane Skinner - b. Jan. 29, 1839 - d. Mar. 23, 1915 - m. Francis Marion Cunningham (see Cunningham Genealogy).
   ii. Sabina Ellen Skinner - b. Feb. 24, 1841 - d. Jan. ——, 1921 - m. John W. Earle, lived at Spencer, Iowa.
   iii. James Thorpe Skinner - b. Feb. 10, 1843 - d. during the Civil War.
   iv. David Skinner - b. Feb. 4, 1845 - d. July ——, 1921.
   v. Jefferson Skinner - died at the age of eight years.
   vi. Abraham Lincoln Skinner - b. Feb. 12, 1849 - d. Dec. 12, 1917.
   vii. Tabitha Skinner - b. Aug. 11, 1851 - d. April 5, 1923.
   viii. John Marshall Skinner - died at the age of two years.
   ix. George Fremont Skinner - b. Feb. 11, 1856 - d. Sept. 18, 1920.
   x. Marcellus Coburn Skinner - b. May 4, 1858 - d. ————.
   xi. Ella Florence Skinner - b. Feb. 13, 1861 - d. 1865.
3. Thomas Jefferson - b. Dec. 1, 1817 - d. June, 1862 - m. Elizabeth Skinner.
4. Michael Pane - b. Sept. 3, 1825 -

139. WILLIAM THORPE (Rheuben - Job) - b. April 26, 1798, in Fayette County, Penn. - d. Oct. 5, 1865, buried near Ohio Pyle, Penn. - m. Marion Mitchell - b. Oct. 21, 1802 - d. Sept. 24, 1865 - buried near Ohio Pyle, Penn., daughter of Thomas Mitchell - b. 1754 - d. Nov. 1, 1831, and Sarah Hyatt Lowell - b. 1757.
   Children:
1. Thomas - b. Sept. 3, 1823 - d. Nov. 2, 1893 - Rebecca Acklin.

2. Tobitha - b. July 20, —— - d. ——————- m. Rev. Swasie.
3. Rheuben - b. Oct. 6, 1826 - d. Jan. 6, 1900 - m. Ann Collins.
4. Sarah - b. Nov. 6, 1831 - d. Aug. 15, 1884 - m. Henry Price.
5. Elisha-b. Nov. 10, 1838- died during Civil War, Jan. 6, 1864.
6. Rachel - b. Feb. 4, 1834 - d. Aug. 20, 1917 - m. William Stull.
7. Elizabeth - b. Aug. 24, 1836 - d. Mar. 2, 1926 - m. Cuthbert Downer.
8. David - b. May 12, 1841 - d. June 14, 1932 - m. Alice Bellsesfield.
9. Brownfield - b. Aug. 9, 1845 - d. Dec. 30, 1924 - m. Margaret Jacks.
10. Margaret - b. Jan. 30, 1850 - living in 1933 - m. William Glotfelty.

1373. THOMAS JEFFERSON THORPE (James - Rheuben - Job) - b. Dec. 1, 1817, at Ohio Pyle, Penn. - d. June 1, 1864, buried in National Cemetery, Vicksburg, Tenn. - Enlisted for service during Civil War, Oct. 3, 1862, at Waukon, Iowa, served with Company A, 27th Regiment, Iowa Vol. - m. Jan. 20, 1839, Elizabeth Skinner - b. May 4, 1820, Mill Run, Penn. - d. June 1897, buried at Decorah, Iowa, daughter of Robert Skinner and Sarah Willis.

Children:

1. Louisa - b. Feb. 28, 1844, at Ohio Pyle, Penn. - d. Sept. 10, 1889, buried in Stevens County, Kansas, at the now abandoned town of Dermot - m. Dec. 25, 1861, at Rossville, Alamakee County, Iowa, by David Skinner, Esq., to DANIEL B. RODERICK - b. May 18, 1839, Fayette County, Penn. - d. June 25, 1911, buried at Sharon, Kan. - of German descent, spelled Rotruck before leaving Pennsylvania. Children:

   i. Willis J. Roderick - b. Dec. 18, 1862 - m. Susan Rule.
   ii. Ida M. Roderick - b. Feb. 4, 1867, Rising Sun, Iowa - m. Nov. 25, 1886, in Polk County, Mo., Ralph H. Knight - living in Windom, Minn.
   iii. Florella V. Roderick - b. Nov. 9, 1868 - d. April 12, 1873.
   iv. Indiana J. Roderick - b. Dec. 6, 1870 - m. W. H. Huffaker, Sharon, Kan.
   v. Phoebe Lillian Roderick - b. July 20, 1873 - d. Aug. 19, 1873.
   vi. Catherine E. Roderick - b. Nov. 10, 1875 - m. L. E. Baker, living in Wildmore, Kan.
   vii. Daniel David Roderick - b. Dec. 28, 1878 - d. Aug. 29, 1879.
   viii. Oscar Claude Roderick - b. Dec. 7, 1885 - d. July 28, 1886.

2. James Madison - b. Sept. ——, 1845 - d. July 4, —— - m. Caroline Holmes.

3. William - b. 1849, Ohio Pyle, Penn. - d. 1850, buried at Dubuque, Iowa.

4. Adaline - b. Apr. 2, 1855, Rossville, Iowa - m. MELVIN BLACKMARR - b. Nov. 6, 1850, Fairfield, Ind., son of Edwin Blackmarr and Annie Washburn. Children:
   i. William Thorpe Blackmarr - b. Sept. 4, 1887, at Decorah, Iowa.

5. David C. - b. Feb. ——. 1860, Rossville, Iowa - d. —————— - buried at St. Louis, Mo. - m. Mattie Gibson. No children.

1391. THOMAS THORPE (William - Rheuben - Job) - b. Sept. 3, 1823, at Ohio Pyle, Penn. - d. Nov. 2, 1893, buried at Ohio Pyle, Penn. - m. Rebecca Acklin - b. Aug. 26, 1826, near Uniontown, Pa. - d. Feb. 28, 1898, buried at Ohio Pyle, Penn.
   Children:
   1. Alice - b. —————— d. —————— - m. Thomas Mitchell.
   2. Mary Edith - b. Feb. 8, 1848, Ohio Pyle, Penn. - d. Dec. 8, 1919, buried in Thorpe Cemetery, Ohio Pyle, Penn. - m. Nov. 6, 1873, ALEXANDER H. COUGHANOUR - b. 1846 - d. 1929, buried in Thorpe Cemetery near Ohio Pyle, Penn.
   3. Ellen - b. —————— - d. —————— - m. Arthur Patten.
   4. John Swayse - b. —————— - d. —————— - m. Phoebe Mitchell.
   5. Carrie - b. —————— - d. —————— - m. Romulous Ritenour.

1393. REUBEN THORPE (William - Rheuben - Job) - b. Oct. 6, 1826, Ohio Pyle, Penn. - d. Jan. 6, 1900, Thorpe Farm - buried in Thorpe Cemetery, Ohio Pyle, Penn. - m. Sept. 11, 1851, at Stonersville, Penn., Ann Collins - b. Jan. 10, 1829 - d. April 28, 1898, buried in Thorpe Cemetery, daughter of Henry Collins and Elizabeth Shaw.
   Children:
   1. William Henry - b. July 28, 1852 - d. Jan., 1928 - m. Jane Rush.
   2. Mary Elizabeth - b. June 23, 1854 - m. James McCartney.
   3. Sarah Jane - b. Mar. 13, 1858 - d. Jan. 17, 1911 - buried in Thorpe Cemetery.
   4. Alfred Mason - b. Sept. 15, 1859 - d. Nov. 11, 1865, buried in Thorpe Cemetery.
   5. Clara - b. Feb. 16, 1866 - m. William Vaughn.
   6. Frances - b. Oct. 26, 1869 -
   7. Moses Fern - b. May 11, 1871 -

1398. DAVID THORPE (William - Rheuben - Job) - b. May 12, 1841, at Ohio Pyle, Penn. - d. June 14, 1932, at Sioux Falls, S. D., buried at Hudson, S. D. - m. Oct. 25, 1869, in Fairview Township, S. D., Alice Irene Bellesfield - b. Mar. 2, 1848, at Stroudsburg, Penn. - d. Sept. 4, 1922, at Sioux Falls, S. D. - buried at Hudson, S. D. - daughter of Peter Bellesfield and Mary Elizabeth Neyhart. David Thorpe and family lived at Eden, Dakota Territory, now Hudson, S. D., and Sioux Falls, S. D. - David Thorpe served during Civil War with Co. K, 62nd Penn. Vol., First Div'n., Fifth Army Corps; Co. B, 155th Penn. Zouaves Inft., 1st Div'n., Fifth Army Corps; and Co. E., 191st Penn. Vol. Inft., First Div'n., Fifth Army Corps, Army of the Potomac.

Children:

1. Mary Elizabeth - b. July 26, 1870, at Eden, S. D. - m. at Hudson, S. D., Nov. 27, 1889, to EMORY DENBOW - b. Feb. 2, 1865, Marshall County, Iowa - d. Aug. 16, 1904 - buried at Hudson, S. D., son of William Denbow and Elizabeth Tate. Lived at Hudson, Lincoln County, S. D. - Children:

   i. Wayne Emory Denbow - b. July 6, 1891 - m. Anna Hilka Michael.
   ii. Annie Lovrene Denbow - b. Sept. 13, 1896 - m. Elmer Ernest Nelson.
   iii. Gertrude Irene Denbow - b. Jan. 30, 1898 - m. Raymond Nelson.
   iv. David Walter Denbow - b. Dec. 17, 1899 - d. Feb. 23, 1905.
   v. Carroll George Denbow - b. Sept. 24, 1901 m. Gladys Howe.

2. Annie Belle - b. July 4, 1873 - d. May 10, 1888, buried at Hudson, S. D.
3. William Walter - b. April 20, 1876 - m. Ida Thorson.
4. Frances Browning - b. Aug. 23, 1877, at Eden, Lincoln County, S. D.
5. George Guerin - b. Aug. 28, 1883 - m. Minnie Smith.
6. Gertrude Guerin (twin) - b. Aug. 28, 1883, Rock Valley, Sioux County, Iowa - m. at Sioux Falls, S. D., June 21, 1919, DONALD HAYES FOX - b. July 17, 1876, at Delevan, Minn. - d. Feb. 19, 1926, buried at Sioux Falls, S. D. - son of Cyrus Augustus Fox and Sarah Harriet Alvey. Served during Spanish American war as Quartermaster Sargent, 1st S. D. Inft. - Residence, 333 North Minnesota Avenue, Sioux Falls, S. D. Children:

   i. Francis Roy Fox - b. Mar. 20, 1920, at Sioux Falls, S. D.

7. Willis Edward - b. Jan. 1, 1885, at Eden, Lincoln County, S. D.

8. Abraham Lincoln - b. Aug. 31, 1885, at Eden, Lincoln County, S. D.

1399. WILLIAM BROWNFIELD THORPE (William-Rheuben Job) - b. Aug. 9, 1854, Fayette County, Penn. - d. Dec. 30, 1924 - buried at David City, Neb. - m. in Seward County, Neb., May 22, 1872, Margaret Jacks - b. June 29, 1851, Chillicothe, Ohio - d. Feb. 24, 1896, buried at David City, Neb. - daughter of Solomon Jacks - b. Jan. 15, 1811 - d. Sept. 20, 1876, from the Carolinas and Lavina McComber - lived in David City, Neb.

Children:

1. Estella - b. May 27, 1872, Seward County, Neb. - m. March 7, 1900, ALFRED KNEELAND SMITH - b. Sept. 8, 1861, Rutland, Vermont - d. Mar. 16, 1929 - conducted banking business in Brainard, Neb. - Residence, Brainard, Neb. - No children.

13913. WILLIAM WALTER THORPE (David - William - Rhueben - Job) - b. April 20, 1876, at Eden, S. D. - m. at Centerville, S. D., December 30, 1899, Ida Thorson - b. May 16, 1878, Christina, Norway - daughter of Andrew Thorson. - Residence, Hudson, S. D.

Children:

1. Ralph David - b. Sept. 20, 1900, Hudson, S. D. - m. Inez Coe.

2. Luverne Arthur - b. July 2, 1902, Hudson, S. D. - m. Mary Ellen James.

13915. GEORGE GUERIN THORPE (David - William - Rheuben - Job) - b. Aug. 28, 1883, at Rock Valley, Sioux County, Iowa - m. at Vermillion, S. D., Jan. 2, 1902, Minnie Smith - b. Oct. 27, 1885, in Ireland. - Residence, Tripp, S. D.

Children:

1. Gladys - b. July 7, 1904, Burbank, Clay County, S. D. - d. Feb. 18, 1906, buried at Burbank, S. D.

JAMES WALLS
OF PISGAH, PRESTON COUNTY (NOW) WEST VIRGINIA, AND SOME OF HIS DESCENDANTS

1. JAMES WALLS and his wife, Deliah, came from Delaware about 1790, and settled on land which included the present site of the village of Pisgah, Preston County, W. Va. He was buried on his farm. The land in recent years has been partly owned by Daniel Ryan. Children:
    1. William - b. ———— - d. 1857 in Kentucky - m. Elizabeth Morrison.
    2. Charles - b. ———— - d. 1853 in Iowa - m. Sarah Forman.
    3. Rebecca - b. 1798 - d. 1851 -m. Samuel Graham - b. 1799 - d. 1881.
    4. Verlinda - b. ———— - d. ———— - m. Thomas Weakley.
    5. Jemina - b. ———— - d. ———— - m. Hezekiah Joseph.
    6. Sarah - b. ———— - d. ———— - m. David Smith.

11. WILLIAM WALLS (James) - b. ———— - d. 1857, in Kentucky - m. Elizabeth Morrison - b. ———— - d. Dec. 25, 1875. Children:
    1. Deliah - b. 1834 - d. Oct. 6, 1896 - m. John Christopher.
    2. Francis M. - b. Feb. 10, 1836 - d. Dec. 22, 1869 - m. Mary Sabina Hall.
    3. William James - b. ———— - d. during Civil War.
    4. Charles - b ———— - d. during Civil War - buried at Pisgah, W. Va.
    5. Elizabeth - b. ———— - d. ———— - single.
    6. Jonathan - b. Sept. 28, 1843 - d. July 31, 1928 - m. Amanda Dillow.
    7. Henry S. - b. July 12, 1845 - d. Apr. 30, 1913 - m. Margaret Huntley.
    8. Millie Jane - b. 1848 - d. 1868, single - buried, Pisgah, W. Va.
    9. Eugene B. - b. Aug. 31, 1849 - d. Aug. 9, 1893 - m. Mary L. Huntley.
    10. Deborah - b. 1852 - d. July 13, 1891 - buried at Smithfield, Penn. - m. Otho Huntley.
    11. Tillie - b. ———— - d. ————.
    12. Emma Jane - b. ———— - d. Jan. 11, 1911 - buried at White Rock, Fayette County, Penn. - m. Jacob Rishel.

12. CHARLES WALLS (James) - b. ———— - d. 1853 - buried in Iowa - m. Sarah Forman - b. Jan. 22, 1791 - d. Jan. 25, 1874 - buried at Pisgah, W. Va. - daughter of Richard Forman - b. 1773 (Robert, 1736 - 1812, and Mary Naylor, 1745 - 1822) and Mary Connor.   Children:
    1. Verlinda - b. Nov. 12, 1822 - d. Mar. 25, 1853 - buried at Mt.

Nebo Church, Preston County, W. Va. - m. ROLLA
JENKINS. - Children:
    i. Verlinda - b. ——————— - m. Randolph Protzman.
 2. Eli J. - b. 1825 - d. 1894 - buried at Pisgah, W. Va. - m. Jane
    Shinnebarger - b. 1828 - d. 1901. No children.
 3. Ami F. - b. Mar. 25, 1828 - d. Nov. 8, 1887 - m. Elizabeth
    Adams.
 4. George W. - b. Apr. 24, 1830 - d. Oct. 4, 1896 - m. Belinda
    Michael.
 5. Mary A. - b. Jan. 14, 1832 - d. Apr. 25, 1872 - buried at Al-
    bright, W. Va. - m. William H. King (see King Genealogy).
 6. Jemina - b. Oct. 29, 1835 - d. Aug. 2, 1872 - buried at Pis-
    gah, W. Va. - m. Aug. 15, 1858, ANDREW S. McNAIR -
    b. Jan. 12, 1836 - d. Apr. 14, 1917 - buried at Bruceton Mills,
    W. Va. Children:
    i. Florence Jane McNair - b. Nov. 26, 1858 - m. James M.
        Smith.
    ii. James Charles McNair - b. Jan. 17, 1861 - m. Virginia
        Yeast.
    iii. Sarah C. McNair - b. Oct. 18, 1862 - d. Nov. 27, 1862.
    iv. Ralph H. McNair (twin) - b. Oct. 18, 1862 - d. Nov. 25,
        1862.
    v. Eugenia Ola McNair - b. Mar. 11, 1864 - m. Frank R.
        Speelman.
    vi. Mary Ann McNair - b. Apr. 3, 1866 - m. James S. Everly.
    vii. Dora Bertha McNair - b. Feb. 14, 1868 - d. May 21, 1868.
    viii. Emma O. McNair - b. Mar. 25, 1869 -
    ix. Emmer O. McNair (twin) - b. Mar. 25, 1869 -
    (See Bible record of Andrew S. McNair for children by his
    second marriage).
 7. Jonathan - b. ——————— - d. ——————— - went west.
 8. William D. - b. ——————— - d. during Civil War, 1861.
112. FRANCIS M. WALLS (William - James) - b. Feb. 10, 1836 -
    d. Dec. 22, 1864, in Libby Prison, Salsbury, N. C. - served with
    Co. H, 3rd Md. Inft. - m. April 5, 1857, Mary Sabina Hall - b.
    Mar. 7, 1841, Bear Creek, lived in Ohiopyle, Penn. - d. May 26,
    1912 - buried at Ohiopyle, Penn. - daughter of Isaac and Nancy
    Hall.   Children:
 1. Sadie M. - b. Nov. 5, 1858, Brandonville, W. Va. - m. J. C.
    Gorden.
 2. William M. - b. Dec. 15, 1861, Beaver Creek Falls, Pa. - d.
    Feb. 14, 1901 - buried at Uniontown, Penn. - m. Mary Mc-
    Cormack.
 3. David Camden - b. May 12, 1864 - m. Gustie M. Briner.

116. JONATHAN WALLS (William - James) - b. Sept. 27, 1843 -
d. July 31, 1928, at Rubles Mill - buried at Smithfield, Penn. -
m. Amanda Jane Dillow - b. ——————— - d. ———————
buried at Smithfield, Penn. - daughter of John and Bettie Dillow.   Children:
1. Albert C. - b. ————, 1867 - d. July 10, 1910 - m. ————
2. George G. - b. ————, 1868 - d. July 24, 1908 - m. ————
3. Andrew C. - b. ——————— - d. ——————— - m. ———————
4. Samuel B. - b. May 5, 1874 - m. Rosa A. McArdle.
5. Walter - b. ——————— - d. Apr. 8, 1908 - m. ———————
6. Nellie May - b. ——————— - d. ——————— - m. ———————

117. HENRY S. WALLS (William - James) - b. July 12, 1845, at
Pisgah, W. Va. - d. April 30, 1913, at Fairchance, Penn. - buried at Smithfield, Penn. - m. in Springhill Township, Oct. 26,
1865, Margaret F. Huntley - b. April 14, 1843, Mononghelia
County, W. Va. - d. Sept. 1, 1910 - buried at Smithfield, Penn. -
daughter of Robert Huntley and Mary McKane.   Children:
1. Mary E. - b. Aug. 12, 1866, near New Salem, Fayette County, Penn. - m. MICHAEL M. SWANEY - b. Aug. 28, 1861,
at Fairchance, Penn., son of Henry Swaney (Joseph) and
——————— Dougherty.
2. Ewing G. - b. Sept. 10, 1868 - m. Sarah E. Cooley.
3. Robert P. - b. July 14, 1872 - m. Lida A. Cooley.
4. Alexander S. - b. Jan. 8, 1875 - d. May 27, 1876 - buried in
Georges Township, Fayette County, Penn.
5. Sarah M. - b. July 14, 1877, Fairchance, Penn. - d. April 26,
1881 - buried at Fairchance, Penn.
6. Lizzie J. - b. Sept. 6, 1878, Fairchance, Penn. - d. May 3,
1881 - buried at Fairchance, Penn.
7. Alice P. - b. Oct. 27, 1886, Fairchance, Penn. - d. Feb. 7, 1887
- buried at Fairchance, Penn.

119. EUGENE B. WALLS (William - James) - b. Aug. 31, 1849 -
d. Aug. 9, 1893 - buried in Walls Cemetery, Pisgah, W. Va. -
m. Mary L. Huntley - b. May 8, 1848 - d. Nov. 23, 1926 - buried
in Sandy Hill Cemetery, Uniontown, Pa. - daughter of Samuel
Huntley and Catherine Deary.   Children:
1. William S. - b. Apr. 3, 1873, Ohiopyle, Penn. - m. Anna M.
Kephart.
2. Alonzo G. - b. Mar. ——, 1875, Spring Hill, Pa., - m. Cora
Metheny.
3. Eli F. - b. Dec. ——, 1878, Pisgah, W. Va. - m. Mollie Rockwell.
4. Catherine E. - b. Aug. ——, 1880, Pisgah, W. Va. - m. Lake
Moore.

5. Samuel H. - b. Sept. ——, 1886, Pisgah, W. Va. - m. Edna
   Lytle.
123. AMI F. WALLS (Charles - James) - b. Mar. 25, 1828 - d.
   Nov. 8, 1887 - buried at Pisgah, W. Va. - m. Elizabeth Adams -
   b. Oct. 4, 1840 - d. July 24, 1913 - buried at Pisgah, W. Va.
   Children:
   1. Abner - b. July 2, 1860 - m. Izura Cale.
   2. George A. - b. Mar. 23, 1862 - m. 1st., Cora B. Snyder -
      2nd., Olive Parks.
   3. Sophronia - b. Jan. 27, 1865 - m. A. D. Lyons.
   4. Chester - b. Jan. 22, 1867 - m. Mattie Gibson.
   5. Rheufus - b. May 15, 1869 - d. Feb. 27, 1871 - buried at Pis-
      gah, W. Va.
   6. Homer - b. Nov. 3, 1871 - m. Disa Wolf (see Wolf Gene).
   7. Charles - b. Apr. 12, 1874 - m. Emma Greathouse.
   8. Margaret - b. Aug. 5, 1882 -
124. GEORGE W. WALLS (Charles - James) - b. April 24, 1830 -
   d. Oct. 4, 1896 - buried at Pisgah, W. Va. - m. Belinda Michael
   - b. Oct. 7, 1829 - d. Mar. 2, 1908 - buried at Pisgah, W. Va. -
   Daughter of Philip Michael - b. 1804 - d. 1892 (William Michael
   - b. 1775 - d. 1854) and Sophia Folk.   Children:
   1. James Harvey - b. Jan. 20, 1855 - d. Sept. 2, 1906 - m. 1st.,
      Phoebe King; 2nd., Phoebe Cale.
   2. Richard Forman - b. Nov. 22, 1856 - d. May 16, 1932 - buried
      at Pisgah, W. Va. - m. 1st., Harriet Gribble; 2nd., Alice
      Ormond.
   3. Philip McCloyd - b. Sept. 6, 1858 - m. Emma ——————— -
      went to South Dakota, and died at Woonsocket, S. D.
   4. Olive Oneda - b. Apr. 18, 1862 - d. Dec. 10, 1931 - m. Evan
      King (see King Genealogy).
   5. Eli Benton - b. July 12, 1864 - m. Minnie Oella Cale.
   6. Joseph Laughlin - b. Nov. 20, 1866 - m. 1st., Mary Clark;
      2nd., Maude Malcomb.
   7. Estella Grace - b. Feb. 9, 1872 - d. Sept. 13, 1896 - buried at
      Pisgah, W. Va.
1123. DAVID CAMDEN WALLS (Francis M. - William - James)
   - b. May 12, 1864, at Monrovia, Md. Residence, 15 Repperd
   Street, Uniontown, Penn. - m. at Ohiopyle, Penn., Sept. 16,
   1884, Gustie M. Briner - b. Aug. 28, 1863, at Roundtop, near
   Ohiopyle, Penn. - d. Feb. 12, 1909, Briar Hill, Penn. - daughter
   of Allen Briner.   Children:
   1. Charles F. - b. April 2, 1886, Dunbar, Penn. - m. Harriet
      Norman.
   2. Lillian M. - b. Mar. 12, 1887, Dunbar, Penn. - d. Nov. 29,
      1918 - m. Charles F. Thompson.

3. Thomas C. - b. April 8, 1889, Ohiopyle, Penn. - m. Annie Rose.
4. Ada B. - b. Feb. 5, 1891, Dunbar, Penn. - m. John Schiffbauer.
5. Daisy L. (twin) - b. Feb. 5, 1891, Dunbar, Penn. - m. Samuel Boyd.
6. Richard A. - b. April 19, 1893, Uniontown, Penn. - m. Agnes Mavehes.
7. Edward E. - b. May 16, 1895, Uniontown, Penn. -
8. Ethel M. - b. Nov. 16, 1900, Uniontown, Penn. - m. Clyde Minerd.
9. Della F. - b. April 11, 1904, New Salem, Penn. - m. Joseph C. Cover.
10. Annabel - b. Feb. 7, 1907, Briar Hill, Penn. -

1164. SAMUEL B. WALLS (Jonathan - William - James) - b. May 5, 1874, Uniontown, Penn. - m. 1895, Rosa A. McArdle - b. June 27, 1874, in England - d. June 28, 1909, Uniontown, Penn. - Daughter of James McArdle and Elizabeth McKinney, in England. Children:
1. Berl Isabell - b. Aug. 24, 1896, Uniontown, Penn. - m. Clyde Kelly.
2. Nellie May - b. July 22, 1898, Fairchance, Penn. - m. Henry Minerd.
3. Arthur B. - b. May 3, 1901, Uniontown, Penn. - m. ———— Fletcher.
4. Mary Elizabeth - b. May 15, 1904, Uniontown, Penn. - m. Paul Miller.
5. Susana - b. May 7, 1906, Uniontown, Penn. - d. ————— - buried in Park Cemetery, Fayette County, Penn.
6. Amana Jane - b. June 18, 1909 - d. June 18, 1909 - buried in Park Cemetery.
7. Margaret Rose - b. Apr. 17, 1907 - m. Harry Fogle.

1172. EWING G. WALLS (Henry S. - William - James) - b. Sept. 10, 1868, at Woodbridgetown, Fayette County, Penn. - Residence, 23 Sheldon Street, Fairchance, Penn. - m. Aug. 17, 1891, Cumberland, Md., Sarah E. Cooley - b. Oct. 9, 1872, at Fairchance, Penn. - d. Sept. 1, 1911 - buried in White Rock Cemetery, near Fairchance, Penn. - daughter of Samuel D. Cooley and Caroline Wilson. Children:
1. Franklin O. - b. Feb. 4, 1892, Fairchance, Penn. - m. Pierie Myers.
2. Samuel H. - b. Feb. 14, 1895, Fairchance, Pa. - m. Alice Barnes.
3. Katie B. - b. May 29, 1896, Fairchance, Penn. - m. Harry Alexander.

4. Jesse C. - b. Aug. 31, 1897, Fairchance, Penn. -
5. Ruth M. - b. Sept. 23, 1898 - d. Mar. 11, 1902 - buried in White Rock Cemetery.
6. Mary E. - b. Feb. 2, 1901, Fairchance, Penn. - m. Edward Myers.
7. Robert P. - b. Jan. 12, 1903 - d. Nov. 6, 1912 - buried in White Rock Cemetery.
8. Ewing E. - b. Sept. 8, 1904, Fairchance, Penn. -
9. Sarah E. - b. Mar. 1, 1906, Fairchance, Penn. - m. William Sturns.
10. Eva B. - b. July 12, 1907, Fairchance, Penn. - m. Joseph Dunham.
11. James S. - b. Sept. 10, 1908, Fairchance, Penn. -
12. Nellie J. - b. July 15, 1911 - d. Aug. 9, 1911 - buried in White Rock Cemetery.

1173. ROBERT P. WALLS (Henry S. - William - James) - b. July 14, 1872, at Smithfield, Penn. Residence, 39 Murphy Street, Uniontown, Penn. - m. at Fairchance, Penn., Sept. 28, 1893, Lida A. Cooley - b. Nov. 12, 1872, Smithfield, Penn. - daughter of Lewis Cooley and Harriett Abel. Children:
1. Arley E. - b. Aug. 26, 1895 - m. Estella Cunningham.
2. Bessie B. - b. Feb. 9, 1897, Fairchance, Penn. - m. July 10, 1923, at Wheeling, W. Va., HOMER I. GRIMM - b. Sept. 20, 1896, Normalville, Penn. - Residence, 11 Murphy Street, Uniontown, Penn. - Son of James B. Grimm and Mary Belle Eicher. Children:
   i. Homer Edwin Grimm - b. May 9, 1925, Uniontown, Penn.
3. Harry M. - b. Nov. 6, 1905 - d. July 6, 1915 - buried in Uniontown, Penn.

1191. WILLIAM S. WALLS (Eugene B. - William - James) - b. April 3, 1873, at Ohiopyle, Penn. - m. April 18, 1897, Kingwood, W. Va., Anna Mary Kephart - b. Mar. 9, 1880, Rohr, W. Va. - daughter of George W. Kephart and Nancy Carr.
   Children:
1. Orian C. - b. Mar. 6, 1898, Pisgah, W. Va. - m. Woneta Most.
2. Goldie G. - b. Mar. 3, 1899, Pisgah, W. Va. - m. Robert Whitby.
3. G. Curtis - b. Sept. 30, 1900 - d. May 13, 1902 - buried at Pisgah, W. Va.
4. Eva M. - b. June 19, 1902, Pisgah, W. Va. - m. Edgar Craft.
5. Edna B. - b. Oct. 20, 1904, Pisgah, W. Va. - m. Robert Kniseley.
6. Doyle G. - b. Sept. 18, 1906 - d. Apr. 14, 1907 - buried at Pisgah, W. Va.

7. Ora H. - b. Apr. 3, 1908, Pisgah, W. Va. - m. Arthur Cramer.
8. Ray W. - b. Mar. 9, 1910, Pisgah, W. Va. - m. Violet Varndel.
9. Avis V. - b. Dec. 18, 1911, Pisgah, W. Va. - m. Clarence Rockwell.
10. Danks - b. Apr. 20, 1914 - d. Apr. 21, 1914 - buried at Pisgah, W. Va.
11. Dorothy W. - b. Feb. 14, 1917 - d. Feb. 19, 1917 - buried at Pisgah, W. Va.
12. Orial W. - b. 1919 - d. Aug. 5, 1919 - buried at Pisgah, W. Va.

1231. ABNER WALLS (Ami F. - Charles - James) - b. July 2, 1860, Pisgah, W. Va. - m. Bruceton Mills, W. Va., Oct. 18, 1891, Izura Love Cale - b. Jan. 23, 1864, near Harmony Grove, Preston County, W. Va. - daughter of Jesse Cale, 1840 - 1899 (Jacob and Sarah Cale) and Martha Liston, 1844 - 1925. Children:
1. Jessie Elizabeth - b. May 15, 1898, Pisgah, W. Va. - m. RAY FURMAN - b. Nov. 10, 1897, Mooresville, W. Va., son of James B. Furman and Sarah Ann Sine. Children:
   i. Donald Ray Furman - b. Jan. 29, 1926, Morgantown, W. Va.

1232. GEORGE A. WALLS (Ami F. - Charles - James) - b. Mar. 23, 1862 - m. 1st., June 23, 1888, Cora Belle Snyder - b. ———— - d. June 19, 1889 - m. 2nd., May 24, 1893, Olive Electa Parks ⁻ daughter of James W. Parks. Children by 1st. marriage:
1. Cora Belle - b. Apr. 19, 1889 - m. Nov. 3, 1910, Forest M. McDaniel.

1236. HOMER WALLS (Ami F. - Charles - James) - b. Nov. 3, 1871 - m. at Albright, W. Va., Disa Wolf - b. Feb. 14, 1878, Rockville, W. Va. - daughter of John A. Wolf and Martha King. (see Wolf Genealogy). Children:
1. Earl - b. Aug. 12, 1900, Pisgah, W. Va. -
2. Elizabeth - b. Dec. 16, 1903, Pisgah, W. Va. - m. Hugh Metheny (page 63).
3. George - b. May 17, 1908, Pisgah, W. Va.

1241. JAMES HARVEY WALLS (George W. - Charles - James) - b. Jan. 20, 1855 - d. Sept. 2, 1906 - buried at Pisgah, W. Va. - m. May 5, 1874, Phoebe King - b. May 16, 1856 - d. Dec. 10, 1896, buried at Pisgah, W. Va. - daughter of Alpheus King (James) and Margaret Jenkins (Evan - Thomas). Children:
1. Adda Belle - b. Oct. 11, 1874 - d. Dec. 30, 1881 - buried at Pisgah, W. Va.
2. William O. - b. Feb. 19, 1876 - m. Georgia A. Cale.
3. Ira Orval - b. Dec. 22, 1877 - m. Pearl Galloway.
4. Marshall F. - b. Feb. 27, 1880 - m. Mary Miller.
5. Ida Coral - b. Oct. 6, 1883 - m. Boyd Parsons.

6. Flora Maude - b. Dec. 9, 1889 - m. Herbert Hauger.
7. Bertha Mary - b. Apr. 2, 1891 - d. ——————— - buried at Pisgah, W. Va.

1242. RICHARD FORMAN WALLS (George W. - Charles - James) - b. Nov. 22, 1856 - d. May 16, 1932 - buried at Pisgah, W. Va. - m. 1st., Harriet Gribble - 2nd., Alice Ormond.
    Children by 1st. marriage:
1. Leona Maude - b. Jan. 7, 1877 - d. Feb. 6, 1879.
2. Nevada Dell - b. Sept. 12, 1878 - d. Dec. 27, 1900.
3. Edison Everett - b. Aug. 6, 1880 - d. Dec. 17, 1900.
4. Savilla Jannette - b. ——————— 1881 - m. WILLIAM ROY PIPER (William) - Children:
    i. Coral Piper - b. Sept. 24, 1901, Pisgah, W. Va. - m. Freeman King.
    ii. Marshall Piper - b. ———————
    iii. Beryl Piper - b. ———————
    iv. Paul Piper - b. ———————
    v. Gladys Piper - b. ———————
5. Phillip Benton - b. Aug. 1, 1883 - d. Nov. 17, 1900.
6. Mona Belle - b. ———, 1886 - m. Harry Rice.
7. Asa Gilbert - b. ———, 1888 - Children by 2nd. marriage:
8. Mary - b. ———————

1245. ELI BENTON WALLS (George W. - Charles - James) - b. July 12, 1864, Pisgah, W. Va. - m. at Pisgah, W. Va., Oct. 28, 1886, Minnie Oella Cale - b. Dec. 18, 1867, near Harmony Grove Church, Pleasant District, Preston County, W. Va. - daughter of Jesse Cale - b. Sept. 2, 1840 - d. May 29, 1899 (Jacob) and Martha A. Liston - b. May 24, 1844 - d. Apr. 5, 1925 (Abraham). Children:
1. Charles Keith - b. Oct. 2, 1895, Pisgah, W. Va. - m. Verna Everly.
2. Hugh Minsel - b. Apr. 20, 1901, Pisgah, W. Va. - m. Pauline Thomas.
3. Nina Mildred - b. Oct. 19, 1905, Pisgah, W. Va. - m. Guy Roby.

1411. JOHN ORMOND WALLS (141, Solomon - b. July 18, 1823 - d. Feb. 1, 1897, son of Verlinda, of James) - b. Mar. 21, 1871 - m. at Laurel Run, Mar. 25, 1911, Maude King - b. Jan. 3, 1884, Laurel Run - daughter of James B. and Cerilda Liston King (see King Genealogy). Children:
1. Wade King - b. June 25, 1916 - d. Oct. 15, 1916 - buried at Pisgah, W. Va.
2. Mary - b. Nov. 4, 1919 - d. Nov. 4, 1919 - buried at Pisgah, W. Va.

11731. ARLEY E. WALLS (Robert P. - Henry S. - William - James) - b. Aug. 26, 1895, Fairchance, Penn. - Residence, 24 Clark Street, Uniontown, Penn. - m. Dec. 12, 1917, Uniontown, Penn., Estella Cunningham - b. May 18, 1902, New Salem, Penn. - daughter of Robert Cunningham and Frances Johnson. Children:
1. Betty Geraldine - b. Nov. 20, 1919, Uniontown, Penn.
2. Robert Arley - b. May 14, 1923, Uniontown, Penn.
3. Harry Raymond - b. Dec. 8, 1925, Uniontown, Penn.
4. David Kenneth - b. Jan. 11, 1928, Uniontown, Penn.
5. Donnie Eugene - b. July 6, 1932, Uniontown, Penn.

12412. WILLIAM O. WALLS (James H. - George W. - Charles - James) - b. Feb. 19, 1876, Pisgah, W. Va. - m. at Rockville, W. Va., Jan. 1, 1899, Georgia A. Cale - b. May 6, 1881, Rockville, W. Va. - daughter of Levi Cale - b. Sept. 18, 1835 - d. Apr. 26, 1897 (John 1790 - 1882 - Christopher 1741 - 1825) and Phoebe Wolf (Augustine - Samuel). Children:
1. Ruth - b. July 15, 1899, Rockville, W. Va.
2. Hazel - b. Sept. 26, 1901, Rockville, W. Va. - m. PAUL GRAHAM - b. Dec. 15, 1902, son of Clinton Graham and Maude Christopher (Jehu - John). Children:
   i. Lucile Graham - b. Sept. 15, 1926 -
   ii. Freda Ruth Graham - b. July 29, 1928 -
3. Gilbert - b. Nov. 30, 1903, Rockville, W.Va. - m. Cora Darby.
4. Irean - b. Aug. 29, 1908, Rockville, W. Va. - m. Feb. 27, 1926, MEARL WENSEL, Greensburg, Pa., son of William C. Wensel. - Children:
   i. Clayton Mearl Wensel - b. June 30, 1926.
5. Carlus - b. June 14, 1910, Rockville, W. Va.
6. Willard - b. Dec. 3, 1914, Rockville, W. Va. - d. Mar. 10, 1916.
7. Helen - b. Apr. 23, 1917, Rockville, W. Va.

12413. IRA ORVAL WALLS (James H. - George W. - Charles - James) - b. Dec. 22, 1877, Pisgah, W. Va. - m. at Hudson, W. Va., Jan. 20, 1901, Pearl Galloway - b. Jan. 20, 1886, daughter of John M. Galloway and Lydia Laub. Children ·
1. Delbert Dwight - b. July 29, 1901 - m. Mabel Herring.
2. Mary Elizabeth - b. May 27, 1905 - m. May 14, 1927, ALSTON C. JENKINS - b. ———— - son of ————
Children:
   i. Melvin K. Jenkins - b. Apr. 30, 1928.
   ii. Willard Curtis Jenkins - b. May 21, 1931.
3. James Harvey - b. June 3, 1907 - m. Lenora Titchnell.
4. Charles Marshall - b. Mar. 25, 1910 - m. Ruby Luesson.

    5. Curtis Paul - b. Oct. 16, 1915 - m. Virgie Merle Arnold.

12414. MARSHALL F. WALLS (James H. - George W. - Charles - James) - b. Feb. 27, 1880, Pisgah, W. Va. - m. at Bruceton Mills, W. Va., Sept. 28, 1904, Mary Miller - b. Oct. 25, 1882, at Bruceton Mills, W. Va., daughter of William H. Miller, b. June 8, 1834 (Joseph N. - b. Dec. 14, 1809 - d. Feb. 6, 1902) and Elizabeth Hardesty (Dennis Hardesty). Children:
    1. William - b. Aug. 4, 1905, Valley Point, W. Va. - m. Dorothy Ramsey.
    2. Helen - b. May 4, 1907 - d. Jan. 8, 1908, buried at Bruceton Mills, W. Va.
    3. Elizabeth - b. Jan. 6, 1910, Valley Point, W. Va. - m. Donald Hartman.

12451. CHARLES KEITH WALLS (Eli Benton - George W. - Charles - James) - b. Oct. 2, 1895, Pisgah, W. Va. - m. Nov. 4, 1914, Verna Everly - b. Mar. 7, 1896, Pisgah, W. Va., daughter of Charles Everly and Cora Galloway. Children:
    1. Harland Voight - b. June 16, 1915 -

124123. GILBERT WALLS (William O. - James H. - George W. - Charles - James) - b. Nov. 30, 1903, Rockville, W. Va. - m. at Greensburg, Penn., Jan. 9, 1927, Cora Maude Darby - b. Nov. 1, 1904, Bruceton Mills, W. Va. - daughter of Herman E. Darby (Samuel T. - John - Samuel) and Isaloma E. King (George H. - Thomas - James). Children:
    1. William Dale - b. Aug. 25, 1927, Bruceton Mills, W. Va.

124131. DELBERT DWIGHT WALLS (Ira O. - James H. - George W. - Charles - James) - b. July 29, 1901 - m. Aug. 18, 1923, Mabel Herring, Morgantown, W. Va. Children:
    1. Betty Jean - b. June 30, 1927.

124133. JAMES HARVEY WALLS (Ira O. - James H. - George W. - Charles - James) - b. June 3, 1907 - m. Nov. 28, 1925, Lenora Titchnell - d. Dec., 1929 - daughter of David Titchnell and Laura Feathers. Children:
    1. Laura Pearl - b. May 25, 1926.

124134. CHARLES MARSHALL WALLS (Ira O. - James H. - George W. - Charles - James) - b. March 25, 1910 - m. June 5, 1926, Newburg, W. Va., Ruby Luesson - b. ——— daughter of ———. Children:
    1. Robert Carl - b. Dec. 26, 1926.
    2. William Marshall - b. June 7, 1928.
    3. Donald Melvin - b. May 14, 1929.

124135. CURTIS PAUL WALLS (Ira O. - James H. - George W. - Charles - James) - b. Oct. 16, 1915 - m. April 9, 1932, Virgie Merle Arnold, of Bruceton Mills, W. Va. - b. ——————— - daughter of ———————.

THE WHEELER FAMILY

IN GRANT DISTRICT, PRESTON COUNTY, W. VA.

1. BENJAMIN WHEELER - married twice, both his wives were named Fickey. He lived near the present St. Peter Church and about the year 1800 owned about one thousand acres of land. The children by his 2nd. marriage:
   1. Smith - b. Feb. ——, 1800 - d. Mar. 29, 1881 - m. Hanna McCollum - b. Oct. 16, 1805 - d. Mar. 27, 1866 - daughter of Daniel McCollum (1754 - 1842) and Sarah Moore. Daniel McCollum was a son of James (1725 - 1800).
   2. Hannah - m. George Maust. Hannah is buried in St. Peter's Church Cemetery.
   3. Rachael - m. George Maust (as 2nd. wife). Both are buried in St. Peter's Church Cemetery, Grant District, Preston County, W. Va.
   4. Susanna -
   5. William - m. Mary Bullion.
   6. Rosanna - b. 1823 - d. 1899 - buried, St. Peter Church.
   7. Elizabeth - m. Gabriel Seese.

15. WILLIAM WHEELER (Benjamin) - m. Mary Bullion and lived in Pennsylvania.
    Children:
    1. Jacob - m. Lucinda Finley.
    2. Hugh - m. Mary Christopher.
    3. Albert - m. ——————— Hibbs.
    4. John - m. Anne Kisner.
    5. Jane - m. ——————— Woods.

151. JACOB WHEELER (William - Benjamin) - m. Lucinda Finley.
     Children:
     1. James -
     2. George -
     3. Robert -
     4. William -
     5. Lilian -

161. JESSE WINFIELD WHEELER (Rosanna - Benjamin) - b. June 10, 1858, at McClellantown, Penn. - m. Sept. 14, 1887, at Bruceton Mills, W. Va., Sarah Belle Cunningham - b. April 11, 1870, at Bruceton Mills, W. Va. - daughter of Thaddeus Cunningham and Eliza Jane Liston (see Cunningham Genealogy).
     Children:

1. Albert Smith - b. June 25, 1888 - d. Aug. 1, 1930 - m. Pauline Dawson Speelman.
2. Roy Thaddeus - b. June 12, 1890 - m. Dacie Ryan.
3. Mary Thankful - b. Aug. 22, 1892 - d. Nov. 27, 1910, buried at Bruceton Mills, W. Va.
4. Wayne Jesse - b. June 24, 1894 - m. Roberta Wiles.
5. Marshall Lloyd - b. Oct. 28, 1898 - m. Evelyn Bucklew.
6. Theodore Emmett - b. Dec. 31, 1901 - m. Nellie Dixon.
7. Paul Spurgeon - b. Feb. 24, 1905 -
8. Emma Clare - b. Sept. 6, 1907 - m. at Oakland, Md., Dec. 6, 1926, EARNEST STANTON - b. Jan. 11, 1894, at Bruceton Mills, W. Va., son of Thomas Stanton and Sarah VanSickle. - Living at Albright, W. Va. Children:
    i. Margaret Belle Stanton - b. Aug. 14, 1927, at Bruceton Mills, W. Va.
    ii. Loretta Grace Stanton-b. Oct. 17, 1928, Albright, W. Va.
    iii. LouWilla Alberta Stanton - b. June 15, 1930, at Bruceton Mills, W. Va.
    iv. Lula Mae Stanton - b. Sept. 30, 1932, Albright, W. Va.
9. Cora Frances - b. Mar. 17, 1910 - m. Aug. 8, 1931, at Morgantown, W. Va., DOUGLAS EARL BUCKLEW - b. Feb. 10, 1911, at Morgantown, W. Va., son of Charles Bucklew and Cora Belle Sisler. Children:
    i. Charles Wayne Bucklew - b. Sept. 20, 1931.

1611. ALBERT SMITH WHEELER (Jesse W. - Rosanna - Benjamin) - b. June 25, 1888, Bruceton Mills, W. Va. - m. at Oakland, Md., Oct. 6, 1917, Pauline Dawson Speelman - b. July 4, 1898, daughter of Rowland Dawson and Leavie Ryan (see Ryan Genealogy). - Enlisted in the Army at Kingwood, W. Va., May 25, 1918. Received his training at Camp Lee, Va.; assigned to the American Expeditionary Forces, July 17, 1918. Was in the following encounters: St. Mehil, Sept. 16 - 30, 1918; Argonne Forest, Oct. 10 to Nov. 1, 1918; and Ardennes, Nov. 5 - 11, 1918. Served in France and Germany until April 28, 1919, and was discharged at Camp Meade, Md., May 15, 1919. He received no wounds and received one gold Chevron. - Carpenter - lived in Uniontown, Penn. - d. Aug. 1, 1930 - buried at Bruceton Mills, W. Va.
    Children:
    1. Warren Gail - b. Nov. 2, 1920, Uniontown, Penn.
    2. Evelyn Louise - b. Jan. 18, 1925, Uniontown, Penn.
    3. Neal Lee - b. Oct. 12, 1929, Uniontown, Penn.

1612. ROY THADDEUS WHEELER (Jesse W. - Rosannah - Benjamin) - b. June 12, 1890, Bruceton Mills, W. Va. - m. at Pisgah, W. Va., Feb. 14, 1915, Dacie Ryan - b. May 14, 1894, at Pisgah, W. Va., daughter of Sanfred Ryan and Ida May Maust (see Ryan Genealogy) - Farmer, living in Bruceton Mills, W. Va.
Children:
1. Dorothy Maebell - b. Dec. 17, 1915 - m. Dec. 20, 1932, to Howard Arford.
2. Eldred Gordon - b. Nov. 2, 1917, Bruceton Mills, W. Va.
3. Ronald Edward - b. Nov. 1, 1919, Bruceton Mills, W. Va.
4. Rex Eugene - b. Sept. 21, 1921, Bruceton Mills, W. Va.
5. Dale Grant - b. Mar. 27, 1924, Bruceton Mills, W. Va.
6. Mary Eva - b. Jan. 7, 1927 - d. Jan. 10, 1927, buried at Pisgah, W. Va.

1614. WAYNE JESSE WHEELER (Jesse W. - Rosannah - Benjamin) - b. June 24, 1894, Bruceton Mills, W. Va. - Enlisted at Kingwood, W. Va., Feb. 25, 1918, served with 22nd Squadron Second Prov. Divn., until Jan. 27, 1919, at Vancouver, Washington. Transferred to Camp Sherman, Ohio, and was discharged Feb. 5, 1919. - m. at Kingwood, W. Va., Jan. 31, 1925, to Roberta Wiles - b. Sept. 29, 1903, at Terra Alta, W. Va. - daughter of Raymond Wiles and Florence Hahn.

1615. MARSHALL L. WHEELER (Jesse W. - Rosannah - Benjamin) - b. Oct. 28, 1898, Bruceton Mills, W. Va. - m. at Oakland, Md., June 8, 1929, Evelyn Bucklew - b. Feb. 10, 1911, at Morgantown, W. Va. - daughter of Charles Bucklew and Cora Belle Sisler.
Children:
1. Jesse Glen - b. June 5, 1931, Morgantown, W. Va.

1616. THEODORE E. WHEELER (Jesse W. - Rosannah - Benjamin) - b. Dec. 31, 1901, Bruceton Mills, W. Va. - m. at Oakland, Md., Mar. 8, 1930, Nellie Dixon - b. Jan. 2, 1910, Friendsville, Md., daughter of Edwin Dixon (of Garrett V. Dixon) and Bertha Fike.
Children:
1. James Emmet - b. Feb. 17, 1932, Friendsville, Md.

SOME DESCENDANTS OF SAMUEL WOLF
OF GRANT DISTRICT, PRESTON COUNTY, W. VA.

1. SAMUEL WOLF - (Cousin to Jacob Wolf) - lived in Grant District and died there about 1832. His wife was a daughter of Michael Teets.
   Children:
   1. Henry - b. ————— - d. ————— - m. Elizabeth Freeland.
   2. Jacob (twin to Henry) - b. ————— - d. ————— - m. Susan Everly.
   3. Michael - b. ————— - d. ————— - m. —————————.
   4. Augustine - b. June 15, 1813 - d. Dec. 10, 1899 - m. Sarah Mosser.
   5. Joseph - b. ————— - d. ————— - m. —————————.
   6. John - b. ————— - d. ————— - m. —————————.
   7. Nancy - b. ————— - d. ————— - m. —————————.
   8. Mary - b. ————— - d. ————— - m. Thomas Warman.
   9. Lydia - b. ————— - d. ————— - m. Joseph Goff.
   10. Peter - b.———, 1822 - d.———, 1895 - m. Louisa Sidwell.
   11. Rebecca - b. ————— - d. ————— - m. 1st., Samuel Shahan, 2nd., ————— Trickett.
   12. Elizabeth - b. ————— - d. ————— - m. Richard Shahan.

14. AUGUSTINE WOLF (Samuel) - b. June 15, 1813 - d. Dec. 10, 1899 - m. Sarah Mosser - b. Sept. 2, 1822 - d. Sept. 6, 1906, both buried near Mt. Nebo Church, Pleasant District, Preston County, W. Va. - Daughter of John Mosser and Susan Frankhouser (Nicholas).
    Children:
    1. William M. - b. Oct. 23, 1840 - d. Mar. 11, 1929 - m. 1st., Hester Jenkins, 2nd., Florence Collins, 3rd., Ola Martin.
    2. Disa (Laodisa) - b. April 11, 1842 - d. Dec. 23, 1906 - m. Forman Jenkins. No children.
    3. John A. -b. June 9, 1844 - d. Jan. 26, 1930 - m. Martha King.
    4. Lehamer - b. Feb. 20, 1850 - d. ————————— - m. Nancy Forman.
    5. Pheobe - b. Mar. 11, 1856-m. 1st., May 8, 1880, LEVI CALE - b. Sept. 18, 1835 - d. Apr. 26, 1897 (John, 1790 - 1882 - Christopher, 1741 - 1825) - m. 2nd., July 24, 1900, JAMES HARVEY WALLS (see Walls Genealogy)-Living in 1933.
    Children by 1st. marriage:

i. Georgia Cale - b. May 6, 1881 - m. William O. Walls.

ii. Oliver O. Cale - b. April 4, 1883 - m. Lillie Welch.

iii. William M. Cale - b. Dec. 14, 1884 - m. Mozori Swart-swelder.

iv. Millie M. Calc - b. July 1, 1887 - single.

v. Lizzie R. Cale - b. July 6, 1889 - m. E. V. Miller.

vi. Frank R. Cale - b. Oct. 4, 1891 - m. Hazel Everly.

141. WILLIAM M. WOLF (Augustine - Samuel) - b. Oct. 23, 1840 - d. Mar. 11, 1929 - buried at Bruceton Mills, W. Va. - m. 1st., Hester Jenkins - b. Sept. 1, 1839 - d. July 7, 1880 - buried in Jenkins cemetery near Mt. Nebo Church - daughter of Graham Jenkins, 1811 - 1869, and Eliza King, 1816 - 1881 (James). - m. 2nd., Aug. 26, 1884, Florence Collins - b. Nov. 19, 1845 - d. 1912, buried at Bruceton Mills, W. Va. - daughter of Andrew Collins, 1811 - 1893 (James) and Olivia McClain, 1824 - 1909 (William) - m. 3rd., Dec. 14, 1919, Ola Martin - b. Oct. 14, 1875 - daughter of Milton Martin, 1832 - 1912 (Jacob - Phillip) and Lydia Forman, 1836 - 1908 (Jesse - Samuel - Robert).

Children by 1st. marriage:

1. Dora Ann - b. Aug. 7, 1869 - d. Dec. 12, 1924 - buried at Bruceton Mills - m. Nov. 22, 1909, OMER Y. SHAW - b. May 21, 1868 - d. Dec. 14, 1931, son of James Shaw - b. July 7, 1811 (Samuel) and Mary Ann Tuttle - b. Sept. 7, 1838 (Eli). - No children.

2. Oliver - b. April 7, 1872 - d. Dec. 1, 1918, buried at Bruceton Mills, W. Va. - Never married.

3. Lucian M. - b. Feb. 9, 1879 - d. Apr. 21, 1929 - m. Hazel Morris.

143. JOHN A. WOLF (Augustine - Samuel) - b. June 9, 1844, at Bruceton Mills, W. Va. - d. Jan. 26, 1930, buried at Pisgah, W. Va. - m. Oct. 25, 1875, Martha King - b. Sept. 25, 1852, at Laurel Run, Grant District - d. Mar. 21, 1931, buried at Pisgah, W. Va. - daughter of Alpheus King (James) and Margaret Jenkins - (Evan - Thomas).

Children:

1. Alta - b. Sept. 22, 1876, Rockville, W. Va. - m. June 20, 1898, at Albright, W. Va., WILBERT L. SMITH - b. Feb. 21, 1874, son of Hadley F. Smith - b. June 3, 1847 - d. Apr. 19, 1927 (John G.) and Malissie Cupp - b. Mar. 26, 1854 - d. July 26, 1915. Children:

i. Virgil - b. July 5, 1899 - d. May 11, 1902.

ii. Ralph - b. Oct. 28, 1901 -

  iii. Bernice - b. Aug. 12, 1906 - d. Aug. 12, 1906.

  iv. Duain - b. Mar. 19, 1911 -

2. Disa - b. Feb. 14, 1878, at Rockville, W. Va.-m. Homer Walls (see Walls Genealogy).

3. Josie - b. April 28, 1880 - d. Jan. 21, 1931 - m. Marshall R. Christopher (see Christopher Genealogy).

4. Anna-b. Jan. 4, 1882, Rockville, W. Va.-m. Charles Forman.

5. Frank - b. July 7, 1884, Rockville, W. Va. - m. Iva Harned.

6. Emma - b. Dec. 8, 1886, Rockville, W. Va. - m. June 26, 1909, at Rockville, W. Va., J. BENTON GRAHAM - b. July 12, 1880, Pleasant District, Preston County, W. Va., son of Jonathan Graham and Mehalia Forman. Children:

  i. Willis Graham - b. Mar. 20, 1913.

7. Roy - b. May 3, 1880, Rockville, W. Va. - m. Sept. 2, 1914, at Morgantown, W. Va., Mary H. Gibson - b. ——————— - daughter of Waitman Gibson and Rebecca Liston. No children.

8. Charles - b. Mar. 20, 1891, Rockville, W. Va. - d. April 2, 1931, at Baltimore, Md. - m. Sept. 22, 1916, at Bruceton Mills, W. Va., Bliss Frankhouser - b. ——————— - daughter of Allen Frankhouser and Rhoda Wolfe (Jacob C. - Jacob - George - Jacob).

9. Nora - b. Mar. 12, 1895 - m. Dec. 30, 1914, at Bruceton Mills, W. Va., EDWARD P. SMITH - b. ——————— - son of Ami Smith and Martha Harned. Children:

  i. Dale Smith - b. ———————.

  ii. Martha Smith - b. ———————.

  iii. Oscar Smith - b. ———————.

  iv. Benton Smith - b. ———————.

144. LEHAMER WOLF (Augustine - Samuel) - b. Feb. 20, 1850 - d. ——————— - buried at Bruceton Mills, W. Va. - m. Nancy Forman - b. ——————— - daughter of Jesse Forman and Susannah Stuck.

  Children:

1. Lora - b. ———————.

2. Dorsey - b. May 8, 1881 -

3. Arley - b. ———————.

1413. LUCIAN M. WOLF (William M. - Augustine - Samuel) - b. Feb. 9, 1879 - d. April 21, 1929 - m. April 23, 1919, at Uniontown, Penn., Hazel Morris - b. April 8, 1893, daughter of Samuel H. Morris - b. Oct. 19, 1861, and Isabella Ariston - b. Sept. 19, 1858 - d. Nov. 25, 1918 - buried at Bruceton Mills, W. Va.

Children:

1. Woodrow W. - b. Feb. 2, 1920, Morgantown, W. Va.
2. Edgar Maurice - b. Mar. 1, 1925, Morgantown, W. Va.
3. Helen Elaine - b. Aug. 10. 1928, Morgantown, W. Va.

THE JACOB WOLFE FAMILY
OF PRESTON COUNTY. WEST VIRGINIA,
AND SOME OF HIS DESCENDANTS

1. JACOB WOLFE - Lived in what is now Preston County, W. Va., in 1782. His wife died about 1824, at the home of her son, Augustine, having attained an extreme age.
   Children:
   1. George - b. 1752 - d. 1827 - m. Catherine Barb.
   2. Jacob - b. 1764 - d. 1834 - m. Christina Wetzel.
   3. Augustine - b. ————— - d. ————— - m. Mary E. Cook.
   4. Clarissa - m. ————— Rodeheaver.

11. GEORGE WOLFE (Jacob) - b. 1752 - d. 1827 - served in the Revolutionary War - m. Catherine Barb, daughter of Isaac Barb and Elizabeth Caulfelt.
    Children:
    1. Jacob - b. 1782 - m. Rachel Briggs.
    2. Daniel - b. Mar. 15, 1794 - d. June 15, 1873 - buried in Parnel Cemetery near Cuzzart - m. 1st., Anne House - b. 1794 - d. Jan. 13, 1864. - m. 2nd., Dorcas Friend.
    3. Christina - b. Sept. 12, 1795 - d. Sept. 12, 1880 - m. 1813, JACOB GUSEMAN - b. Feb. 14, 1786 - d. Mar. 15, 1878. - Children:
       i. Mary Guseman - b. Oct. 8, 1817 - d. Mar. 16, 1909 - m. Samuel Matlick.
       ii. Susan Guseman - b. Oct. 7, 1819 - d. Aug. 27, 1902 - m. William Kelley.
       iii. Sophia Guseman - b. Apr. 1, 1822 - d. Feb. 27, 1888 - m. Samuel F. Connor - (see Connor Genealogy).
       iv. Abraham Guseman - b. July 31, 1824 - d. June 6, 1825.
       v. Isaac Guseman - b. May 16, 1826 - m. ————— Michael.
       vi. John Wesley Guseman - b. June 25, 1828 - m. Eleanor Drabell.
       vii. Joseph Guseman - b. Nov. 14, 1830 - m. Mary Haze.
       viii. Jacob Guseman - b. Aug. 8, 1835 - m. Lavina Connor.
       ix. Amos Guseman - b. Dec. 26, 1839 - m. ————— - went west.
    4. Henry - b. ————— - went west in 1835.
    5. Anthony - b. Dec. 12, 1799 - d. May 12, 1843 - buried in Parnell Cemetery near Cuzzart, Pleasant District, Preston County, W. Va. - m. Mary Matlick - b. 1804 - daughter of Joseph S. Matlick.
    6. Martin - b. ————— - m. Elizabeth Sine.

7. Sarah - b. ——————— - m. Emanuel Harned.
8. Susan - b. ——————— - m. Jacob Feather (Jacob) - 1796 -
   1864.
9. Abigail - b. ——————— - m. John Sine.
12. JACOB WOLFE (Jacob) - b. 1764 - d. 1834 - Served in the
    Revolutionary War. Lived near Lennox, Preston County, W.
    Va.; later near Zanesville, Ohio, and died in Preston County,
    near Piney Knob - m. Christina Wetzel.
    Children:
    1. Susan - b. ————, 1775 - d. Mar. 11, 1853 - m. LEONARD
       CUPP (Peter, 1750 - 1835) - b. April 8, 1776 - d. 1871 - both
       are buried in Cupp Cemetery on the Victor Cupp farm about
       three miles southeast of Brandonville, W. Va., in Pleasant
       District. Children:
       i. Catherine Cupp - b. Feb. 25, 1802 - d. Oct. 15, 1876 - m.
          Jacob Barb - b. 1799 - d. 1875 - son of Isaac Barb.
       ii. George Cupp - b. ——————— - m. Christina Kelley -
           went to Indiana.
       iii. Mary Cupp - b. ——————— - m. Solomon Wilhelm.
       iv. Jacob Cupp - b. 1807 - d. 1890 - m. Clemena Keller - b.
           1811.
       v. John L. Cupp - b. 1809 - d. 1880 - m. Mary Wilhelm.
       vi. Eve Cupp - b. 1818 - d. 1915 - m. Moses Silbaugh.
       vii. Sarah Cupp - b. May 16, 1821 - d. Apr. 23, 1909 - m.
            James J. Benson - b. Jan. 5, 1810 - d. Mar. 23, 1890 -
            both are buried in Cupp Cemetery.
    2. John - b. ——————— - m. Mary Teets - daughter of Mich-
       ael Teets, Sr.
    3. George - b. ——————— - m. Elizabeth Teets - daughter of
       Michael Teets, Sr.
    4. Elizabeth - b. ——————— - m. John Teets - son of Michael
       Teets, Sr.
    5. Louise C. - b. ——————— - m. Henry Sine.
    6. Lewis - b. 1804 - d. 1866 - m. Hannah Falkenstine.
    7. Augustine - b. Aug. 11, 1810 - d. Dec. 26, 1859 - m. Julia A.
       Everly.
    8. Jacob - b. Nov. 14, 1814 - d. Jan. 22, 1895-m. Lorana Zweyer.
    9. Nancy - b. ——————— - m. Phillip Lewis, of Pennsylvania.
    10. Sarah - b. ——————— - m. Henry Lewis, of Pennsylvania.
13. AUGUSTINE WOLFE (Jacob) - m. Mary E. Cook - b. 1766 -
    d. 1844.
       Children:
    1. Phillip - b. 1794 - d. 1877 - m. 1st., Christina Miller - b. 1797 -

d. 1844 - daughter of John Miller - m. 2nd., Drusilla Rohr-
baugh.

2. George - b. ————————— - m. —————————.
3. David - b. ————————— - went west.
4. Joseph - b. ————————— - m. Catherine Nine.
5. Anne - b. ————————— - m. Jacob Moyers.
6. Mary A. - b. 1802 - d. 1849 - m. John J. Cuppett - b. 1802 -
d. 1871 - (son of John Cuppett, 1775 - 1855, and Susan
Spahr).

111. JACOB WOLFE (George - Jacob)-b. 1782-m. Rachel Briggs.
Children:

1. Jacob C. - b. May 16, 1828 - d. Nov. 17, 1905 - m. Lucinda
Frankhouser.
2. Anthony - b. in Preston County - m. ————————— Budd. -
buried in Washington County, Penn.
3. Mary Ann - b. in Preston County - buried at Streator, Ill. -
m. James Martin.
4. Sarah - b. in Preston County - buried at Pittsburgh, Penn. -
m. ————————— Leadbeter.
5. David - b. in Preston County - died single.
6. George - b. in Preston County - went west during California
gold rush in 1849.
7. John - b. in Preston County - went west during California
gold rush in 1849.
8. Martin - b. in Preston County - went west.
9. Henry - b. in Preston County - m. Julia Matlick.
10. Joseph - b. in Preston County - buried in Pennsylvania - m.
Malinda —————————.

121. JOHN WOLFE (Jacob - Jacob) - b. ————— - d. ————— -
m. Mary Teets - b. ————— - d. ————— - daughter of Michael
Teets.
Children:

1. Amos - b. ————————— - m. Nancy Sine.
2. Alfred - b. —————————.
3. Urias - b. ————————— - m. Mahala Sine.
4. Clara - b. 1820 - d. 1891 - m. George Sisler - b. 1819 - d. 1889
- son of Samuel Sisler, 1786 - 1870.
5. Catherine - b. ————————— - d. —————————.

123. GEORGE WOLFE (Jacob - Jacob) - b. ————— - d. —————
- m. Elizabeth Teets - b. ————————— - d. ————————— - daughter
of Michael Teets.
Children:

1. Levi - b. ————————— - m. Eve Wilhelm.
2. Rachael - b. ————————— - m. Christian Wilhelm.

3. Matilda - b. ——————— - m. Bethlahem Hileman.
4. Huldah - b. ——————— - m. Lewis VanSickle.
5. Margaret - b. ——————.
6. Mary - b. ——————— - m. Ephriam Conway.
7. Christina - b. ——————— - m. James Metheny (see Metheny Genealogy).
8. Leonard - b. ——————.
9. John E. - b. ——————.

126. LEWIS WOLFE (Jacob - Jacob) - b. 1804 - d. 1866 - m. Hannah Falkenstine - b. 1805 - d. 1874 - daughter of Lewis Falkenstine - b. 1777 - d. 1856.
     Children:
   1. Eugenus - b. 1828 - d. 1884 - m. Rachel Bishoff.
   2. Lucinda - b. Mar. 5, 1830 - d. Aug. 13, 1893 - m. Jonas DeBerry - b. Sept. 18, 1828 - d. Sept. 30, 1884.
   3. David - b. 1832 - d. ——————— - m. 1st., Elizabeth Faulkner - m. 2nd., Ann Shaw Jenkins.

127. AUGUSTINE WOLFE (Jacob - Jacob) - b. Aug. 11, 1810 - d. Dec. 26, 1859 - buried on the Jehu King farm near Laurel Run Church, in Preston County, W. Va. - m. Julia A. Everly - b. 1812 - d. Feb. 3, 1888, daughter of Henry Everly - b. 1785 - d. 1855.
     Children:
   1. Elizabeth - b. Aug. 30, 1833 - d. Apr. 1, 1900 - m. Edward D. Ryan. (see Ryan Genealogy).
   2. Jasper - b. ——————— - m. Sarah Jane Dillow.
   3. Mary - b. ——————— - m. David Yohey - b. Dec. 23, 1830 - d. Aug. 23, 1898 - buried on Mintare Everly farm near Greenville, Grant District, Preston County, W. Va.
   4. Sarah - b. ——————— - m. James D. Benson.
   5. Henry - b. ——————— - m. Sarah Mathews.
   6. Jacob - b. ——————— - m. Elizabeth Darnell.
   7. Thomas - b. ——————— - single.
   8. Joan - b. ——————— - single.

128. JACOB WOLFE (Jacob - Jacob) - b. Nov. 14, 1814 - d. Jan. 22, 1895 - m. Lorana Zweyer - b. Aug. 12, 1820 - d. Oct. 13, 1888 - both are buried on the Jehu King farm near Laurel Run Church, Grant District, Preston County, W. Va. - daughter of Adam Zweyer - b. Mar. 11, 1772 - d. June 30, 1833, and Mary Cale, 1786 - 1878 (Christopher).
     Children:
   1. Adam - b. Mar. 27, 1841 - d. Sept. 22, 1926 - m. Harriett Street.

2. Martha - b. —————————— - m. William Darnell.
3. Albert - b. Sept. 15, 1845 - d. Oct. 18, 1926 - m. Sarah Frances Haines.
4. Christina - b. —————————— - m. William Cleaver.
5. Nancy - b. —————————— - m. John Hart.
6. Jacob - b. —————————— - buried at Confluence, Penn. - m. Rebecca Hyatt.
7. Sophia - b. —————————— - m. Jacob Coffman.
8. Mary - b. —————————— - m. Jack McCann.
9. Anna - b. —————————— - m. Joseph McCann.
10. Eliza C. - b. —————————— - m. Abraham Liston - b. Mar. 26, 1854 - d. Aug. 28, 1900.
11. Elizabeth - b. —————————— - d. single.
12. John - b. —————————— - d. single.
13. James B. - b. —————————— - d. single.

1111. JACOB C. WOLFE (Jacob - George - Jacob) - b. May 16, 1828 - d. Nov. 17, 1905 - buried at Centinary Church, Pleasant District, Preston County, W. Va. - m. 1st., Nov. 27, 1851, Lucinda Frankhouser - b. Feb. 20, 1830 - d. Jan. 19, 1874 - buried at the Old Brick Church cemetery near Brandonville, in Grant District, Preston County, W. Va. - daughter of Daniel Frankhouser - b. Nov. 28, 1791 - d. Jan. 22, 1873 (Nicholas) and Elizabeth Moyers - b. Jan. 14, 1791 - d. Nov. 25, 1876 (Jacob Moyers) - m. 2nd., Mary Edwards.
    Children:
    1. Eugenius - b. Feb. 21, 1851 - d. Apr. 12, 1852 - buried in Old Brick Church Cemetery.
    2. Charles E. - b. Oct. 8, 1853 - d. Mar. 18, 1854 - buried in Old Brick Church Cemetery.
    3. William Addison - b. Apr. 18, 1855 - m. Sarah J. Guseman.
    4. Laura E. J. - b. May 2, 1860 - d. Nov. 14, 1880 - buried in Old Brick Church Cemetery.
    5. Rhoda C. - b. Apr. 22, 1862 - m. —————————— - ALLEN FRANKHOUSER.

11113. WILLIAM ADDISON WOLFE (Jacob C. - Jacob - George - Jacob) - b. Apr. 18, 1855 - d. June 30, 1933 - m. Jan. 16, 1881, Sarah J. Guseman - b. Oct. 28, 1854 - daughter of John W. Guseman - b. 1828 (Jacob, 1786 - 1878) and Elanorah Drabelle - b. 1837. - Residence, Cuzzart, W. Va.   No children.

1281. ADAM WOLFE (Jacob - Jacob - Jacob) - b. Mar. 27, 1841 - d. Sept. 22, 1926 - buried at Pisgah, W. Va. - Served during the Civil War, Corporal, Co. C, 3rd. W. Va. Cavalry. - m. Harriet Street - b. Apr. 26, 1849 - d. Jan. 1, 1927 - daughter of George

Washington Street (Jackson) and Ethelinda Kelley (see Street Genealogy). - Lived near Pennsylvania state line in Grant District, Preston County, W. Va.

Children:

1. Judson - b. ————————— - m. Kate Morrison.
2. Albert - b. ————————— - m. Cora Wolf.
3. Jesse - b. ————————— - m. Millie Maust.
4. Laura - b. ————————— - m. 1st., Harlan Orndoff; 2nd., George Turner.
5. Lulu - b. Sept. 22, 1874 - d. Jan. 12, 1914 - buried at Pisgah, W. Va. - m. Charles Stuart.
6. Thurman - b. Mar. 23, 1877 - m. Flora Everly.
7. Minnie Ollie - b. April 12, 1878 - d. Nov. 17, 1895 - buried near Laurel Run Church on Albert Metheny farm.

1283. ALBERT WOLFE (Jacob - Jacob - Jacob) - b. Sept. 15, 1845 - d. Oct. 18, 1926 - buried at Pisgah, W. Va. - m. Nov. 4, 1871, Sarah Frances Haines - b. Oct. 13, 1855 - living in 1933 - daughter of Silas K. Haines and Mary Yohey Haines.

Children:

1. Bruce H. - b. Aug. 23, 1873 - d. May 25, 1904 - single.
2. Herman Benton - b. Mar. 23, 1876 - m. Birdie Everly - no children.
3. Harvey Astaley - b. Aug. 18, 1878 - m. Grace Gribble.
4. Mary Lou Reiney - b. Dec. 6, 1880 - d. ————————— - m. July 17, 1898, CHARLES M. GRIBBLE - b. Sept. 20, 1872 - son of John J. Gribble (Archibald) and Lucinda Ringer. Children:
   i. Albert Gribble - b. Dec. 24, 1900 - m. Irene Church May.
   ii. Herman Gribble - b. Nov. 9, 1908 -
5. Virginia Belle - b. Nov. 17, 1883 - m. at Bruceton Mills, W. Va., Nov. 12, 1902, FRANK FIKE - b. Nov. 16, 1880, at Brandonville, W. Va. - son of Samuel Fike (Jacob) and Malinda Shaffer (David) - Children.
   i. Paul Fike - b. July 9, 1903 - m. Lillian Whitesell.
   ii. Margaret Fike - b. Aug. 13, 1915 -

12816. THURMAN WOLFE (Adam - Jacob - Jacob - Jacob) - b. Mar. 23, 1877 - m. at Bruceton Mills, W. Va., Jan. 4, 1904, Flora Everly - b. Aug. 20, 1887, daughter of T. C. Everly (John L.) and Emma Galloway (John). Residence, near Greenville, Grant District, Preston County, W. Va.

Children:

1. Evalyn Pearl - b. July 19, 1905 - m. Charles S. Christopher - 179 -

2. Walter Samuel - b. Mar. 23, 1907 - m. Ethel Forman.
3. Emma Harriet - b. May 23, 1911 -
4. Vernis Louise - b. Sept. 23, 1912 -
5. Guy Isador - b. Sept. 2, 1914 -
6. Zora Virginia - b. Sept. 23, 1916 -
7. Inez Eleanor - b. July 11, 1918 -
8. Roxa Maxine - b. Oct. 26, 1922 -
9. Oval Dale - b. Mar. 23, 1925 -
10. Wilford Gay - b. Jan. 11, 1927 -
11. Willard Ray (twin) - b. Jan. 11, 1927 -
12. Curtis Hoover - b. April 2, 1928 -

12833. HARVEY ASTALEY WOLFE (Albert - Jacob - Jacob - Jacob) - b. Aug. 18, 1878 - m. May 16, 1903, at Bruceton Mills, W. Va., Grace Gribble - b. Nov. 18, 1877 - daughter of John J. Gribble (Archibald) and Lucinda Ringer.
      Children:
1. Ruth - b. July 25, 1904, at Bruceton Mills, W. Va. - m. John Benson.
2. Ruby - b. Apr. 9, 1908, at Bruceton Mills, W. Va. - m. Ralph Thomas.
3. Sidna - b. Aug. 25, 1916, at Bruceton Mills, W. Va.

CHURCH RECORDS

AS RECORDED IN AN OLD CHURCH BOOK OF THE BRANDONVILLE (W. VA.) M. E. CHURCH

Names of Probationers.

* *

1853, Elmira Guthrie, Little Sandy.
1853, Lucinda Jeffreys, Little Sandy.
1853, Danl. Herron, Little Sandy.
1853, Sarah Herron, Little Sandy.
1853, Elizabeth Frankhouser, Brandonville.
Mar. 15, 1853, Hanna Groves, Beech Run.
Wm. A. Miller, Beech Run.
John A. Miller, Beech Run.
Elvira Miller, Beech Run.
Cindavilla Harned, Beech Run.
John G. Harned, Beech Run.
Jesse Groves, Beech Run.
Saml. Groves, Beech Run.
Catherine Groves, Beech Run.
Moses Tichnell, Beech Run.
Michl. Tichnell, Beech Run.
Salatheal Tichnell, Beech Run.
Oliver S. Horr, Beech Run.
Ebenezar Liston, Beech Run.
Elisha Mason, Beech Run.
Geo. M. Metheny, Beech Run.
Elizabeth Metheny, Beech Run.
Danl. McNear, Beech Run.
Rachel McNear, Beech Run.
Amanda Fickey, Beech Run.
Benj. Martin, Beech Run.
Eve Martin, Beech Run.
Shelva Metheny, Beech Run.
William Bishoff, Dougherty Ridge.
Anne Colbert, Dougherty Ridge.
Absalom Metheny, Dougherty Ridge.
DeKalb Mason, Dougherty Ridge.
Albert Mason, Dougherty Ridge.
Alpheus D. Shafer, Shafer School House.
John Shafer, Junr., Shafer School House.

William Shafer, Shafer School House.
Charles Dean, Crawford School House.
Margaret Dean, Crawford School House.
January, 1853, Andrew J. Dean, Crawford School House.
Mary Crawford, Crawford School House.
Isabell Crawford, Crawford School House.
Alpheus Brook, Michaels School House.
Ruhama Trowbridge, Michaels School House.
Wm. Armstrong, Michaels School House.
James Michael, Junr., Michaels School House.
Philip Michael, Junr., Michaels School House.
Sophia Michael, Michaels School House.
Cornwell McClelland, Bruceton.
Ruth Guthrie, near Brandonville.
Lucy Robinson, near Brandonville.
Sarah Brobst, near Brandonville.
Sept. 23, 1853, Magdalen Seese, Crawford School House.
Elizabeth Dean, Crawford School House.
H. P. Crawford, Crawford School House.
Catherine Scott, Michaels School House.
A. Brook, Michaels School House.
Geo. Armstrong, Michaels School House.
Geo. Severe, Michaels School House.
Math Brook, Jr., Michaels School House.
Naoma Michael, Michaels School House.
Albert Collins, Bruceton.
Andrew Chidester, Bruceton.
Delilah Irvin, Little Sandy.
Nicholas Lee, Beech Run.
Wm. Forker, Forkers School House.
Amanda A. Jenkins, Harmony Grove.
Mary Vaughen, Crawford School House.
Oct. 15, 1853, Adaline Mason, Dougherty Ridge.
Nov. 15, 1853, Benj. Michaels, Laurel Run.
Jane Michaels, Laurel Run.
Mary J. Street, Laurel Run.
Elizabeth Wolf, Laurel Run.
Amanda Yoe, Laurel Run.
Mary A. Yoe, Laurel Run.
Mary Jane Tichnell, Beech Run.
Jan. 1, 1854, James Pulliam, Crawford School House.
Jan. 22, 1854, Margaret Silbaugh, Brandonville.
Elizabeth H. Street, Brandonville.

Sarah J. Silbaugh, Brandonville.
Jane Fitzbaugh, Brandonville.
Francina Spahr, Brandonville.
Amelia Hetherington, Brandonville.
Mary Ann Robinson, Brandonville.
Emily Robinson, Brandonville.
Barbara E. Frankhouser, Brandonville.
Roda J. Frankhouser, Brandonville.
Rachel Stewart, Brandonville.
Wm. H. Hagans, Brandonville.
Samuel Spiker, Bruceton.
Wm. T. Jnks, Bruceton.
John Biggs, Bruceton.

May 7, 1854, Mary Cramer, Forkers School House.
Sept. 3, 1854, Lucian Martin, Forkers School House.
Mary Martin, Forkers School House.
Lavina Conner, Forkers School House.
Elizabeth Forker, Forkers School House.

Oct. 15, 1854, Isabells Sliger, Crawford School House.
Martha Yeast, Crawford School House
Mary A. Dean, Crawford School House.
Edward Dean, Senr., Crawford School House.
Edward Dean, Junr., Crawford School House.
Henry Sliger. Crawford School House.
Lydia Sliger, Crawford School House.

Dec. 3, 1854, Thomas I. Welch, Wesley Chapel.
Isaac B. Feather, Wesley Chapel.
Jacob H. Welch, Wesley Chapel.
Rebecca Lewis, Wesley Chapel.
Lydia Feather, Wesley Chapel.
Mary Ann Feather, Wesley Chapel.
Saml. Welch, Wesley Chapel.
Mary A. Welch, Dougherty Ridge.
Maria Welch, Dougherty Ridge.
Eleanor J. Guthrie, Brandonville.

Dec. 26, 1854, Althalinda Sickle, Brandonville.
Jan. 14, 1855, Jane Sickle, Bruceton.
Naoma Forker, Gusemans School House.
Elizabeth Fike, Sandy School House.
Louisa J. Fike, Sandy School House.

Feb. 1, 1855, Elisha Bishoff, Dougherty Ridge.
William Poston, Dougherty Ridge.
John N. White, Dougherty Ridge.

Mary Jane Shaw, Dougherty Ridge.
Belinda Jane Feather, Dougherty Ridge.
Lydia C. White, Dougherty Ridge.
Elizabeth E. McKnight, Dougherty Ridge.
Guy Allen Bishoff, Dougherty Ridge.
Isaac C. Wetzell, Dougherty Ridge.
Mary E. Poston, Dougherty Ridge.
Margaret Bishoff, Dougherty Ridge.
Asa Kelly, Dougherty Ridge.
John Francisco, Dougherty Ridge.
Thomas White, Dougherty Ridge.

*　　*　　*　　*

Record of the first classes in the church book of the Brandon-ville (W. Va.) M. E. Church, their leaders and places of meeting. List made by E. McCarty, an early minister of the church.

HARRISON HAGANS, LEADER, CLASS NO. 1, MEETS AT BRANDONVILLE.

Jane Hagans	Lydia Hethrington
William Hagans	Milinda Kimberly
Isabella Hagans	Mary Ann Crane
Virginia E. Hagans	A. D. Crane
J. W. Leach	Milinda Casteel
Elizabeth Leach	Lucy Robinson
Thomas Scott	Leanora Pedan
Sarah McCollum	Joseph H. Gibson
Thos. L. Stewart	Ann Gibson
Mary Stewart	Jane E. Gibson
Wm. McKee	Cath Stewart
Mary McKee	

WILLIAM ROBINSON, LEADER, CLASS NO. 2, MEETS AT BRANDONVILLE.

William Guthrie	Richard Forman
A. D. Hagans	Nancy Forman
Lydia C. Hagans	Cathe Fike
Jared E. Hagans	Ruth Guthrie
Amanda J. Hagans	Elizabeth Myers
A. C. Leach	John Davidson
Catherine Leach	Rebecca P. Davidson
Jane A. Leach	Rhoda J. Frankhouser
Isaac McGrew	Barbara E. Frankhouser
Margaret McGrew	Sarah J. Silbaugh
Moses Silbaugh	Mary Ann Robinson
Eve Silbaugh	

GEORGE BOWERS, LEADER, CLASS MEETS AT FORKER'S SCHOOL HOUSE.

Cassaphia Bowers
Joseph N. Miller
Elizabeth Forker
Sarah Ann Forker
Eugenius Forker
Salathial Forker
Mary Ann Forker

Margaret Hartzel
Sarah Martin
William Conner
Sarah Rigg
Mary Rigg
Mary Ann Metheny
Catharine A. Martin

SAMUEL FORKER, LEADER. CLASS MEETS AT LITTLE SANDY MEETING HOUSE.

Isabella Forker
William Glover
William Fike
Edmond Jeffreys
Nancy Jeffreys
Celia Jeffreys
Emily Jeffreys
Alex Harvey
Minerva Spurgin

Ann Harvey
Elizabeth Jeffreys
Benj. Jeffreys
Elizabeth Jeffreys, of Amos
Rachel DeBerry
Christian Guthrie
George Spiker
Nancy Spiker
Mrs. Elizabeth Guseman

HENRY CHIDESTER, LEADER. CLASS MEETS AT UNION CHAPEL.

Conrad Ringer
Mary Ringer
John Kelly, deceased
  Sept. 9, 1854.
Catherine Kelly
Bertha Kelly
Archibald DeBerry
Isaiah Armstrong
Elizabeth Armstrong

Rebecca Spiker
Henry Spiker
Mary Spiker
Mary Jane Ringer
William Boger
Robert Ross, deceased,
  July, 1854.
James Feathers
Christiana Feathers

CLASS MEETS AT WESLEY CHAPEL.

James Feathers
Christiana Feathers
Melinda Feathers
Amos Dodge
Louisa Feathers
Abraham Feathers
Elizabeth Feathers
Joseph Hartman
Frances Trimbley

Margaret Lewis
Mary Lewis
Catherine Lewis
Jane Lewis
Jacob Feathers
Catherine Feathers
Frederick Cramer
Roanna Rodeheaver
Rachel Feathers

Rebecca Feathers
John Lewis
Eve Lewis
Melinda Crane

Harrison Feathers
Jane Feathers
Sarah Ann Smith
John P. Crane

JOHN P. MILLER, LEADER, CLASS NO. 1.
MEETS AT BEECH RUN.

Sarah Miller
Revd. Danl. Tichnell
Ann Tichnell
James Tichnell
Judah Tichnell
Sarah Tichnell
Stephen Tichnell
Lydia Tichnell
John Groves
Margaret Groves
Elenor May
Rebecca Groves
Isabell May
Lydia Lee

Mary Sypolt
John G. Mason
Mrs. Forker went west.
Jeremiah Forker went west.
John A. Miller
John G. Harned
Amanda Fickey
Samuel Groves
Moses Tichnell, of Danl.
Salathiel Tichnell
Melinda Crane
Elisha Mason
Rebecca Mason

JONAH HORR, LEADER, CLASS NO. 2,
MEETS AT BEECH RUN.

Rebecca Horr
Catherine Sylpolt
Elisha Liston
Margaret Liston
Rebecca Lee
Peter Metheny
Eve Harned
Wm. H. Horr
Lucinda Horr
Lydia Groves
Levi May
Jane May
Jacob Groves

Hannah Groves
Wm. A. Miller
Cindavilla Harned
Jesse Groves
Catherine Groves
Oliver S. Horr
Absalom Metheny
Lydia Liston
Nathan Groves
Moses Silbaugh
Eve Silbaugh
Sarah J. Silbaugh

JOHN H. M. POSTON, LEADER. CLASS MEETS
AT DOUGHERTY RIDGE.

Harriet Poston
William Bishoff
Catherine Bishoff
Leonard Poston

Margaret Poston
Lydia Bishoff
David O. White
Mary White

Christiam Sylpolt
Mary Sylpolt
John H. Miller
Geo. W. White
Susan Bishoff
Charlotte Poston
Marion Boyland
George Miller

Mary Miller
Isaac Irvin
Rachel Irvin
William Jones
Belinda Jones
Wm. Bishoff, Junr.
Albert Mason

LEVI GIBSON, LEADER. CLASS MEETS AT HARMONY GROVE.

Elizabeth Gibson
Jonathan Jenkins
Abram Liston
Elizabeth Liston
John Jenkins
Eliza Jenkins
Christiana Everly
Graham Jenkins

Hanah Boylan
Maria Daniels
Mary Cale
Wm. Shineberger
Catherine Shineberger
William Cupp
Charlotte Smith
Elizabeth Gibson

MILES SCOTT, LEADER. CLASS MEETS AT SHAFER'S SCHOOL HOUSE.

Catherine Scott
Revd. John Shafer
Mary Shafer
Hannah Wheeler

Charlotte Shafer
Melissa Benson
Abigail Myers
Elizabeth Shafer

JAMES C. CRAWFORD, LEADER. CLASS MEETS AT GLOVER SCHOOL HOUSE.

Margaret Crawford
Rachel Crawford
Anthony Hardman
Mary Hardman
Ham P. Crawford

Isabell Crawford
A. J. Dean
Elizabeth Dean
Margaret Dean

REVD. JOHN SHAFER, LEADER. CLASS MEETS AT LAUREL RUN.

Chas. Walls,
    deceased, 1853.
Sarah Walls
Jane King
Ammi Walls
Geo. Walls

Eli Walls
Mary Jane Walls
Absalom G. Brandon
Delilah Gribble
Margaret King
William King

John Chidester

Christiana Chidester

Charlotte Michaels

Sarah Chidester

Jemima Walls

Persis King

Christiana Cupp

A. J. BELL, LEADER, REMOVED TO MINNESOTA. ELIPHALET CHIDESTER, LEADER. CLASS MEETS AT BRUCETON.

John C. Forman

Ann Forman

Frances Forman

N. R. Harding

Sarah Harding

Joseph Conner

Ann Conner

Elizabeth McClelland

James C. McClelland

J. H. Spiker

Elizabeth Spiker

Malvina McCarty

Elizabeth Guseman

Mary Casteel

Louisa F. Hoffman

A. D. Casteel

Elizabeth Bell

Cath'e Watson

Elizabeth Biggs

James S. Moorehead

John McCarty

Mary Greer

Josephine Moorehead

Mary Ann Moorehead

ISAAC ARMSTRONG, LEADER. CLASS MEETS AT SCOTT'S SCHOOL HOUSE.

Frances Armstrong

Wm. Michaels

Rachel Michaels

John Michaels

Ruth Michaels

Philip Michaels

Mrs. Sophia Michaels

Melinda Walls

Sam'l Smith

Elenor Smith

John Michaels, of Philip

James Michaels

Mary Michaels

Sophia Michaels

James Michaels of Philip

——————————, LEADER, CLASS NO. 2, MEETS AT NEW CHURCH, BRANDONVILLE.

Henry Spiker

Mary Spiker

William Spiker

Robert Spiker

Sarah S. Spiker

Jos. N. Miller, Stw.

Mary A. Miller

Jane Miller

John Ringer

Elizabeth Ringer

Mary A. Metzler

Sarah Metzler

John Rodeheaver

Mary Rodeheaver

Sarah Rodeheaver

Clenina Cupp

Hannah Cupp

Sarah E. Cupp

James Benson

Sarah E. Benson

John Jenkins

Wm. F. Kibber

William Ringer

Susan Benson

Mary Rodeheaver

WILLIAM RINGER, LEADER, CLASS NO. 3, MEETS AT
UNION CHURCH, RINGER NEIGHBORHOOD.

Mary A. Ringer

Henry Chidester

Conrad Ringer

Mary Ringer

Wm. M. Smith

Eliz. K. Smith

Benj. Awman

Julia A. Awman

Alexander Shafer

Mary J. Shafer

James Feather

Christena Feather

Emma J. Chidester

Catherine Smith

Rebecca Kelly

MARRIAGE RECORDS
IN THE OLD CHURCH BOOK OF THE BRANDONVILLE
M. E. CHURCH.

MARRIAGES BY E. McCARTY.

Jan. 15, 1854, Josiah Smith and Lucinda Cuppett, at Bruceton.

Aug. 13, 1854, Silas Haines and Mary Yoe, at Bruceton.

Aug. 31, 1854, Thomas Reed and Christina Cupp, at Bruceton.

Mar. 22, 1855, Oliver L. Horr and Mara Magdalen Deets, at Bruceton.

May 1, 1855, John A. Bowermaster and Amanda Jenkins, at Bruceton.

MARRIAGES BY JOS. B. FEATHER.

April 25, 1867, Burbridge Frailey and Susannah Silbaugh, near Brandonville.

June 2, 1867, Jacob W. Feather and Sallie Michaels, near Bruceton.

June 20, 1867, Henry E. Engle and Mary M. Casteel, at Dougherty Ridge.

Sept. 5, 1867, Jeremiah Cross and Emma J. Chidester, at Morgans Glade.

Sept. 22, 1867, James W. Gibson and Abagail Jenkins, at Col. Jenkins.

Oct. 13, 1867, Henry Harner and Sarah Cupp, at Bruceton.

Nov. 20, 1867, John M. Wirsing and Ellen Haines, at Wirsing.

Dec. 21, 1867, Irvin Christopher and Mary C. King, at Thomas Kings.

Dec. 24, 1867, Zac Feather and Nancy Metzler, at John Metzlers.

Jan. 5, 1868, Wm. H. Metheny and Emma King, at Laurel Run.

Jan. 12, 1868, James M. Silbaugh and Alberta Shaffer, at David Shaffers.

Jan. 29, 1868, Isaac N. Forman and Martha M. Jenkins at Parsonage.

Mar. 26, 1868, Pat M. Morgan and Eusebia McCollum, at Brandonville.

Mar. 29, 1868, Jonathan Gibson and Mary F. Smith, at widow Smiths.

Apr. 9, 1868, John F. McGrew and Malissa J. Saggell, at Wm. Hagans.

Apr. 16, 1868, Jos. W. Michael and Maggie C. Feather at Parsonage.

May 3, 1868, Saml. B. Lee and Martha A. Liston, at Beech Run.

June 25, 1868, Hugh W. White and Jane Frazer, at Dunkard Flats.

Oct. 4, 1868, Jacob Stokes and Nancy M. Feather, at Craborchard.

Oct. 18, 1868, John McElroy and Sarah Rigg, at Jno. W. Riggs.

Oct. 18, 1868, Benjamin Liston and Margaret J. Martin, at Jesse Martins.

Oct. 24, 1868, Henry M. Wright and Sarah J. Chidester, at Cuppett neighborhood.

Nov. 12, 1868, John K. Liston and Matilda H. Arnold, at Snatchburg.

Nov. 26, 1868, John J. Spiker and Lucinda Spindler, at Morgans Glade.

Dec. 24, 1868, Silas M. Metheny and Mary A. King, at Hester Kings.

Dec. 24, 1868, Wm. M. Wolf and Hester A. Jenkins, at Graham Jenkins.

Jan. 14, 1869, David O. Feather and ——————— Albrights, at Danl. Albrights.

Jan. 14, 1869, Charles G. Shaw and Mollie Huggins, at widow Huggins.

Feb. 18, 1868, Jos. J. Welch and Hannah E. Smith, at Jacob Smiths.

Apr. 25, 1869, Wm. H. Garner and ——————— Spurgin, at F. Spurgins.

July 1, 1869, Samuel Fike and Melinda Shaffer, at Brandonville.

Aug. 3, 1869, Milton Kemp and Sarah Harader, at John Haraders.

Aug. 12, 1869, Henry A. Smith and Malissa Hartman, at bride's house.

Dec. 23, 1869, John Cale and Sophia H. Michael, at Wm. Michaels.

Dec. 30, 1869, Francis J. Kern and Sarah O. White, near Selbyport, Md.

Jan. 11, 1870, Lloyd Loudersmith and Sarah M. Riley, near Selbyport, Md.

* * * *

MARRIAGES BY J. P. THATCHER.

——————, 1870, H. J. Boatman and Elma Forman, at R. Formans.

——————, ——, ——————— Cale and ——————— Cale at H. Cales.

Jan. 1, 1871, ——————— Groves and ——————— Cassiday, at P. Hill Church.

March —, 1871, Ralph Hoff and Louisa Freeland, at Freelands.

Apr. 26, 1871, J. C. Painter and M. J. Hagans, at Brandonville.

May 4, 1871, Harrison Smith and Mollie Forquer, near Brandonville.

Aug. —, 1871, James King and Serilda Liston, at Abraham Listons.

Oct. —, 1871, J. Stockman and Ann Wilson, at William Wilsons.

Dec. —, 1871, Nelson Gibson and Jennie Falkenstine, at David Falkenstines.

Jan. 5, 1872, John Christopher and ——————— Streets, at Eliz. Kings.

Jan. 11, 1872, Obediah Metheny and Nancy Otto, at Edmond Ottos.
Mar. 20, 1872, William H. Millqr and Lizzie Chidester, at Brandonville.

*　　*　　*　　*

MARRIAGES BY GEO. CROSFIELD.

May 30, 1872, Allen Forman and Caroline Forquer, at Brandonville.
Sept. 11, 1872, John R. Scott and Sarah M. Feather, at Brandonville.
June 14, 1873, Jacob S. Protzman and Mollie E. Spindler, at Par-
sonage.
Nov. 27, 1873, Andrew McNear and Sophia Michael, at Bruceton.
Mar. 1, 1874, Col. Wm. H. King and Elma McCollum, at Albrights-
ville.

*　　*　　*　　*

MARRIAGES BY WM. J. SHARPES.

April 4, 1874, ———— Sampson and Rebecca Hagans, at Brandonville.
May 10, 1874, James H. Walls and Pheby King, at Laurel Run.
Aug. 13, 1874, Singleton Schrock and Elizabeth J. Shaw, at Harmony Grove.
Aug. 13, 1874, Louis F. Cale and Sabina E. Benson, at Harmony
Grove.
————, 1874, Jacob Guseman and Eliza Arnold, at Hopewell.
————, ——, John Wolf and Miss King, at Laurel Run.
————, ——, Geo. Jeffries and Miss Colins, at Mt. Moriah.
————, 1875, Hamon Rodeheaver and Miss Feather, at Centinary.
————, 1875, Rev. R. P. VanMeter and Mollie Feather, at Pleasant Valley.
————, 1875, Edwin Brooks and Sallie Scott, at Bruceton.
————, 1875, Geo. Jeffreys and Mattie Colins, at Valley Point.
————, 1875, Geo. W. Mathey and Elizabeth Darnell, at Sugar
Valley.
————, 1875, Evan Bowermaster and Hulda Liston, at Brandonville.
————, 1875, Isaac N. Forman and Elizabeth Hartman, at Sugar
Valley.
————, 1875, John S. Mitchel and Mattie Spurgin, at Glade Farm.
————, 1875, Brooks Metheny and Miss Sarah Martin, at Elijah
Methenys.
————, 1875, Randolph Protzman and Verlinda Jenkins, at Laurel
Run.
————, 1875, Mr. Mires and Miss Fear, at Glade Farm.
————, ——, P. Bunker Michael and Sarah Walls, at Pleasant
Hill.
(Some pages gone).

*　　*　　*　　*

HISTORICAL RECORDS
OF THE METHODIST EPISCOPAL CHURCH
OF BRUCETON MILLS, W. VA.

From an Old Church Book.

The Bruceton Mills Charge of the Oakland District, West Virginia Conference, was taken in 1894 from the Brandonville charge which is one of the very oldest in the state. It covers the southern and western portions of Grant District and a considerable area in the west of Pleasant. It reaches to Cheat River and Laurel Ridge and even extends into Fayette County, Penn. Its territory has no equal in Preston County in point of beauty and fertility. Its undulating expanse is seldom too broken for successful farming and the graceful ***(illegible) is dotted with spacious and comfortable farm houses, the inviting appearances of which is easily understood when one gazes over the well tilled fields. An Occasional border of woodland adds beauty to the summer scenery. The people are intelligent and thrifty. The very poor are scarcely found among them. They are well informed of the current news of the day and progressive in the matter of schools. The proportions of resident teachers holding first grade certificates is greater than any where else in the county. Ever since the separate existance of this charge it has been ministred to by Rev. Charles E. Feather, the fact that he has been returned for four successive years is of itself an eloquent witness to the ability, faithfulness and zeal which he has devoted to those under his care.

There are eight appointments. Bruceton Mills, Sugar Valley, Harmony Grove, Pisgah, Laurel Run, Hopewell, Faulkenstine, and Wirsing. At all but the last two are church buildings, their aggregate value being $5000.00. None are more than fifteen years old, all are well looked after and in size, appearance and condition, there is little to choose between them. The membership of the charge is about 400 and is made up of the best element of the community. Revival meetings have been held every year with good results. During these four years 100 persons have been added to the fold. At Bruceton Mills a pleasant little village of well painted houses and lying on the banks of Big Sandy sixteen miles from Kingwood. The church edifice stands on the border of the town and will seat 450 people. Not infrequently it is well filled although in the village itself the number of inhabitants is not above 100. The class leader for the entire four years has been J. P. Bowermaster. That as many as 50 persons often attend the class meetings is an effective testimonial to his acceptability. He is miller, squire and landlord. Another prominent member is T. S. Cunningham a prosperous farmer and member of the district board of education. The oldest member at the date of organization of this work was Joseph Feather a wealthy citizen who died June 29, 1896 aged 80 years. Mrs. T. S. Cunningham is the present stewardess and Mrs. J. H. Feather the present Sunday school superintendent. T. S. Cunningham was Superintendent during the years 1894 to 1897. Ella DeBerry was president of the Epworth League in 1894 and Mrs. Lizzie Miller in 1895, since then the league has not been maintained.

Sugar Valley is three and one half miles south of Bruceton Mills on the Kingwood pike. The trustees are Hadey Smith, A. A. Bishopp, Staley Liston and Marshall A. Wolfe. G. A. Bishopp is also steward. P. B. Michael is also class leader. John G. Cale was Sunday school superintendent in 1895, Mrs. P. B. Michael in 1896 and M. A. Wolfe since then. G. A. Bishopp, P. B. Michael and Allen Miller are among the leading members. They are all farmers. The first is district steward, the last was steward in 1895.

Harmony Grove lies four miles south east of Sugar Valley among the Cheat River hills. The trustees are John Galloway, Elisha Jenkins, Henry Seal, Thompson Graham and Nelson Gibson. John Galloway is Class leader and Henry Seal steward. John Galloway was Sunday school superintendent in 1895. Abraham Gibson in 1896. Thatcher Cale in 1897 and Chas. Beerbower in 1898. Henry Seal in an old worker and an earnest advocate for christian interests. Another father in this church was James Shaw who died at the age of 84.

Pisgah is six miles from Harmony Grove and by the Morgantown pike seven miles from Bruceton Mills. The trustees are Ervin and J. Christopher, Jesse Cale, R. F. and Abner F. Walls, George King and Jonathan Gibson. Irvin Christopher is class leader and D. A. Ryan steward. R. F. Walls was president of the league in 1896, Jonathan Gibson since then. Daniel Ryan was Sunday school superintendent in 1895, E. B. Walls in 1896 and 1897, Newton Rogers in 1898. R. F. Walls is a leading farmer and a great church worker. He is a son of George Walls who was class leader thirty years and died two years ago. E. Benton Walls is a merchant.

Laurel Run is two miles from Pisgah on the way to Bruceton. The trustees are Obediah Metheny, Sanfred Ryan, Wm. Metheny, Hosea King and R. F. Walls. The latter is also class leader. Sanfred Ryan is steward, Hosea King was Sunday school superintendent in 1895 and Sanfred Ryan from 1896 to 1898. Obediah Metheny was president of the league in 1895 and 1896 and Hosea King in

1897 and 1898. Wm. Metheny, Hosea King and Sanfred Ryan all farmers are among the most active workers.

Hopewell also on the Morgantown pike is two miles from Bruceton and three miles from Laurel Run. The trustees are A. S. McNair, T. S. Cunningham, and John Collins. Thurman King is steward and A. S. McNair has been class leader for twenty years. Frank Speelman was Sunday school superintendent in 1895, Thurman King in 1896, John Collins in 1897 and Thurman King in 1898. A. S. McNair and John Collins all farmers are among the leading members.

Falkenstine is five miles north west of Bruceton Mills. At this point a commodious school house is used in place of a church. Joseph Reckard is class leader assisted by L. Warman. Samuel Nedro is steward. Charles Thomas was Sunday school superintendent in 1895 and 1896. L. Warman in 1897 and Abner Liston in 1898. Joseph Reckard a wealthy farmer and an old time Methodist and John Spiker also a farmer are leading members.

Wirsing lies two and one half miles north east from Falkenstine and just beyond the Pennsylvania line. This appointment is now suspended since by the laws of that state, that school houses may not be used for public worship. Efforts are being made to have a church building provided. John Wirsing is class leader. Mansel Wirsing is steward and since 1895 Sunday school superintendent.

(signed) C. E. Feather.

T. R. Faulkner took charge of the work in 1901 following E. P. Idleman. It consisted of eight appointments viz: Bruceton, East View, Hopewell, Laurel Run, Pisgah, Harmony Grove, Sugar Valley and Pleasant Valley. Protracted meetings were held at all of the appointments and each appointment had preaching once in three weeks on the sabbath. The same pastor was reappointed to the charge for another year. During the year a lot was bought and paid for in Bruceton for the purpose of building a church. A church here has been a felt need for some time. It is to be hoped in the near future that Bruceton will be able to boast of a neat, comfortable and attractive church. Several hundred dollars have been subscribed and some of it paid for this purpose. The Conference returned me for the third time. We had some good meetings this year. A number were converted and a fine class of probationers were received into full membership at Laurel Run. The Bruceton church has been in process of erection but not completed. Special mention should be made of Sister Cochran of Dawson, Penn., who contributed $150.00 toward the church. Sister Maria Ringer of Terra Alta, W. Va. presented a fine pulpit suite and brother J. W.

Feather of Mountain Lake Park, Md. donated ***(illegible) for the church and parsonage. The Terra Alta Marble works donated the corner stone. I close this the third year of my pastorate with gratitude to God and to my brethren, to Him for sustaining grace and to them for sympathy and co-operation in the work. May God's riches and blessing rest upon them. May prosperity attend the charge in all the future.

(signed) T. R. Faulkner.

*   *   *   *

MARRIAGE RECORDS

IN AN OLD CHURCH BOOK OF THE BRUCETON MILLS M. E. CHURCH.

Marriages by C. E. Feather.

Dec. 16, 1894, Charles C. Everly and Cora L. Galloway, at Hudson.

Dec. 25, 1894, Harry L. Smith and Mattie M. Cale, at Pisgah.

Dec. 25, 1894, John F. Cress and Nancy J. Piper, at Pisgah.

Feb. 24, 1895, Sanfred McKinney and Anna E. Rogers, at Pisgah.

Jan. 8, 1895, Frederick Copeman and Virginia Miller, at Bruceton Mills.

Mar. 17, 1895, Wm. A. Taylor and Anna E. Ormond, at Pisgah.

Sept. 4, 1895, Franklin Jenkins and Dora Cale, at Oakland, Md.

Sept. 4, 1895, William Bowermaster and Ida Harden, at Oakland, Md.

Apr. 8, 1896, William Spiker and Birdie Liston, at Bruceton Mills.

Apr. 15, 1896, Arthur D. Teets and Louisa Liston, at Bruceton Mills.

Oct. 20, 1896, Jesse Englehart and Sarah Graham, at Bruceton Mills.

Nov. 11, 1896, John G. Graham and Bertie C. Cale, at Bruceton Mills.

Nov. 24, 1896, Thos. B. Falkenstine and Nina B. McMillen, at Rockville.

Feb. 4, 1897, Charles Miller and Laura Wolf, at Valley Point.

Jan. 2, 1897, Frank Nedro and Clara Collins, at The Valley.

Apr. 15, 1897, Ebon Liston and Artie Wilson, at Bruceton Mills.

May 20, 1897, John A. Graham and Maggie E. Harned, at Bruceton Mills.

May 23, 1897, Franklin Cunningham and Jessie B. McNair, at Bruceton Mills.

May 29, 1897, David Graham and Sallie Protzman, at Albrightsville.

Sept. 2, 1897, Thaddeus S. Benson and Grace King, at Laurel Run.

Jan. 24, 1898, Alvin D. Lyons and Safrona Walls, at Pisgah.

May 25, 1898, John William Idleman and Edna E. McNair, at Bruceton Mills.

May 28, 1898, William H. Adams and Nora Walls, at Bruceton Mills.

May 4, 1898, Albert Collins and Goldie Hicks, at Bruceton Mills.

July 17, 1898, Chas. Gribble and Mollie Wolfe, at Bruceton Mills.

Sept. 22, 1898, Thornton Wells and Maud L. Wilson, at Hudson.

Marriages by E. P. Idleman.

Dec. 17, 1899, Judson Gooding and Mary Metheny, at Bruceton Mills.

Mar. 24, 1900, Isaac B. Smith and Effie C. Gribble, at Bruceton Mills.

Aug. 15, 1900, Orval D. Cuppett and May Forman, near Lennox.

Aug. 30, 1900, Marshall J. Falkenstine and Sarah V. Frankhouser, at Bruceton.

Oct. 10, 1900, James H. Smith and Minnie M. Glotfelty, at Bruceton Mills.

Nov. 20, 1900, Allen L. Uphold and Dora Benson, at Hopewell Church.

Nov. 22, 1900, Lawrence F. Smith and Metta L. Liston, at Bruceton Mills.

Dec. 30, 1900, Bruce H. Gibson and Lillie B. King, at Pisgah.

Jan. 20, 1901, Orval Walls and Pearl J. Galloway, at Rockville.

Feb. 23, 1901, J. Hite Garner and Bessie Metheny, at Bruceton Mills.

Mar. 10, 1901, J. Marshall Collins and Emma Darby, at Bruceton Mills.

Mar. 14, 1901, Eugene B. King and Ida B. Gribble, at Bruceton Mills.

Mar. 16, 1901, Howard D. Cupp and Effie May Galloway, at Rockville.

Apr. 27, 1901, Thurman W. Gibson and Mattie M. Graham, at Harmony Grove.

Aug. 20, 1901, Stephen G. Ashby and Mary Agnes Freeland, at Bruceton Mills.

Sept. 22, 1901, Clarence H. Titchnell and Emma L. Rodeheaver, at Bruceton Mills.

Marriages by T. R. Faulkner.

Oct. 31, 1901, Jacob D. Martin and Mary L. Westerman, near Albright.

Feb. 27, 1902, Chester A. Wolfe and Matilda A. Frankhouser, at Bruceton Mills.

Mar. 1, 1902, Gilbert M. Grimm and Lillie Friend, at Bruceton Mills.

April 18, 1903, Arthur Galloway and Florence L. Christopher, at Bruceton Mills.

May 2, 1903, Chas. R. Forman and Sallie E. Metheny, at Rockville.

Nov. 25, 1903, Orval Jackson and Laura V. Titchnell, at Bruceton Mills.

Nov. 26, 1903, Wm. J. Bowermaster and Emma Miller, at Bruceton Mills.

Jan. 6, 1904, Thurman W. Wolf and Flora B. Everly, at Bruceton Mills.

Jan. 18, 1904, Hiram A. Grimm and Rosa J. Emerson, at East View.

Jan. 27, 1904, Silas Beerbower and Effie J. Frankhouser, at Brandonville.

Aug. 24, 1904, Chas. H. Seal and Rhuea V. Harned, at Bruceton Mills.

Aug. 24, 1904, Frank Wolf and Iva M. Harned, at Bruceton Mills.

Sept. 14, 1904, Benj. R. Spiker and Isaphine Copeman - (no information).

Sept. 28, 1904, M. F. Walls and Mary B. Miller - (no information).

Jan. 29, 1905, Charles B. Goodwin and Tina E. Tichnell - (no information).

Feb. 19, 1905, Edward F. Titchnell and Louise C. Austin - (no information).

Oct. 12, 1905, George Bice and Evalina Griffith - (no information).

Apr. 4, 1906, Marshall O. Harned and Hannah S. Graham - (no information).

Apr. 16, 1906, William A. Nehls and Alice L. Caton - (no information).

Apr. 26, 1906, C. G. Teets and M. J. Spiker - (no information).

July 4, 1906, J. G. Spiker and M. Wilson - (no information).

* * * *

HAZEL RUN BAPTIST CHURCH

The only indications to be found today, of the old Hazel Run Baptist Church is the stone foundation on which it stood. It is located about three and one-half miles northwest of Bruceton Mills, Preston County, W. Va., on a three-cornered lot at the junction of three roads leading from it to Mountain Grove Church, and to the White School and to Bruceton Mills.

The following information regarding the history and membership of the Church is found in the old Church Book, which fortunately has been well preserved for nearly eighty years. The book contains seventeen year's records of the activities of the church and it is regretted that space does not permit publishing the complete record.

The membership seems to have been scattered over a large territory, when a glance at the list of names and where they lived at that time, would indicate.

At a meeting of the church, July 1, 1856, the Church Covenant and Rules were adopted and signed by the following persons: Catherine Strawser, Margaret Brown, Catherine Bright, Hanah Wheeler, Sarah Ann Connelly, Eliza Smith, Mary Ann Harned, Catherine A. Fuller, Hanah Bright, Sarah M. Wheeler, Sarah Myers, Sally M. Laub, Nancy Jane Haines, Phebe Wheeler, Nancy Myers, Charles Connelly, Phillip Pringey, George W. Myers, Jacob Mosser, Phebe Mosser, and Jane Bright.

August 23, 1856, among other business transacted, it was resolved "that this church be called The Hazel Run Church" and again at the meeting on Nov. 15, 1856, "Resolved that the Hazel Run Church be dedicated Nov. 30, 1856. Resolved that we invite Bro. I. D. King to preach the dedication sermon."

The ministers and the years they served were: P. G. Sturgis, 1856 to 1858; Geo. W. Hertzog, 1858 to 1869; P. G. Sturgis, 1869 to 1870; John Williams, 1870 to 1871; Benjamin Brown, 1871 to 1873.

The following persons were the trustees and deacons of the church: Jacob Mosser, Charles P. Connely, Wm. Harned, Frederick Pringey, John Sommers, Phillip Pringey, J. Colyer, Martin Luthern, J. Smith.

"Saturday, June 20, 1857 * * * Resolved that the deacons Jacob Mosser and Chas. P. Connely be the Trustees of the Hazel Run Baptist Church and that they be and are now authorized to get the deed for the land given the said church by James Benson the deed to be made to the said deacons and their successors in office for the above named church."

The records for the years following indicate that the church evidently prospered under the leadership of the ministers and officers already mentioned. Protracted meetings were held nearly every year which added new names to the membership. On the other hand many members were excluded from the church for various offenses, in some cases the offense is mentioned and in others no reason is stated for the member being "excluded.' For instance, one member is excluded for "conduct unbecoming a Christian," and another for "imbracing Cambelite's doctrine," and another "for immoral conduct," and "anyone knowing to be intoxicated shall be excluded from the fellowship of the church."

"Aprile the 4th A. D. 1868 * * * On motion Bro. R. Miller & R. Arnold were appointed to make a trade of land with Bro. William

Harned for hitching purposes. Approved by the church the trade was made and confirmed."

Other denominations evidently used this church building. At the meeting on July 15, 1868, "the Church authorized the trustees to see the other denominations using the house heretofore care an equal share of repairs or they will be deprived of preaching in our church."

The last two entries in the original church book are as follows: "August the 23 1873. Brother Jacob Mosser, moderator. Moved and seconded for Brothers J. Sumy, Luther Collins, Samuel Rayman, Rev. B. F. Brown to be sent as delegates to the association with the Indian Creek Church. Carried. Moved and seconded to remodel this church book. Carried. And this constitution. Moved and seconded to appoint a committee to raise balance of money needed to pay for repairing this church. Committee names Brothers Jacob Mosser, Samuel Romesburg, Wm. Smith. Adjourned to meet Saturday, Sept. the 3, 1873 at lamp liting."

"September the 3 1873. Church met. Moderator, Brother Jefferson Sumy. Letter was read before the church, approved. * * * Moved and seconded to approve the new constitution and articles of faith to be attached. Moved and seconded to retain this book as reference. Moved and seconded to have church meeting the second Sunday of September at 11 o'clock at Center."

ORIGINAL CHURCH LIST

A list of the member's names and dates as they were received into the church:

1856. Jacob Mosser, Phillip Pringey, George W. Myers, Nancy Myers, Chas. P. Conly, Sarah A. Conly, Phebe Mosser, Catherine Strawser, Margaret Brown, Hanah Wheeler, Catherine Bryte, Eliza Smith, Mary A. Harned, Catherine Fuller, Hanah Bryte, Sarah, M. Wheeler, Sarah Myers, Sally Laub, Nancy Hains, Jane Bryte, Phebe Wheeler, Eliza Fuller, Fredk. Pringey, Josephine Spahr, Drusella Fuller, Harriet Hannah, Susanah Maust, Joseph A. Benson, Abraham Maust, Alfred Spahr, Smith Wheeler, Daniel Myers, George Burk, Alpheus Wheeler, Mary A. Benson, Elizabeth King, John Myers, Jr., John Myers, Harriet Myers.

1858. Anne Smyth, Olly Collins, Josiah Smith, Lucinda Smith, Andrew Collins, Martha Jones, Delmont Jones, Lydia Laub, William Harned, Mary Ann Benson, Isreal Fuller.

1861. Milo Jenkins, Thos. Jeff. Collins, Saml. Myers, Canadee Pringey, Mary Smith, John Summers, Elizabeth Mosser, Isaac Frazey.

Feb. 11, 1862. Sarah Worsing, Elmira Maust, Elizabeth Luthern, Margaret Broucher, Maria Frazy, Triphena Myers, Elan Smith, Julia A. Mosser, Florence Collins, Martha Collins, Caroline Jenkins, Margt. Galoway, Marshal Woolf.

May 4, 1862. James Williams, Rebecca Williams, Sarah Williams, Martha Williams, Eliza Williams, Jane Frazy, Mary J. Fuller.

Mar. 8, 1865. Mathias Fry, Mary Fry, Mary Justing, Mary Luthern, Martin Luthern, Amanda Miller, Nancy Williams, Jonathan Beeghley, Robt. Arnold, Harriet Arnold, Eliza A. Arnold.

Feb. 14, 1866. Samuel Koontz, John Herod, Henson Liston, Anna B. Smith, Sarah Jane McCollum, Eve Liston, Elizabeth Williams, Wm. Maust.

June 30, 1866. Simon R. Martin, Sarah Martin, Jacob T. Martin, Caroline Dastine.

Jan. 30, 1867. Julia A. Pringey.

Feb. 3, 1867. Jacob Caton, Geo. W. Rishel, Thomas Collins, Asenius King, Robert John Arnold, Mary A. King, Nancy Mosser, Caroline Collins, Caroline Rishel, Samantha J. Rishel, Elizabeth Caton, Sarah J. Coontz, Abbigail Martin, Lucinda Martin.

May 19, 1867. Hugh Miller, Mary Miller, Robert Miller.

July 21, 1867. Louis A. Maust.

Feb. 2, 1868. Mandy J. Brown, Emma Brown, Mary Melery, Elizabeth Sliger, Isarel Miller, Alexander Miller, Samuel Romesburg, Jackson Collier, Jane Caton, Sarah Harider, John Ringer, John Sliger, Harrison Spurgeon, Mary Holland, Mary J. David, Harrison Tuttle, Sarah Sliger, Mary Colyer, Enoch Davit, Margaret J. Davit, Nancy Spurgeon, Delila Sumy, Jonas Maust, Walter Wallace, Samuel Sliger, Watson White, David Seese, William Seese, Parsee Anne Romsburgh, Eliza White, B. Ringer.

SALEM CHURCH OF THE BRETHREN.

The early history of the Salem Church of the Brethren dates back to about 1830. At that time there was no church building for meetings and the occasional visits into the community by ministers were always occasions for services, which were held in homes of the early settlers. School houses, and even barns were used for services for large gatherings.

One of the homes used for these meetings during the early period of the church was the home of Jacob M. Thomas, who became one of the first ministers. Jacob M. Thomas was born March 15, 1795, and died Nov. 21, 1881, and was buried on his own farm near Salem Church. He was the oldest son of Michael Thomas, of Welch descent, and Magdalena Maust, of German descent, and was reared on his father's farm at Markleysburg, Penn., near the West Virginia state line. In 1818 he married Mary Fike, bought a farm in Grant District, Preston County, W. Va., and lived there the rest of his life. After the death of Mary Fike Thomas he married Hepsy Davis.

At the age of thirty-five, Jacob M. Thomas united with the church, and became an earnest Bible student from the start. He could read English and German equally well, had a wonderful memory, and soon possessed a store of helpful biblical knowledge. In 1836 he was called to the ministry in the Sandy Creek congrgation, which was organized in 1835. In 1841 he was ordained, the first Bishop in the First District of what is now West Virginia. For forty-five years he preached a free gospel, and gave practically all his energies to the Master's work. When eighty-five, Bishop Thomas, by special request, preached the first sermon, the Saturday evening before the dedication, in the large church in Markleysburg, Penn.

Salem Church is located in Grant District, Preston County, W. Va., about four miles northeast of Brandonville. The first church house was built about 1842. It was forty by eighty feet in size. The old Salem church was replaced by the present one in 1890. It was first built thirty-five by fifty feet, and later to accommodate the growing congregation, a wing twenty-five by thirty-five feet was added to it.

When this first church was built there were two ministers, Jacob M. Thomas, and John Boger, who did the preaching. John Boger preached in German and was well versed in the Scripture. Boger wrote a small book in German on the Second Coming of Christ. He died in 1852.

ST. PETERS EVANGELICAL LUTHERAN CHURCH
GRANT DISTRICT, PRESTON COUNTY, W. VA.
ORGANIZATION, FOUNDERS AND BUILDING.
Prepared by Samuel T. Wiley and D. W. Sechler.

The Lutheran Church which takes to herself the high appellation of the Mother of Protestants and claims to have successfully laid a doctrinal liturgical and government basis which leaves no possible excuse for sectarianism, has today millions under her spiritual care and training. Ranks today in order of the religious denominations of the United States.

The Lutheran Churches of north and eastern Preston County, West Virginia, were included in the Brandonville charge of the Virginia Synod. One of these is St. Peters, now (1933) sixty years old. This Church at present is not supplied with a minister, but maintains a fine Sunday School. The territory of this Church membership extends from Hopewell to Clifton Mills and Wirsing (Penn.) and membership was made up mostly of persons living between Hazel Run and Mary's Run, western tributaries of Big Sandy.

Up to 1850 no Lutherans were residents on the west side of Big Sandy Creek, but in that year, John Haines, whose father came from Germany, came here from Centerville, Somerset County, Penn., and with his five sons, Jonas, Jacob, Henry, Silas and John, and also two son-in-laws, Jonathan Laub and Jonathan Nedrow, purchased a tract of nearly five thousand acres of land in the Hazel Run settlement, and the edge of Pennsylvania. They were the first Lutherans in that section and were later followed by the Spindlers and Philip Gardner, of Clifton Mills, W. Va., and the Hartmeyers, of Hopewell. This respectable Lutheran element sought to secure a church service nearer than the Crab Orchard and The Frankhouser settlement, and secured occasional preaching by Rev. Nicksdorf, in the old Hazel Run School House, which was located on the left side of the road leading from the mountain to Bruceton Mills. It was destroyed by fire about 1912. These frequent services occurred between 1850 and 1856. The pioneer Lutherans contributed to the building of the Hazel Run Baptist Church, in which they organized and worshiped there up to 1870. The old Hazel Run Church is now out of existence, it being sold to a Mr. Molsby, who removed the building and rebuilt it for a farm building on the farm formerly owned by George Maust.

In 1870, when an account of conflicting services of other denominations, it was deemed advisable to build a Church of their own. Three sites were selected, one near Joseph Dillows, another near Kantner School House, and the third where the church now stands, being the site finally selected. The ground was donated by George Maust and John Haines.

Andrew Spindler was the contractor who erected the church building for the sum of thirteen hundred and sixty dollars. The Church was dedicated Dec. 18, 1870, by the Rev. J. G. Cambell, president of the Synod, assisted by Rev. J. H. Cupp and Rev. J. W. Tressler. The building is thirty-six by forty-eight feet in size, is built on a cut stone foundation. The material in the building is all hard wood. Has a very fine pulpit, now covered with a black and red Brussells carpet, which was donated by Smith W. Hill, who also donated the five chandeliers. Seating capacity is two hundred and fifty people.

On the ground adjacent to the church a cemetery was opened and the first interment was the body of Jacob Haines in the spring of 1871.

The St. Peters Church was organized Dec. 27, 1861, by Rev. J. R. Melhorn, of Pennsylvania, and the original members and officers were:

Jonas Haines and George Beerbower, Elders;
Jacob Haines and Andrew Spindler, Deacons;
George Laub, Secretary, served from 1870 to 1900.

John Haines
Rebecca (Cupp) Haines
Jacob Haines
Elizabeth (Mitts) Haines
John Spindler
Ellen Wyant Spindler
Jonathan Laub
Elizabeth Haines Laub
Conrad Raymond

Catherine A. (Haines) Raymond
Christopher Hartmeyer
Louisa Hartmeyer
(Two sons and three daughters of Christian Hartmeyer)
William Hartmeyer
Christian Hartmeyer
Marria Louise Hartmeyer
Lydia Haines Nedrow

The principal subscribers to the church building were in the order named, as follows:

George Maust
Jonas Haines
Andrew Spindler
Jacob Haines
Henry Haines
George Laub
John Galloway
Mrs. Elizabeth Laub
Joseph Haines

Hugh Hastie
John Spindler
Mrs. Susan Maust
John Wirsing
Robert Arnold
George Evans
John Evans
Rev. D. H. Myers
Rev. Tressler

Many others were also contributors to the church building, the names being unknown, as the original subscription list has been lost.

The following is a partial list of members soon after dedication of the church December 18th, 1870, other than original names.

Lydia (Haines) Myers
Lavinna (Haines) Gribble
John Mosser
Philip Gardner

Christian Gardner
Hugh Hastie
John Galloway
Lydia (Laub) Galloway

Sarah M. (Laub) Beerbower
Sarah M. Haines
Nancy J. (Haines) Spindler
Joseph Haines
Lucinda R. (Haines) Wheeler
Hester A. (Strauser) Guseman
Lucy (Wyant) Waddell
R. B. Waddell
Andrew J. Spindler
Mary S. Spindler
Daniel Barkley

Sarah (Strauser) Conn
Catherine Barkley
Mary Ann Barkley
Catherine (Haines) King
Henry Haines
Mary A. (Gardner) Haines
Mary C. Guseman
George Laub
Mary Laub
Jacob Dull
Mary Dull

MINISTERS BETWEEN THE YEARS 1861 AND 1905.

J. K. Melhorn, 1861 - 1865
S. H. Swingle, 1865 - 1868
John W. Tressler, 1869 - 1872
J. H. Cupp, 1872 - 1873
D. B. Floyd, 1873 - 1874
A. M. Smith, 1875 - 1877
Vacant, 1877 - 1878
J. H. Gilbrath, 1878 - 1879
Jacob Summers, 1879 - 1882

W. D. Beerbower, 1882 - 1884
R. G. Rosenbaum, 1884 - 1885
J. W. Smith, 1886 - 1891
W. H. Berry, 1891 - 1893
R. L. Bane, 1893 - 1894
W. H. Berry, 1894 - 1897
Rev. Petra, 1897 - 1903
Rev. First, 1904 - 1905

Rev. Summers, Cupp, and Beerbower all died in 1884.

The following from a letter by D. W. Sechler in connection with St. Peters Church:

"For the past twenty-five years the Church has been without a pastor, due to the fact that few Lutherans remain in that section of the County. Much credit is due Mrs. Mary Thornton, wife of David Thornton, who gave much of her time from about 1906 to 1915 keeping the Church in repair. She also had a fence constructed to enclose the cemetery and church building. Mrs. Thornton died about 1927, at the home of Mrs. I. E. Haines, and was buried in the St. Peter Cemetery. A funeral unattended by relatives.

"In the year of 1927, after seeing the condition of the cemetery and Church, my mother, Mrs. Martha Bell (Maust) Sechler, daughter of George Maust, who donated the ground for the Church, persuaded me into trying to repair the building and cleaning of the cemetery. I secured all the names of those who had relatives buried there and wrote them asking for donations towards the work, and the same plan has been followed each succeeding year, and at the present time we have the cemetery in fine condition and all graves cared for and well marked. Two Civil War soldiers are buried in the cemetery. "Colonel" William Adey and Samuel Wheeler husband of Lucinda R. Wheeler, one of the first members of the church.

"The Church building is in fine state of repairs. The foundation repaired, new chimney built, new stone steps, the interior has been papered and all wood-work painted, and new carpet furnished.

"I truly think that this is an old land mark that the people of that section should be very anxious to preserve."

(signed) D. W. Sechler.

OLD BIBLE RECORDS

Records from the Jehu Christopher family Bible, no date or names on title page, now owned by a son Thurman Christopher living near Pisgah, W. Va.

CERTIFICATE OF MARRIAGE.

Jehu H. Christopher of Preston Co. W. Va. and Isabelle M. Street were united by me together in Holy Matrimony on the 6th day of January in the year of our Lord One thousand eight hundred and seventy two in the presence of T. E. Christopher and Adam Wolf. (signed) J. P. Thatcher Minister of the Gospel.

OTHER MARRIAGES.

Shiloah Christopher married March 21, 1894.
Lester Christopher married July 7, 1899.
Maude Christopher married Dec. 26, 1901.
Thurman Christopher married Mar. 20, 1909.
Sylvester Christopher married July 4, 1917.
Elizabeth Christopher married Nov. 15, 1917.
Minnis Christopher married Sept. 20, 1924.

BIRTHS.

Jehu H. Christopher was born Aprile the 12 in the year of our Lord 1839.

Isabelle M. Christopher was born Feb. the 18 in the year of our Lord 1853.

Shiloah M. Christopher was born December the 27 in the year of our Lord 1872.

Lester L. Christopher was born Feb. the 13 in the year of our Lord 1874.

Ruther Ford H. Christopher was born Dec. the 31 in the year of our Lord 1876.

Lizzie J. Christopher was born Jan. the 6 in the year of our Lord 1879.

Virginia M. Christopher was born Sept. the 30 in the year of our Lord 1880.

Siota E. Christopher was born Dec. the 2 in the year of our Lord 1882.

Sylvester F. Christopher was born Aprile the 12 in the year of our Lord 1885.

Hosea T. Christopher was born December the 11 in the year of our Lord 1888.

Guy B. Christopher was born October the 25 in the year of our Lord 1892.

Junior Christopher was born October the 19 in the year of our Lord 1895.

Minnis M. Christopher was born March the 28 in the year of our Lord 1898.

DEATHS.

Jehu H. Christopher died Feb. 23, 1916. Rutherford H. died Dec. 16, 1891.

Siota E. Christopher died July 11, 1898. Junior Christopher died Oct. 11, 1896.

Guy B. Christopher died Sept. 20, 1918.

     *   *   *   *

Family Bible of Andrew Collins, published by Domestic Bible Publishing Co. No date, now owned by Mr. and Mrs. Ashbul Collins, Route 1, Bruceton Mills, W. Va.

CERTIFICATE OF MARRIAGE.

This certifies that Andrew Collins and Olivia McLain were joined together by me in the Bonds of Holy Matrimony at Petersburg, Pa. on the 23rd day of November in the year of our Lord one thousand eight hundred and forty one in the presence of Wm. Reynolds, Elmira Reynolds and others

(signed) Rev. Sawhill.

BIRTHS	MARRIED	DEATHS
Andrew Collins July 22, 1811. in Monongahela Co. Va. now Marion Co. W. Va.	Nov. 23 1841.	Nov. 6, 1873.
Olivia McLain Oct. 29, 1824. in Somerset Co. Pa.		Oct. 30, 1909.
Charles Collins Aug. 13, 1843. in Preston Co, W. Va.		Dec. 8, 1845.
Florence Collins Nov. 19, 1845	Aug. 26, 1884.	
Martha Collins May 5, 1846.		
Thomas Collins July 24, 1848.	July 19, 1881.	
Caroline Collins Dec. 28, 1849.	Nov. 14, 1872.	May 17, 1885.
Luther Collins Jan. 7, 1852.	Sept. 10, 1877	
Emily Collins Oct. 18, 1853.		Oct. 12, 1857.
Mary A. Collins July 21, 1855.	Jan. 17, 1877	
Marshall Collins Aug. 5, 1857.	Sept. 16, 1880.	
Eliza Jane Collins Mar. 5, 1859.	Sept. 5, 1881.	Dec. 24, 1893.
Walter Collins Mar. 15, 1861.		
Clara Collins Dec. 15, 1863.		
Ashbel Collins June 17, 1865.		
Albert Collins July 29, 1867. Married Aggie Yeast.	April 4, 1900.	July 17, 1918.

     *   *   *   *

The family Bible record of Thaddeus S. Cunningham, now owned by Mrs. Sarah Belle Wheeler, a daughter living near Bruceton Mills, W. Va. Route No. 1. Bible printed by Zeigler and McCurdy, Philadelphia and title page bears the date 1871.

MARRIAGES.

Thaddeus S. Cunningham and Eliza Jane Liston were united in the Holy bonds of Matrimony December 22, 1867 by J. Williams Esq.

BIRTHS.

Katie Cunningham was born Feb. 2, 1869.
Sarah Belle Cunningham was born April 11, 1870.
Emma O. Cunningham was born Jan. 12, 1873.
Francis M. Cunningham was born Mar. 31, 1874.
Edward E. Cunningham was born Sept. 17, 1876.
Albert D. Cunningham was born Mar. 20, 1878.
Alfred E. Cunningham was born Dec. 15, 1882.

DEATHS.

Thaddeus S. Cunningham died Jan. 22, 1924 aged 82 yr. 3 mo. & 6 days.

* * * *

The family Bible of John J. Gribble, printed by the American Bible Society, New York, dated 1863, now owned by a son Hosea Gribble living Route No. 1, Bruceton Mills, West Virginia.

BIRTHS.

John J. Gribble born June 22, 1832.
Lucinda Ringer Gribble born Nov. 22, 1839.
William H. Gribble born April 2, 1864.
Virginia B. Gribble born Dec. 23, 1865.
Philip L. Gribble born Oct. 7, 1867.
Rebecca M. Gribble born Aug. 19, 1870.
Charles M. Gribble born Sept. 20, 1872.
Mary O. Gribble born June 18, 1875.
Annie G. Gribble born Nov. 18, 1877.
Hosea Gribble born Oct. 14, 1879.
Ruey M. Gribble born Feb. 9, 1884.

DEATHS.

John J. Gribble died Dec. 9, 1920.
Lucinda Ringer Gribble died Sept. 16, 1905.
Ruey M. Gribble died Apr. 25, 1911.

The family Bible of Jesse Forman printed in 1826 for "The American Bible Society" by E. & J. White, New York, now (1933) owned by Ola Martin Wolf, Bruceton Mills, W. Va.

Robert Forman born 17th of 7th Mo. 1736, died 4th of 2nd Mo. 1812.

Mary Naylor Forman wife of Robert Forman was born the 20th of 7th Mo. 1745 and died the 14th of 5th Mo. 1822 aged 76 y. 9 mo. 24 days. Children of Robert and Mary Forman.

John Forman born 21st of 1st Mo. 1767.

Elizabeth Forman born the 12th of 2nd Mo. 1769.

Joseph Forman born the 24th of 3rd Mo. 1771.

Richard Forman born the 22nd of 8th Mo. 1773.

Samuel Forman born the 9th of 7th Mo. 1775.

Rachel Forman born the 8th of 6th Mo. 1777.

Jane Forman born the 9th of 7th Mo. 1779.

Mary Forman born the 29th of 7th Mo. 1781.

Isaac Forman born the 11th of 3rd Mo. 1784.

Rebecca Forman born the 23rd of 5th Mo. 1786.

Joseph Forman son of Robert and Mary Forman married Margaret Connor. Their children were Elizabeth, Mary, Marguarette (married to Jacob F. Martin), Rebecca, and Robert.

Samuel Forman son of Robert and Mary Forman married Elizabeth Willet. Their children were Debby, Ann, Hannah, Rhoda, Ellis, Richard, James, and Jesse.

Jesse Forman, son of Samuel (1775) was born June 2 A. D. 1805.

Susannah Stuck was born Sept. 30 A. D. 1813 and we were united in marriage Nov. 17, 1831. Children.

Lydda Forman was born Dec. 28 A. D. 1836.

Nancy Forman was born ————— Married Lehamer Wolf.

Mathias Forman was born ————— Married Alcinda Jenkins.

Amon Forman was born Feb. 8, 1841. Married Mary Cale. 2nd Orrie Huggins.

Samuel Forman was born ————— Married Savilla Everly.

Jehu Forman was born 1849 married Melzina Liston.

Ephriam Forman was born ————— Single.

Elizabeth Forman was born 1856. Married Newton Graham.

*   *   *   *

Family Bible of Henry Harrison Gribble, stereotyped for the American Bible Society by D. & G. Bruce, New York, 1829, and now owned by a grand daughter Mrs. Effie Smith, Pisgah, West Virginia.

Henry Harrison Gribble was born Aprile the twenty Eight Day in the year of our Lord 1826, a son of Archibald Gribble and Margaret Gribble his wife.

Deborah Ione Gribble was born July the first Day in the year of our Lord 1829.

John Jacob Gribble as one of the above mentioned parents was Born Jan. the twenty first day in the year of our Lord 1832.

James Madison Gribble as one of the above mentioned parents was born January the Twenty Sixth Day in the year of our Lord 1835.

Harriet Ann Gribble a Daughter of the above Mentioned parents was Born May the twenty first Day in the year of our Lord 1837.

Jefferson Thompson Gribble as one of the above Mentioned parents was Born November the Twenty fourth in the year of our Lord one thousand Eight hundred and forty 1840.

Marcellus K. Gribble was Born November the Third in the year of our Lord 1843.

Manerva Gribble was Born August the fourth in the year of our Lord One thousand Eight hundred and forty Six and she departed this life January the third one thousand Eight hundred and forty Seven age four months and thirty days.

*   *   *   *

Family Bible of Jefferson T. Gribble, the title page of which has no names or dates, and is now owned by his daughter Mrs. Effie Smith, Pisgah, West Virginia.

MARRIAGES.

Jefferson T. Gribble and Frances A. Michael married at Wm. Michaels' by The Rev. ——————— of the Luthern Church.

Daniel S. Gibson and Zettie May Gribble married at Jefferson T. Gribbles' by the Rev. Jas. E. Darby of the Baptist Church.

BIRTHS.

Jefferson T. Gribble Born Nov. 24, 1840.

Frances A. Gribble Born Dec. 23, 1849.

Zettie May Gribble Born March 25, 1870.

William Russell Gribble Born Dec. 29, 1871.

Ina Gertie Gribble Born Dec. 19, 1873.

Effie C. Gribble Born Oct. 5, 1875.

Birdie W. Gribble Born Feb. 13, 1878.

Forest Cleveland Gribble Born Oct. 18, 1884.

*   *   *   *

Family Bible of George H. King, now owned by a daughter Mrs. Lillian Gibson, Pisgah, West Virginia. The fly leaf reads, "Geo. H. and Frances A. King's Bible 1892". Printed by National Publishing Co. 724 Cherry St., Philadelphia, Penna.

CERTIFICATE OF MARRIAGE.

This is to certify that George H. King and Frances A. Christopher were joined in marriage by me at Albright on the 28th day of February 1862 in the presence of Wm. King and Jehu and Irvin Christopher. (sined) Rev. G. W. Arnold, Minister, M. E. C.

BIRTHS.

George H. King Oct. 4, 1837.

Frances A. King Sept. 2, 1836.

Lowry C. King Jan. 20, 1863.

Isaloma E. King Oct. 1, 1864.

Ulyssus G. King Jan. 29, 1867.

Nora J. King Feb. 3, 1869.

Ida C. King Apr. 18, 1872.

Marshall S. King Nov. 24, 1874.

Lillian B. King Dec. 17, 1875.

DEATHS.

George H. King Sept. 12, 1915.

Frances A. King June 1, 1907.

Nora J. King Feb. 12, 1872.

Marshall S. King Jan. 11, 1875.

Lowry C. King Jan. 10, 1878.

Ulyssus G. King Jan. 22, 1878.

Ida C. King Jan. 28, 1878.

MARRIAGES.

Herman E. Darby and Isaloma E. King were married Oct. 29, 1885 by Rev. D. Flannigan.

Bruce H. Gibson and Lillian B. King were married Dec. 30, 1900 by Rev. E. P. Idleman.

BIRTHS.

Bruce Herbert Gibson June 29, 1879.

Lilian Blanche Gibson Dec. 17, 1875.

Mabel Frances Gibson May 23, 1902.

Dwight King Gibson Apr. 23, 1903.

George Herbert Gibson July 7, 1915.

*   *   *   *

Family Bible of Elizabeth Street King, Printed by Henry S. Goodspeed and Co. No. 14 Barclay Street, New York, no date. Now owned by Scott King, a grandson living near Bruceton Mills, W. Va. Route No. 1.

William J. King and Elizabeth H. Street were married June 13 A. D. 1854, by Rev. Daniel Smith of Uniontown, Penna.

BIRTHS.

William J. King was born Oct. the 20 A. D. 1832.

Elizabeth H. King was born Dec. the 14 A. D. 1833.

E. P. King was born April the 14 A. D. 1855.

M. H. King was born November the 7, 1856.

Z. K. King was born Oct. the 15, 1858.

Ethelinda J. King was born April the 30, 1861. Died May the 18 A. D. 1862.

T. M. King was born March 20, 1863.

CERTIFICATE OF MARRIAGE.

This is to Certify that Thurman M. King of Bruceton Mills and Katie Cunningham of Bruceton Mills were by me united together in Holy Matrimony on the 18th day of October in the year of our Lord One Thousand Eight Hundred and 91 in presence of Abner Walls and Izura Cale. (sined) Rev. W. H. Berry. Bruceton Mills, W. Va.

BIRTHS.

Edward T. King was born Sept. 25, 1895.   Hazel M. King was born June 23, 1897.

Wm. Scott King was born Aug. 10, 1899.   Lydia H. King was born Jan 19, 1907.

*   *   *   *

Family Bible of Everhart Liston, published by Case, Lockwood & Co. Hartford, 1866. Owned by a grand daughter, Mrs. Belle Wheeler, Route 1, Bruceton Mills, W. Va.

MARRIAGES.

Everhart Liston and Thankful Thorp were married March 8, 1846.

BIRTHS.

Everhart Liston was born March 22, 1822.

Thankful Thorp was born Jan. 10th, 1816.

Martha M. Liston was born January 16, 1847.

Eliza Jane Liston was born Dec. 3, 1849.

John M. Liston was born Aug. 4, 1852.

Hulda A. Liston was born Nov. 7, 1855.

George A. Liston was born Sept. 29, 1858.

DEATHS.

Everhart Liston died May the 9th 1888, aged 66 years 1 Mo. and 20 days.

Thankful Thorp Liston died Dec. the 18, 1901 aged 85 years 11 months and 8 days.

Martha M. Liston Graham died December 19, 1909 aged 92 years 11 months and three days.

John M. Liston died Sept. 2nd, 1925 aged 74 years and 1 month.

Eliza Jane Liston Cunningham died March 6, 1930 aged 80 yr. 3 mo. 3 days.

Minnie C. Liston died June the 8th, 1900 aged 41 years 9 months 5 days.

*   *   *   *

Family Bible of William Michael, title page gone, now owned by a daughter, Mrs. Cora Metheny, Route 1, Bruceton Mills, W. Va.

CERTIFICATE OF MARRIAGE.

This is to Certify that William Michael of Bruceton Mills, W. Va. and Rachel Forman of Bruceton Mills, W. Va. were by me joined together in Holy Matrimony on the 10th day of December, 1868 at Albrightsville, W. Va. in the presence of William King and Mary A. King, (sined) Rev. Felix Elliott.

OTHER MARRIAGES.

Albert F. Metheny and Cora A. Michael were married March Thirtieth Eighteen Hundred and Ninety Two.

Walter C. Pell and Ella F. Michael were married April Twenty eighth Eighteen Hundred and Ninety Seven.

BIRTHS.

William Michael born May 4, 1823.

Rachel Michael born March 6, 1838.

Cora A. Michael born June 7, 1870.

Ella F. Michael born Sept. 18, 1872.

Amanda R. Michael born June 17, 1874.

John R. Michael born April 9, 1878.

Albert F. Metheny born Mar. 3, 1870.

Walter C. Pell born July — 1870.

Ralph Metheny born Aug. 2, 1893.

May (Mae) Metheny born Mar. 12, 1895.

Hugh Metheny born June 14, 1898.

R. Wane Pell born July 6, 1898.

Guy M. Metheny born Sept. 14, 1900.

Ray S. Metheny born Dec. 23, 1904.

DEATHS.

William Michael died June 6, 1898.

Rachel Michael died April 1st, 1920.

Ralph E. Metheny died Sept. 30, 1922.

* * * *

The Mosser family Bible records now owned by Mrs. Edna Mosser King, a grand daughter of Jacob Mosser, living at Bruceton Mills, W. Va. Route No. 1. The title page bears no date and was stereotyped by E. White, New York, published and sold by Kimber and Sharpless at their book store No. 8 South 4th Street, Philadelphia, Pa.

Births of children born to Nicholus V. Mosser Snr.

(Apparently omitted).

Anne Fike born February 16, 1779.

Children born of Christian & Anne Mosser.

John was born June 30th, 1807.

Mary was born November 15th, 1808.

Jacob was born November 8th, 1810.

Christian was born October 30th, 1812.

Peter was born ――――――――.

Phebe Watson daughter of James and Mary Watson was born on the third day of March One thousand Eight Hundred and Seventeen.

Jacob Mosser and Phebe Watson were married by the Rev. Wynn on the tenth day of November in the year One thousand Eight hundred and thirty nine.

Births of children born to Jacob & Phebe Mosser.

Julia Ann was born the 13th November 1840.

William was born the 23rd November 1842.

Mary Ellen was born the 11th April 1845.

Nancy Ann was born the 1st January 1850.

DEATHS.

Christian Mosser son of Nicholas departed this life ――――― aged ―.

Anne Mosser departed this life March 15th 1873 aged 94 years 27 days.

Jacob Mosser son of Christian Mosser departed this life April 30 1883 aged 72 ys. 5 m. 22 days.

Phebe Watson Mosser wife of Jacob Mosser departed this life March 22 1897 aged 80 years & 18 days.

*   *   *   *

The family Bible of William Clark Myers, owned by a son Charles F. Myers, Route No. 1. Bruceton Mills, W. Va.

Wm. Clark Myers and Emma K. Street were married at the home of Isaac Armstrong on the 25th day of July, A. D. 1865 in presence of Harriet S. Street and Wm. Armstrong.

BIRTHS.

Amelia Jane Myers born Dec. 22, 1865.

Edgar Grant Myers born Oct. 1, 1867.

Rufus Colfax Myers born June 3, 1870.

Lauretta Alice Myers born Oct. 12, 1872.

Mary Ethelinda Myers born Dec. 12, 1874.

Harrison Elza Myers born April 21, 1877.

Joseph Claude Myers born Oct. 9, 1879.

James Washington Myers born Oct. 18, 1882.

Hannah E. Maude Myers born Mar. 16, 1885.
Charles F. Myers born July 16, 1887.
Perry Russell Myers born Dec. 1, 1889.
William Clark Myers born Dec. 3, 1841.
Emma K. Street Myers born April 23, 1846.

DEATHS.

Edgar Grant Myers died Dec. 11, 1896.
Hannah E. Maude Myers died Feb. 25, 1894.
James Washington Myers died Aug. 9, 1905.
Rufus Colfax Myers died Aug. 13, 1914.
William C. Myers died May 22, 1916.
Lauretta Alice Myers died   *   *   *
Perry Russell Myers died ――――――――, 1922.
Amelia Jane Turner died April 15, 1925.
Mary Ethelinda Murphy died Oct. 7, 1929.

*   *   *   *

Family record of Andrew S. McNare furnished by Mrs. Jessie
McNair Cunningham, a daughter living Route No. 1, Bruceton
Mills, W. Va. and, who also owns the Family Bible containing
records of Andrew C. McNair. His name is spelled McNare and
McNair in these records.

MARRIAGES.

Andrew S. McNair and Jemima Walls were married Aug. 15,
1858 by Rev. F. Bell.

J. C. McNair and Virginia Yeast were married Jan. 21, 1883 by
Rev. F. G. W. Ford.

Florence J. McNair and Jas. M. Smith were married Oct. 29, 1885
by Rev. L. W. Roberts.

Eugenia O. McNair and F. R. Speelman were married April 12,
1888 by Rev. L. W. Roberts.

Mary A. McNair and Jas. S. Everly were married Mar. 30, 1890
by Rev. A. S. Arnett.

BIRTHS.

Florence Jane McNare daughter of Andrew and Jemima McNare
was born November the 26th 1858.

James Charles son of Andrew and Jemima McNare was born January the 17th 1861.

Sarah Casandre and Ralph Houston son and daughter of Andrew and Jemima McNare was born October the 18th 1862.

Eugenia Ola daughter of Andrew and Jemima McNare was born March the 11th 1864.

Mary Anne McNare daughter of Andrew and Jemina McNare was born April the 3rd, 1866.

Dora Bertha McNare daughter of Andrew and Jemina McNare was born February the 14th, 1868.

Emma O. and Emmer O. son and daughter of Andrew and Jemina McNare was born March the 25, 1869.

DEATHS.

Jemima McNare died Aug. the 2, 1872 aged 37 years 9 Months & 2 days.

Ralph Houston McNare died November the 25th, 1862.

Sarah Casandre McNare died November the 27th, 1862.

Dora Bertha McNare died May the 21st, 1868.

The Family Bible of Andrew S. McNair was printed by National Printing Co., 724 - 728 Cherry St., Philadelphia, Penn. No date when printed. The fly leaf reads, "Presented to Sophia E. McNair by Andrew S. McNair Jan. 16, 1892."

CERTIFICATE OF MARRIAGE.

This Certifies that Andrew S. McNair of Fayette County, Penn., and Sophia E. Michael of Preston County, W. Va., were joined together by me in the Bonds of Holy Matrimony at brides home on the 20 day of November on the year of our Lord 1870, in presence of G. W. Walls and Jos. W. Michael. (signed) Rev. G. W. Crossfield.

BIRTHS.

Jessie B. McNair was born May the 20, 1876.

Edna E. McNair was born Oct. 8, 1879.

Andrew S. McNair born Jan. 12, 1836, died Apr. 14, 1917 aged 87 years 3 months 2 days.

Sophia E. McNair born Aug. 6, 1836, died Mar. 16, 1927 aged 90 years 7 months 10 days.

* * * *

Bible records of Family Bible once owned by Thankful Thorp Liston, a grand daughter of Rheuben Thorp, Revolutionary Soldier, and Bible is now owned by Edward Thorp King, great grand son of Thankful Thorp Liston. Bible published by McCarty and Davis No. 171 Market Street, Philadelphia, I. Ashmead and Company, printers, title page bears date 1831.

MARRIAGES.

Rheuben Thorp the son of Job Thorp was married to Hannah Lobdell Aug. 23, 1778.

James Thorp the son of Rheuben Thorp was married to Huldah Rush March the 16, 1815.

Thankful Thorp daughter of James Thorp was married to Everhart Liston March 8, 1846.

Adaline Thorp daughter of James Thorp was married to Sylvester Skinner January 20, 1839.

Jefferson T. Thorp son of James Thorp was married to Elizabeth Skinner February —— 1839.

BIRTHS.

The ages of Job Thorp's children:

Mary Thorp was born April 31, 1752.

Hannah Thorp was born Oct. 12, 1753.

Rheuben Thorp was born Jan. 16, 1755.

Jennet Thorp was born Mar. 21, 1757.

Benjamin Thorp was born Feb. 23, 1759.

Eunes Thorp was born June 19, 1761.

Then Jobe Thorp died and the widow married William Spencer. These are the children by Spencer.

Nathan Spencer was born July 9, 1764.

Icabod Spencer was born Feb. 4, 1766.

Sarah Spencer was born Oct. 18, 1767.

William Spencer was born Nov. 25, 1770.

Elizabeth Spencer was born July 15, 1772.

Morris Spencer was born Oct. 26, 1775.

Sarah the wife of Job Thorp then of Wm. Spencer was born April 7, 1733.

William Spencer was born May 8, 1739.

Hannah Lodbell consort of Rheuben Thorp was born Sept. 11, 1760.

The ages of the children of Rheuben Thorp son of Job Thorp.

Hannah Thorp was born May 25, 1779.

David Thorp was born March 9, 1781.
Mary Thorp was born July 26, 1783.
John W. Thorp was born July 4, 1785.
Reuben Thorp was born July 24, 1787.
Job Thorp was born Mar. 6, 1790.
James was born June 28, 1793.
Asa Thorp was born Feb. 22, 1796.
William Thorp was born Apr. 26, 1798.
Huldah Rush wife of James Thorp was born Sept. 11, 1796.
Michael Pane Thorp was born Sept. 3, 1825.
Adaline Thorp was born June 4, 1830.
Thankful Thorp daughter of James Thorp was born Feb. 10, 1816.
Thomas Jefferson Thorp was born Dec. 1, 1818.

DEATHS.

Hannah Thorp wife of Rheuben Thorp departed this life Nov. 14, 1826.

James Thorp died July 30, 1881 aged 88 years 1 month 2 days.

Huldah wife of James Thorp died July 28, 1878 aged 80 years 10 mo. 17 days.

Jefferson Thorp son of James Thorp died June — 1862 aged 45 years.

Sylvester Skinner died Jan. 17, 1870 aged 51 years 9 months 5 days.

Everhart Liston died May 9, 1888 aged 66 years 1 month 17 days.

Thankful Thorp Liston daughter of James Thorp died Dec. 18, 1901 aged 85 years 11 months 8 days.

David Thorp son of Reuben Thorp died Feb. 2, 1828.

John W. Thorp son of Reuben Thorp died Feb. 10, 1839.

Hannah Graham died Oct. 10, 1851.

＊　　＊　　＊　　＊

This record was copied from an old paper (in fragments) of the family of Philip Michael son of William Michael, 1776 - 1858.

Philip Michael was born March 14th 1804.
Sophia Michael was born May 25th 1806.

　　　Their children:
Eugenius Michael was born February 13, 1826.
William Michael was born Aprile 24, 1827.
Bolinda Michael was born October 7, 1828.
Philip Michael was born December 21, 1829.
Edgar Michael was born September 24, 1831.

John Michael was born February 7, 1833.

James Michael was born August 1, 1834.

Sophia Michael was born August 6, 1836.

Naomi Michael was born Aprile 4, 1838.

Rachel Michael was born May 13, 1840.

Mary Michael was born January 12, 1842.

George G. Michael was born June 22, 1844.

Joseph W. and Benjamin A. Michael was born December 24, 1845.

Sarah A. Michael was born Aprile 20, 1850.

* * * *

Family Bible of George W. Walls, no date of publication, and was found stored in a Lodge building at Pisgah, W. Va.

BIRTHS.

George W. Walls was born Aprile the 24th A. D. 1830.

Belinda Walls was born Oct. the 7th A. D. 1828.

James Harvey Walls was born January the 20th, 1855.

Richard Forman Walls was born November the 22nd, 1856.

Phillip McCloyd Walls was born September the 6th A. D. 1858.

Olive Oneda Walls was born Aprile the 18th A. D. 1862.

Eli Benton Walls was born July the 12 A. D. 1864.

Joseph Laughlin Walls was born November the 20th, 1866.

Estella Grace Walls was born February the 9 A. D. 1872.

* * * *

Family Bible of William Alexander Yeast now owned by a daughter, Effie Cunningham, 48 Delaware Avenue, Uniontown, Penn. Bible published by T. Coulton & J. Porter, 200 Mulberry St., New York. No date.

BIRTHS.

William Alexander Yeast son of Adam and Susan Yeast was born Sept. 25, 1829. in Allegany County Maryland.

Martha Ellen Yeast formerly Martha Ellen Dean daughter of Edward and Mary Ann Dean was born May 18, 1833 in Fayette County, Penn.

Catherine Jane Yeast formerly Catherine Jane Ross was born July 30, 1842 in Allegany County Maryland.

John Wesley Yeast son of William and Martha Ellen Yeast was born Dec. 13, A. D. 1854 in Preston County, Virginia.

Mary Ann Yeast daughter of William and Martha E. Yeast was born Nov. 16, A. D. 1856 in Preston County, Virginia.

Martha Jane Yeast daughter of William and Martha Ellen Yeast was born June 7, 1858 in Preston County, Virginia.

Virginia Yeast daughter of William and Martha Ellen Yeast was born March 9, A. D. 1860 in Preston County, Virginia.

Archey Yeast son of William and Martha Ellen Yeast was born April 30, A. D. 1862 in Preston County, Virginia.

Ellsworth Yeast son of William and Martha Ellen Yeast was born Nov. 8, A. D. 1863 in Preston County, West Virginia.

Joseph Heaster Yeast son of William and Catherine Jane Yeast was born Jan. 30 A. D. 1867 in Preston County, West Virginia.

Emma Alice Yeast daughter of William and Catherine Jane Yeast was born July 12, 1869 in Preston County, West Virginia.

William Bruce Yeast son of William A. and Catherine Jane Yeast was born Mar. 2, 1871 in Preston County, West Virginia.

Arminta Ann Yeast daughter of William and Catherine Jane Yeast was born August 27, 187— in Preston County, West Virginia.

James Albert Yeast son of William A. and Catherine Jane Yeast was born April 2, 1878.

Agnes Edna Yeast daughter of William A. and Catherine Jane Yeast was born Sept. 8, 1880.

Effie Pearl Yeast daughter of William A. and Catherine Jane Yeast was born Feb. 6, 1883.

DEATHS.

Martha Ellen Yeast departed this life Nov. 29, 1863 aged 30 years 6 months & 11 days.

Mary Ann Yeast daughter of William and Martha E. Yeast departed this life Dec. 2, A. D. 1862 aged 6 years & 16 days.

Martha Jane Yeast daughter of William and Martha E. Yeast departed this life Dec. 4, A. D. 1862 aged 4 years 5 mo. & 23 days.

Archey Yeast son of William and Martha E. Yeast departed this life Dec. 24, 1862 aged seven months and 24 days.

Ellsworth Yeast son of William and Martha Ellen Yeast departed this life Nov. 23, 1863 aged 15 days.

William Bruce Yeast son of William and Catherine Yeast departed this life Dec. 30, 1871 aged 9 mo. & 28 days.

Annie Yeast daughter of William and Catherine Yeast died Oct. 12, 1872.

William Alexander Yeast died May 26, 1906 aged 76 years 8 Mo. 1 day.

MARRIAGES.

William Yeast and Martha Ellen Yeast formerly Martha Ellen Dean were married Feb. 26, A. D. 1854.

William Yeast and Catherine Jane Yeast formerly Catherine Jane Ross were married Feb. 4th, A. D. 1864.

CEMETERY RECORDS

Cemetery at Sugar Valley Church, located on highway about three and one-half miles south of Bruceton Mills, W. Va., and in Pleasant District, Preston County.   Copied July 4, 1931.

Ezra M. Falkenstein Jan. 23, 1840 - Feb. 16, 1916. Lydia his wife Oct. 18, 1841 - Apr. 26, 1919.

Four graves unmarked.

Iona B. dau. of H. E. & I. E. Shields Apr. 18, 1907 - Apr. 21, 1907.

Marcelite dau. of H. E. & I. E. Shields June 26, 1908 - May 21, 1909.

Frederick P. son of E. F. & H. E. Colebank Mar. 16, 1910 - Apr. 1, 1910.

One grave unmarked.

Rolla Liston 1852 - 1922. Esther his wife 1856 - 1921.

Zelima V. Miller Sept. 30, 1857 - Feb. 27, 1908 age 50 yrs. 4 mo. 27 days.

May dau. of A. H. & V. Miller Feb. 9, 1889 - Apr. 2, 1911.

Mildred B. Miller June 19, 1907 - Dec. 2, 1907.

One grave unmarked.

Jacob Cale 1809 - 1862. Sarah his wife 1816 -1894. (Loose stone lying at foot of above stone, Jacob Cale died Sept. 13, 1862 aged 53 years 4 mo. 2 days.

Julianna dau. of J. &. S. Cale died May 26, 1859 aged 3 yrs. 5 mo. 22 days.

Catherine Cale born April 1, 1892 died April 25, 1918.

William T. Cale 1871 - 1916. Elizabeth his wife 1871 - ——.

One grave unmarked.

William Floyd Frankhauser Sept. 25, 1877 - Jan. 28, 1930.

One grave unmarked.

Ira Graham 1870 - 1876.

Father, Ebenezer Graham 1834 - 1926. Mother Elizabeth Cale 1838 - 1926.

John M. Smith Sept. 22, 1818 - May 3, 1867. Charlotte his wife June 24, 1822 - Mar. 3, 1912. Samuel their son Feb. 2, 1855 - Dec. 16, 1903.

Harrison H. son of J. M. & G. Smith died Jan. 10, 1854 aged 6 yrs. 23 days.

One grave unmarked.

Son of S. F. & E. L. Cale born Oct. 3, 1905 died Nov. 22, 1906 aged 1 year 1 mo. 19 days.

Avis dau. of John L. & Laura Keenan born Mar. 26, 1896 died June 29, 1902.

Four graves unmarked.

Isaac Newton Forman Nov. 6, 1853 - June 14, 1921. Francis A. his wife Oct. 5, 1854 -July 31, 1897.

One grave unmarked.

J. W. Jackson 1862 - 1918. Sarah S. Jackson 1858 - 1929.

Amir Smith 1863 ———. Martha A. his wife born Feb. 27, 1861 died Dec. 3, 1928.

John A. Light June 23, 1860 - Dec. 1, 1913. Effie D. Light June 16, 1864 - ———.

J. Frank Loraw 1884 - 1928. his wife G. Hazel 1895 - ———.

Charles W. Forman Jan. 6, 1875 - ———. Ivy M. his wife June 15, 1873 - Mar. 27, 1918.

Welington G. S. son of T. M. & A. E. Everly May 8, 1916 - Aug. 15, 1916.

Elijah C. Metheny born July 16, 1818. His wife Christena born Oct. 7, 1820 died Mar. 12, 1902.

Harmon B. son of E. C. & C. A. Metheny died Nov. 2, 1875 aged 19 yrs. 4 mo. 7 days.

Sarah J. dau of E. C. & C. A. Metheny born Feb. 14, 1842 died Jan. 17, 1893.

Two graves unmarked.

Mattie wife of H. G. Jenkins died Dec. 17, 1877 aged 22 yrs. & 11 mo.

Lewis W. Wolf died Oct. 4, 1876 aged 25 years 10 mo. & 1 day.

Mary A. dau. of L. W. & I. Wolf died July 23, 1875 aged 14 days.

Charles F. son of L. W. & I Wolf died Jan. 13, 1872 aged 1 yr. 7 mo. 16 ds.

Hannah H. wife of H. Rumble died Nov. 25, 1874 aged 87 yrs. & 28 days.

Four graves unmarked.

W. Marshall son of W. C. & S. C. Smith Sept. 6, 1888 - Jan. 10, 1896.

Mathias Forman 1844 - 1917. Alcinda his wife 1846 - 1927. J. Franklin 1887 - 1888.

One grave unmarked.

Jacob Frankhouser born Dec. 22, 1823 died Sept. 10, 1897.

Elizabeth Frankhouser born May 30, 1835 died April 22, 1905 age 69 yrs. 10 mo. 22 days.

William A. son of J. & E. Frankhouser died Aug. 8, 1890 aged 24 yrs. 2 mo. 10 days.

William son of J. S. & Jennie Teets died Jan. 27, 1898 age 5 yr. 7 mo. 4 ds.

Peter Spahr died Mar. 4, 1901 aged 80 years.

Mary Barb wife of Peter Spahr born May 26, 1825 died Mar. 27, 1895.

Martha P. dau. of Mary A. Wilson born Aug. 20, 1884 died May 15, 1892.

Esta L. dau. of Mary A. Wilson born Nov. 4, 1882 died May 2, 1892.

J. A. Jacobs born July 10, 1871 died June 11, 1899.

William Wilson Mar. 20, 1826 - Jan. 31, 1911. Martha A. his wife Apr. 9, 1828 - June 23, 1903.

Raymond C. Bishop 1862 - ———. Laura E. his wife 1864 - 1929. Two graves unmarked.

Marshall A. Wolf 1855 - 1917.

J. Allen Miller born Jan. 21, 1837 died June 4, 1900 aged 63 years 4 mo. 14 days.

Catherine A. wife of J. A. Miller born Jan. 14, 1837 - ———.

George W. son of Wm. H. & S. E. Harner born July 12, 1881 died Jan. 8, 1882 age 5 mo. 2 days.

Wm. H. Harner 1844 - 1895. Sarah E. his wife 1849 - ———.

Hadley F. Smith June 3, 1847 - Apr. 19, 1927, Malissa J. Smith Mar. 26, 1854 - July 26, 1915.

Roy J. son of H. F. & M. J. Smith born & died Mar. 10, 1882.

Henry E. Cale Feb. 18, 1836 - Apr. 29, 1905. Sarah E. Cale May 16, 1840 - May 6, 1882.

Philip B. Michael Nov. 13, 1837 - Dec. 15, 1924. Lavinia A. his wife Jan. 18, 1835 - May 18, 1908.

Mollie E. wife of Dr. E. T. Martin born Jan. 30, 1865 died June 6, 1894.

Carrol son of Dr. E. T. & M. E. Martin born June 5, 1894 died Oct. 7, 1894.

Maud dau. of J. M. & C. J. Metheny died Sept. 28, 1881 aged 1 yr. 8 days.

George A. son of J. M. & C. J. Metheny died Nov. 28, 1871 aged 10 mo. 16 ds.

Guy A. Bishop Oct. 23, 1835 - Apr. 9, 1924. Sarah J. his wife Nov. 24, 1840 ———.

Mary wife of Benj. Trembley died May 12, 1878 aged 63 yrs. 2 mo. 15 days.

Sarah Ann Smith Nov. 5, 1819 - May 15, 1886.

John G. Smith died June 24, 1874 aged 69 yrs. 11 mo. 7 days.

Mary wife of John G. Smith born Dec. 28, 1806 died ———1, 1902.

Louis C. Frankhouser Nov. 8, 1849 - Nov. 6, 1909. Dellie his wife May 9, 1859 - ———.

George W. Miller 1846 - 1921. Hattie his wife 1855 - 19—. One grave unmarked.

Norman R. son of B. A. & C. E. Liston June 6, 1917 - Sept. 23, 1917.

Norma Delphine Liston Dec. 8, 1922 — Jan. 2, 1923.

Two graves unmarked.

Elmer C. Wilson 1876 - ———. Minerva S. his wife 1878 - 1925.

Alonzo Reese son of E. C. & M. S. Wilson June 18, 1899 - Aug. 31, 1903.

Lilly F. dau. of E. K. & E. J. Wilson died Sept. 16, 1888 aged 12 yrs. 5 mo. 15 days.

Alice Falkenstine 1846 - 1914.

Flora M. dau. of L. N. & M. V. Groves born June 13, 1888 died Aug. 3, 1888.

LaFayette N. Groves born Sept. 4, 1862 died June 11, 1888.

Elle A. Davis died Apr. 1, 1876 aged 5 yr. 1 mo. 10 days.

Mary E. H. wife of James E. Jackson June 22, 1840 - Mar. 13, 1917.

Mary Rebecca dau. of J. W. & M. C. Michael died May 26, 1881 aged 5 yrs. 5 mo. 15 days.

Bertie D. son of S. E. & M. M. Kelly died Sept. 23, 1889 aged 5 yrs. 11 mo. & 28 days.

Jefferson Cuppett died Oct. 28, 1892 aged 60 yr. 7 mo. 10 days.

Margaret wife of Jefferson Cuppett died Nov. 29, 1893 aged 56 years 10 mo. 29 days.

Harrison M. Smith born May 6, 1825 died Nov. 21, 1895 aged 70 yrs. 6 mo. 15 days.

Elizabeth Smith born Apr. 9, 1825 died Sept. 18, 1895 age 70 years 5 mo. 9 days.

Elmer I. Titchnell 1840 - 1922.

Cornelia J. dau. of M. & A. I. Titchnell born Oct. 14, 1880 died Sept. 21, 1889.

Samuel Groves died June 11, 1883 aged 55 yrs. 10 mo. & 15 days.

Rebecca wife of Samuel Groves died Jan. 26, 1892 aged 70 years 11 mo. 15 days.

Jacob Groves Dec. 2, 1823 - Sept. 14, 1875.

Hannah wife of Jacob Groves Nov. 26, 1833 - Feb. 19, 1923.

William A. Loraw died Sept. 18, 1895 aged 62 yrs. 13 days. Elvira wife of Wm. A. Loraw born Mar. 24, 1842 died Jan. 12, 1919.

Benjamin Liston died Nov. 1, 1922 aged 76 yrs. 9 mo. 7 days.

Margaret J. Liston died Oct. 14, 1908 age 59 yrs. 9 mo. 9 days.

Loose stone lying in northeast corner of cemetery, Sarah E. wife of H. E. Cale died May 6, 1882 aged 42 yrs. 1 mo. & 20 days.

*   *   *   *

Cemetery at Mt. Moriah Church on Highway three-fourths of a mile south of the village of Valley Point, Pleasant District, Preston County, W. Va.   Copied July 4, 1931.

Mary B. dau. of G. O. & R. M. Fortney Jan. 24, 1920 - Mar. 7, 1920.

Ester Ruth Fortney Nov. 18, 1927 - Nov. 18, 1927.

Four graves unmarked.

Evelyn Marguerite dau. of O. R. & B. E. Martin Oct. 15, 1920 - Jan. 18, 1922.

Norman Roy son of C. D. & N. F. Groves July 16, 1924-Dec. 11, 1926.

Six graves unmarked.

Noah Liston July 3, 1857 - Jan. 19, 1929, Mary E. Liston Sept. 13, 1859 - ———.

Walter D. Liston 1879 - ———. Mary E. his wife 1879 - 1919.

Freda Olive Liston Mar. 21, 1916 - Apr. 28, 1916.

Three graves unmarked.

Virginia dau. of C. D. & H. S. Lewis 1927 - 1930.

Isaac N. Graham 1847 - 1895. Martha M. 1847 - 1909.   Edith 1885 - 1911.

David Graham Sept. 17, 1822 - Feb. 14, 1906.

Harrison Teets Feb. 12, 1821 - Sept. 18, 1898.

Amos Teets born Aug. 25, 1848 died Dec. 14, 1900. Ruhama Teets born Nov. 14, 1848 - ——————.

Benjamin S. son of A. & R. Teets died Aug. 4, 1890 aged 8 yrs. 6 mo. 7 days.

Rachel S. J. dau. of A. & R. Teets died Jan. 2, 1880 aged 4 yrs. 2 mo. 6 days.

Perry D. son of A. & R. Teets born July 30 died Apr. 15, 1902.

One grave unmarked.

Carl B. son of J. W. & Lettie Goff Apr. 20, 1892 - Sept. 29, 1913.

Cora Ethel wife of C. D. Blake Dec. 3, 1889 - May 28, 1916.

J. J. Martin born Nov. 16, 1832 died July 8, 1918 aged 85 yrs. 7 mo. & 22 days. Sarah wife of J. J. Martin born Dec. 5, 1840 died May 11, 1896 age 55 yrs 5 mo. 6 days.

Four graves unmarked.

Jerome L. Falkenstine died Apr. 23, 1898 aged 46 yrs. 3 mo. & 23 days.

Mary E. wife of J. L. Falkenstine died May 9, 1886 aged 33 yrs. & 21 days.

Noah Z. Liston 1856 - 1930. Elizabeth M. his wife 1856 - 1929.

Laura B. Metheny born July 4, 1876 died Feb. 22, 1894.

Letitia C. wife of J. E. Liston Apr. 22, 1878 - June 7, 1903.

Lewis Smith July 27, 1834 - June 25, 1929. Lydda A. his wife Dec. 2, 1836 - Apr. 8, 1913.

Stephen Martin Feb. 16, 1827 - ——————.   Phebe his wife Oct. 13, 1829 - Nov. 24, 1908 age 79 yrs. 1 mo. 11 days.

One grave unmarked.

Daniel H. Martin born Sept. 10, 1823 - ——————.   Catherine wife of D. H. Martin born May 6, 1827 died Jan. 22, 1881 age 53 years 8 mo. 16 days.

Sara Jane wife of J. W. Thomas born Nov. 2, 1844 died Apr. 14, 1894 aged 49 years 5 mo. 12 days.

Anna G. dau. of Smith & Mary J. Martin died Sept. 15, 1913 aged 19 yrs. 7 mo. 18 das.

David M. Martin 1853 - 1931. Martha A. his wife 1858 - 19—.

Asbury Liston born Feb. 23, 1861 died —————. Ida A. wife of Asbury Liston born June 1, 1864 died Nov. 7, 1900 aged 36 yrs. 4 mo. 6 da.

Sheridan D. son of A. & I. Liston born Feb. 21, 1896 died Oct. 16, 1897 aged 1 yr. 7 mo. 25 da.

Three graves unmarked.

Leona Titchnell Walls born Jan. 12, 1908 died Dec. 4, 1929.

Junior infant son of Guy & Effie Crane Sept. 21, 1918 - Oct. 3, 1918.

Arlie E. son of J. S. & Eva Smith Apr. 17, 1894 - Mar. 4, 1911.

James K. Martin died July 21, 1900 aged 68 yrs. 9 mo. 4 days.

Margaret Martin born June 21, 1834 died Jan. 4, 1905.

Alpheus Metheny July 11, 1848 - Jan. 6, 1920. Nancy Ann his wife Apr. 2, 1855 - Nov. 20, 1900.

John A. Lamberd 1861 - 19—. Emma J. his wife 1862 - 1927.

James H. Lamberd 1887 - 1927.

John A. Conner Jan. 26, 1862 - Sept. 22, 1909.

Jane DeVall Aug. 24, 1830 - Oct. 23, 1906.

Thomas J. Walls Feb. 15, 1859 - Apr. 24, 1901.

One grave unmarked.

Earnest B. Walls born Apr. 5, 1896 died Aug. 16, 1900.

Hazel G. wife of A. F. Teets Feb. 22, 1894 - Dec. 2, 1918.

One grave unmarked.

Joel Titchnell Aug. 23, 1848 - —————. Sarah Lee his wife June 21, 1853 - July 6, 1920.

Martha E. dau. of J. M. & H. C. McNear died Nov. 30, 1900 aged 18 yr. 10 mo. 23 da.

Lucy V. wife of W. H. Rhodeheaver born Dec. 5, 1871 died Oct. 3, 1903 aged 31 yrs. 9 mo. 28 da.

Alston Dayton son of W. H. & L. V. Rhodeheaver born Aug. 22, 1900 died Dec. 2, 1902.

Daniel McNear Mar. 10, 1829 - Aug. 14, 1906 age 77 yrs. 5 mo. 4 days. Rachel wife of Daniel McNear Sept. 15, 1836 - Aug. 2, 1906 age 69 yrs. 10 mo. 17 days.

Isaac L. Wilson Mar. 11, 1828 - July 18, 1909.

Catherine wife of Isaac Wilson Jan. 1, 1841 - Feb. 17, 1917.

Eben S. Liston 1877 - —————. Artie his wife 1877 - 1926.

Two graves unmarked (recent).

Hallie O. son of J. A. & Daisy C. Martin Feb. 25, 1901 - Feb. 5, 1904.

Christian W. Martin 1850 - 1927. Louvenia A. his wife 1857 - —————.

*   *   *   *

The Cress Cemetery near Mt. Nebo Church about one and one-half miles south of Rockville, and in Pleasant District, Preston County, W. Va. Copied July 5, 1931.

Levi A. Cale Apr. 3, 1864 - ———. Martha V. Cale July 3, 1861 - Dec. 2, 1908.

William H. Jenkins Oct. 4, 1832 - July 1, 1909. Louisa J. his wife July 16, 1832 - Jan. 16, 1910.

Ten graves unmarked.

Erma Aldona Groves 1906 - 1909.

Emma J. Galloway died Sept. 15, 1903 aged 14 days.

Isaiah Metheny born Nov. 3, 1817 died Sept. 30, 1893. Elizabeth wife of I. Metheny born Apr. 8, 1820 died Jan. 29, 1891.

Jacob N. Cress 1829 - 1908. Lucinda his wife 1823 - 1901.

Simon P. son of J. A. & M. A. Cress Jan. 15, 188— - May 2, 1881.

Delila Cale June 14, 1839 - Sept. 17, 1890. Erected by her brother Elijah Cale.

Wilbert F. son of A. A. & P. J. Christopher Oct. 1, — Dec. 28, 1896.

Three graves unmarked.

Lewis Soverns born Nov. 13, 1828 died July 15, 1913. Sophia his wife born Apr. 6, 1823 died Mar. 22, 1904.

Everhart Liston born Mar. 22, 1822 died May 9, 1888.

Thankful Liston born Jan. 10, 1816 died Dec. 18, 1901.

John M. Liston 1852 - 1925.

Azareel Cale Co. E 3rd Reg. Md. Vol. 1836 - 1923. Emily A. his wife 1847 - 19—.

Three graves unmarked.

John H. son of A. Z. & E. A. Cale died Apr. 22, 1897 aged 10 yr. 3 mo. 10 days.

Elijah Cale Oct. 14, 1830 - Nov. 24, 1915. Co. A 7th W. Va. Inft.

Lizzie B. dau. of J. P. & A. A. Bowermaster died May 12, 1883 aged 14 yr. 5 mo. 2 days.

Mary H. dau. of J. P. & A. A. Bowermaster born June 3, 1862 died Feb. 21, 1873.

Levi Gibson died Apr. 6, 1884 aged 74 yr. 10 mo. 5 da. Elizabeth Gibson died Apr. 3, 1888 aged 72 yr. 5 mo. 18 da.

Elizabeth wife of James Gibson died May 20, 1857 aged 69 years.

Mary Smith wife of the Rev. Jonathan Smith was born Feb. the 28, 1762 and departed this life Mar. 30th 1827 aged 65 yrs. 2 mo. "The tender parent wails no more her loss nor labors more beneath lifes heavy load. The anxious soul released from fears and woes has found her home her children & her god."

Sylvanus son of L. & E. Gibson died Nov. 10, 1836 aged 6 mo. 7 days.

One grave unmarked.

Ludema dau. of L. & E. Gibson died Mar. 10, 1861 aged 13 yr. 11 mo. 9 days.

William son of L. & E. Gibson died Mar. 17, 1861 aged 6 yr. 11 mo. 12 days.

James E. son of L. & E. Gibson died Sept. 27, 1862 aged 18 yrs. 7 mo. 21 days.

Martin son of L. & E. Gibson Sergeant of Co. H. 3rd P. H. B. Md. Inft. died Nov. 28, 1863 aged 23 yr. 11 mo. 4 days.

Nelson H. Gibson 1837 - 1912. Virginia his wife 1847 - 1917.

Harry E. son of W. E. & Ella O. Kidwell April 13, 1907 - Oct. 3, 1907.

One grave unmarked.

J. M. Light Dec. 27, 1856 - ————. Maggie J. May. 17, 1851 - Mar. 19, 1926.

Eliza F. Jenkins born July 14, 1817 died Feb. 16, 1903.

Victoria E. wife of J. J. Jenkins born Apr. 13, 1864 died Dec. 24, 1898.

Three graves unmarked.

Roxey D. dau of M. J. & A. E. Christopher Nov. 26, 1892 - Feb. 3, 1893.

Alcineous J. son of S. J. & S. E. Hileman born Apr. 21, 1870 died May 9, 1887.

Three graves unmarked.

Elizabeth wife of John G. Smith died May 21, 1850 aged 66 yr. 6 mo.

Agnes Smith died May the 24 1827 aged Fifty 6 years wife of the Rev. John G. Smith. - Joshua 23 - 8 But cleave unto the lord your god as ye have done unto this day. Remember man as you pas By, as you are now So once was i. as i am now So you must be * * * yourself (unreadable) * * * me.

Eight graves unmarked.

John Liston died november 19, 1831 aged 64 yr. 8 mo. Dath is a Dat to Nater due That i have paid and so must you.

Eve J. Smith 1859 - 1883. Wm. Ira Smith born & died 1882.

Asa Metheny died July 21, 1883 aged 63 y. 3 m. 4 d.

Augustine Wolf Jan. 25, 1832 - June 12, 1902. Sarah his wife June 12, 1831 - Apr. 6, 1905.

Virgil M. son of W. L. & Alta Smith July 5, 1899 - May 11, 1902.

R. F. Jenkins Apr. 13, 1842 - Mar. 10, 1918. Laodicea wife of R. F. Jenkins Apr. 11, 1842 - Dec. 23, 1906.

Gilbert G. Wolf Apr. 1, 1907 - Jan. 2, 1910.

Baby (girl) Wolf died Jan. 29, 1930.

Loose stone near gate, Azareel Cale 1836 - 19—.

*   *   *   *

Abandoned cemetery on farm originally owned by Robert Cunningham, now owned by Ivan Bishop, on top of hill about two miles west of Rockville, in Pleasant District, Preston County, W. Va. Copied July 5, 1931.

Peter Lambert Co. H 3rd Md. P. H. B. Inft.

Jacob G. son of J. G. & M. Smith died Oct. 5, 1854 aged 18 yr. 8 mo. 6 d.

Mary A. dau. of J. G. & M. Smith died Feb. 23, 1826 aged 1 mo. 25 days.

Phebe dau. of J. G. & M. Smith died May 10, 1865 aged 13 yr, 10 mo. 5 da.

Nathan Metheny died Feb. 21, 1856 aged 74 yrs. 5 mo. 7 da.

Mary Ann wife of Nathan Metheny died Sept. 5, 1854 aged 70 yrs. 8 mo. 13 da.

Allen son of A. & N. Metheny died Oct. 6, 1851 aged 13 yr. 1 mo. 2 da.

Peter Everly died agu 10th in 1819 aged 70 years.

Caty Everly died dec the 1 day in 1820 aged 72 years. "& Rose the Man the Evning Come and death did Vale my Evning Sun."

Henry Everly died Mar. 31, 1851 aged about 77 yrs.

Robert Cunningham died June 7, 1889 in his 81 year. Sarah P. wife of Robert Cunningham died June 9, 1880 in her 72 year.

Thirty-seven graves unmarked except for flat field stones marking head and foot of graves.

*   *   *   *

Cemetery at Bruceton Mills, Grant District, Preston County, W. Va.   Copied July 6, 1931.

Mary M. wife of C. M. Swift 1890 - 1918.

Three graves unmarked.

Milton F. Martin June 29, 1832 - Jan. 30, 1912. Lydia Martin Dec. 28, 1836 - Feb. 4, 1908. Eliza A. Martin June 22, 1864 - May 7, 1901. Nailor E. Martin Nov. 2, 1868 - Aug. 11, 1912.

Five graves unmarked.

S. H. Morris 1861 - ———. Isabella Morris his wife 1858 - 1918.

Allen Smith aged 72 yrs. Margaret J. Smith born Aug. 3, 1835 died Sept. 12, 1900. Nancy Metheny aged 80 yrs. Elizabeth Saucer aged 75 yrs. Mahala Metheny aged 70 yrs.

Mrs. Belle Wilt wife of Rev. S. W. Wilt died Oct. 19, 1895.

Rebecca J. dau. of J. & E. Guseman died Dec. 29, 1891 aged 28 yr's.
10 mo. & 22 ds.

J. A. Rodeheaver died Feb. 18, 1905 aged 49 y. 7 m. & 6 d's.

Synthy E. wife of J. A. Rodeheaver died July 26, 1891 aged 35 y's.
7 mo. & 7 d's.

One grave unmarked.

David B. Rodeheaver born Apr. 4, 1887 died Nov. 24, 1904.

Levi Cale died Apr. 26, 1897 age 61 ys. 7 ms. 8 ds.

Jacob Prinkey 1827 - 1922. Ann his wife 1833 - 1905.

Andrew S. McNare 1836 - 1917. Sophia E. his wife 1836 - 1927.

One grave unmarked.

Charles W. Cramer 1860 - 1917. Lida his wife 1859 - ———. (recent
grave).

Our darling Baby Collins.

Wm. C. Armstrong 1831 - 1907. Lee Anne his wife 1845 - ———.

Anna wife of G. R. Armstrong 1885 - 1908.

Three graves unmarked.

John J. Spiker Feb. 21, 1835 - ———. Co. E 6th W. Va. Vol. Cav.

Lucinda wife of John J Spiker Feb. 11, 1836 - Nov. 4, 1904.

Amos Goodwin born July 13, 1837 died Apr. 12, 1900. Sarah J. wife
of Amos Goodwin born Dec. 27, 1842 died Dec. 11, 1914.

Helen Clair dau. of M. F. & Mary B. Walls May 4, 1907 - Jan. 6,
1908.

Ida wife of Wm. J. Bowermaster born July 27, 1872 died March 24,
1901.

John P. Bowermaster Sept. 5, 1833 - Feb. 20, 1911.

Isaac Guseman 1826 - 1911. Elizabeth 1826 - 1867. Susanna 1848 -
1903. Rebecca J. 1863 - 1891.

John M. Collins 1845 - ———. Sarah A. 1850 - 1917. Joseph H. 1870 -
1915. Elizabeth 1879 - 1899. Clarence 1884 - 1915. Marie 1890 -
1916.

Otis R. son of H. & A. M. Benson died Dec. 13, 1897 aged 16
ms. 4 ds.

One grave unmarked.

Margaret M. wife of T. D. Dye 1901 - 1927.

Emma J. Evans born May 10, 1864 died May 29, 1895 dau of J. P.
& D. D. Bowermaster. Fannie A. Evans born Apr. 21, 1895 died
Aug. 15, 1895.

Wm. H. Miller June 8, 1834 - Feb. 16, 1920. Elizabeth his wife Oct.
29, 1852 - May 10, 1930. Laurin Lovell son of W. H. & L. Miller
born Nov. 24, 1876 died Aug. 12, 1893.

One grave unmarked.

Benj. Ross Spiker 1856 - 1925.

Jacob Bowman Co. G 67 Pa. Inft.

Two graves unmarked.

B. Merle dau. of F. M. & J. B. Cunningham born Oct. 12, 1899 died
Aug. 4, 1901.

One grave unmarked.

Anna M. Benson Apr. 25, 1873 - Dec. 9, 1907.

Samuel Sliger 1831 - 1913.

One grave unmarked.

Joseph C. Carroll 1850 - 1922. Mary C. his wife 1862 - 19—.

Mary T. Wheeler Aug. 22, 1892 - Nov. 28, 1910.

Infant son of J. W. & S. B. Wheeler Feb. 7, 1901.

Albert S. Wheeler 1888 - 1930. Pauline M. his wife 1898 - ——.

Joseph W. Michael 1845 - 1910. Mary R. 1875 - 1881.

Luther Collins 1852 - 1926. Lizzie Collins 1856 - 1913. Hosea Collins
1879 - 1905.

William M. Wolf 1840 - 1929. Florence C. his wife 1845 - 1912.
Oliver - son - 1872 - 1918.

Andrew Collins born July 22, 1811 died Nov. 5, 1893. Olivia Collins
born Oct. 29, 1824 died ———.

James M. Collins born Aug. 5, 1858. Ada F. wife of J. M. Collins
born May 19, 1861 died Nov. 15, 1895.

James A. son of J. M. & A. F. Collins born July 23, 1891 died Dec.
15, 1892.

Isaac Armstrong born Nov. 5, 1823 died Apr. 5, 1887. Minerva Ellen
1826 - 1911. Jennie H. 1860 - 1898.

Lorna Beth dau. of H. C. & N. Herring Jan. 4, 1919.

Glen son of J. W. & M. A. Haines Oct. 28, 1906 - Mar. 17, 1907.

Dr. Milton S. Bryte 1846 - 1902. Body interred in National Cemetery, Dayton, Ohio. Georgiana F. his wife 1853 - 1901.

Hannah Bryte born Jan. 21, 1821 died Jan. 20, 1892. Jane Bryte born
Nov. 26, 1825 died Jan. 22, 1892.

Samuel Koontz born Jan. 7, 1800 died Jan. 15, 1895.

Children of J. T. & S. J. Smith. Robert R. born Aug. 19, 1887. Herbert A. born July 21, 1896 died Aug. 7, 1896.

Josiah T. Smith Feb. 17, 1852 - Nov. 22, 1905.

Josiah Smith Oct. 12, 1811 - May 31, 1899. Lucinda C. wife of Josiah
Smith Mar. 13, 1830 - Oct. 5, 1911. Mary J. Cuppett Jan. 23, 1840
- May 14, 1901.
Sept. 5, 1855 - July 26, 1893.

Ralph E. son of R. H. & L. L. Myers July 24, 1910 - Sept. 22, 1910.

Mary Ann Caton born Aug. 3, 1866 died Apr. 18, 1888 aged 21 yrs. 8 mo. 15 ds.

Philip Michael born Mar. 14, 1804 died Feb. 2, 1892. Sophia Michael born May 25, 1806 died Feb. 27, 1895.

Frederick Copeman 1849 - 1926.

Sabina Cale Copeman 1860 - 1892.

Wm. Cloyd Copeman 1892 - 1892.

James Walter son of J. & S. J. Brooks died Jan. 22, 1892 aged 9 ms. 17 ds.

Thaddeus S. Cunningham 1842 - 1925.

Eliza . Cunningham 1849 - 1930.

Mildred dau. of W. L. & E. O. Conner born Nov. 12, 1900 died Nov. 26, 1900.

Albert Collins 1867 - 1918. Darwin - son - 1918 - 1920.

Thurman M. King 1863 - 1930.

Emma wife of W. M. Smith Aug. 2, 1857 - May 28, 1900.

One grave unmarked.

Infant son of R. A. & L. M. Smith 1920 - 1920.

Sarah Etta wife of John M. McNair born May 26, 1871 died Oct. 5, 1894 aged 23 ys. 4 mo. 10 ds.

Two graves unmarked.

Samuel T. Darby Sept. 6, 1827 - May 24, 1907. Susanna wife of S̃. T. Darby May 15, 1832 - Dec. 14, 1902.

Emma S. dau. of C. & M. S. Kantner died Jan. 8, 1871 aged 9 ys. 2 ms. 23 ds.

Three graves unmarked.

Samuel Wiles born Jan. 21, 1821 died Sept. 15, 1898. Sophrona J. wife of S. Wiles born Dec. 24, 1830 died Mar. 17, 1873.

Eight graves unmarked.

Omar Y. Shaw 1868 - 19—. Dora W. 1869 - 1924.

William Shaw born April 1827 died Dec. 30, 1896 aged 69 ys. 3 ms.

One grave unmarked.

James W. Shaw July 4, 1811 - Jan. 29, 1896. Mary A. his wife Sept. 23, 1838 - Sept. 24, 1913. Cameron W. Aug. 17, 1865 - Oct. 26, 1888. Georgia A. Oct. 3, 1879 - Sept. 24, 1907.

Wayne son of J. S. & A. V. Nedrow died Jan. 11, 1892 aged 1 yr. 8 mo. 19 d. Nina Claire dau. of J. S. & A. V. Nedrow died Mar. 14, 1892 aged 4 yr. 8 m. 10 d. Edith Pearl dau. of J. S. & A. V. Nedrow died Mar. 26, 1892 aged 6 yrs. & 21 d.

Sophiah G. wife of S. F. Conner died Feb. 27, 1888 aged 65 y. 10 m. & 26 ds.

Henry Smith Dec. 7, 1805 - July 29, 1862.

Martha Smith Apr. 30, 1807 - Sept. 20, 1882.

Lucian H. Smith Aug. 4, 1830 - July 2, 1905.

Persis A. Smith Mar. 23, 1843 - Jan. 26, 1909.

Emma A. Smith Mar. 12, 1841 - Mar. 14, 1922.

W. Winfield Smith Oct. 9, 1848 - Sept. 7, 1911.

Martha Ann wife of Dr. Jesse Beerbower Dec. 12, 1836 - May 28, 1906. Zoie Beerbower May 12, 1860 - Dec. 31, 1879.

Blanche E. dau. of C. A. & J. Kaiser died Sept. 11, 1875 aged 6 mos. & 3 ds.

John Gibson of Co. D 1st. Regt. Md. Vol. born July 7, 1833 died June 15, 1880. Mary wife of John Gibson born Mar. 15, 1838 died May 7, 1881.

William A. Yeast Sept. 25, 1829 - May 26, 1907. Catherine J. Yeast July 30, 1842 - ————.

William B. son of W. & C. J. Yeast died Dec. 30, 1871 aged 9 mo. 28 ds.

Albert Yeast 1876 - 1899.

Dora M. dau. of E. D. & E. C. Benson died Aug. 1, 1867 aged 8 mos. 24 ds.

Mollie L. Benson 1876 - 1922.

Albert son of G. W. & M. A. Burke died July 21, 1870 aged 3 ms. 1 dy.

John H. son of G. W. & S. A. Burke died July 26, 1867 aged 16 yrs. 6 ms.

Milo Jenkins died May 23, 1872 aged 37 years 9 months & 16 days.

Willie S. son of Milo & Annie Jenkins died Nov. 22nd 1871 aged 7 years 6 months & 26 days.

Joseph Feather 1816 - 1895. Lydia Feather 1819 - 1898. Elizabeth Feather Cale 1882 - 1909. John H. Feather 1842 - 1894 1st. Sergt. Co. I 17th Regt. W. Va. Vol. U. S. Inft. Mizpah.

Louanna wife of Chas. Spindler died Apr. 22, 1897 aged 24 ys. 8 ms. 3 ds.

Joseph W. son of B. W. & S. J. Arnold died July 21, 1876 aged 3 m. 20 d.

Archibald T. Arnold died Apr. 16, 1881 aged 33 ys. 1 m. 18 d.

Robert Arnold died July 7, 1902 aged 85 y. 7 m. 21 d. Harriet Arnold died Feb. 27, 1890 aged 78 y. 8 m. 23 d.

William H. McGibbons Feb. 24, 1832 - Aug. 7, 1912.

Eliza S. wife of Wm. H. McGibbons July 26, 1837 - June 9, 1914.

D. T. Scott. Nov. 9, 1862 - Feb. 3, 1916.

Otho S. Mitchell died March 26th 1881 aged 73 years 10 mos. & 8 days.

Susan wife of Otho S. Mitchell died July 27th 1884 aged 76 years 4 mos. & 15 days.

Missouri A. wife of Abraham Benson died Jany. 7, 1882 aged 19 years 8 mo. & 3 days.

Harold D. Son of A. L. & M. B. Benson Feb. 25, 1899 - Aug. 13, 1906.

James Benson died Mar. 31, 1879 aged 84 y. 9 m. 7 d.

Sarah wife of James Benson died Dec. 19, 1877 aged 77 y. 8 m. 2 d.

Lewis F. Cale died Oct. 22, 1899 aged 49 ys. 10 ms. & 20 ds. Sabina E. wife of L. F. Cale died June 22, 1886 aged 28 ys. 2 m. & 6 ds.

(Another stone) Sabina E. Cale wife of Lewis F. Cale born April 16, 1858 died June 22, 1886.

Amelia I. dau. of M. M. & S. L. Benson died Dec. 14, 1877 aged 3 y. 3 m. 29d.

George H. Armstrong died Oct. 14, 1886 aged 60 years & 7 days.

Catherine Armstrong died Nov. 14, 1907 aged 74 years 4 mo. & 13 days.

Large iron fence enclosure contains the following markers.

John C. Forman born May 31, 1809 died Sept. 7, 1883. Ann wife of John C. Forman born June 11, 1811 died Apr. 23, 1875.

Edgar W. son of John C. & Ann Forman born March 20, 1836 died April 24, 1836. Martha M. dau. of John C. & Ann Forman born Dec. 8, 1842 died April 19, 1851.

George R. son of John C. & Ann Forman born July 24, 1848 died Dec. 5, 1860.

Emma A. 1846 - 1886.

Jane Friend born Jan. 1, 1841 died Oct. 31, 1863.

John F. son of A. & A. Reckard died Feb. 26, 1886 aged 2 years 1 mo. & 26 ds.

Dr. Francis C. Shepherd 1829 - 1872.

Noland R. Harding born November 25th, 1826 died September 26th, 1865.

Loose stones in northwest corner of iron fence enclosure.

Edgar W. Forman died April 24, 1836 aged 1 month & 4 days.

Martha M. Forman died April 19, 1851 aged 8 years 4 months & 11 days.

George B. son of J. C. & A. Forman died Dec. 5, 1860 aged 12 y. 4 m. 11 ds.

*   *   *   *

Cemetery at Brandonville, Grant District, Preston County, W. Va. Copied July 6th and 7th 1931.

Sacred to the Memory of Caroline G. Hagans consort of Alpheus D. Hagans who departed this life June 3rd 1847 in the 21st year of her age.

Delia Ella dau. of Jared E. & Amanda J. Hagans died June 2, 1855 aged 2 yrs. 10 days.

Infant son of J. E. & A. J. Hagans.

Margaret I. dau. of Dr. A. S. & S. J. Warder born Feb. 8, 1853 died Feb. 14, 1853.

William Michael died Aug. 25, 1854 aged 79 yrs. 5 mos. 27 ds.

Rachel wife of William Michael died De. 29, 1858 aged 82 years.

(Stone lying on ground)) Samuel M. Smith died Jan. 2, 1878 aged 84 yrs. 4 m. 28 d.

Mary wife of Samuel M. Smith died June 3, 1834 aged 36 ys. 1 mo. 4 d.

Martha Anne dau. of H .M. & E. Smith died Dec. 21, 1860 aged 9 ys. 6 mo. 4 ds.

William A. son of H. M. & E. Smith died Dec. 24, 1860 aged 5 ys. 8 mo. 7 ds.

Annette dau. of A. J. & Elizabeth Bell died Sept. 17, 1849 aged 1 yr. 5 mo.

Missouri Eliza wife of Wm. H. McGibbons died Sept. 29, 1857 aged 25 yrs. 4 mo. 29 ds.

John A. son of J. H. & E. J. Gibson born April 14, 1850 died Mar. 22, 1852.

Joseph Ritenour died April 12, 1872 aged 76 yrs.

Elizabeth wife of J. Ritenour died Dec. 13, 1875 aged 83 yrs.

Joseph son of Samuel & Rachel M. Peder died Feb. 27, 1852 aged 3 yrs. 4 mo. 27 da.

Alpheus Michael died Oct. 26, 1891 aged 58 ys. 9 mo. 3 ds.

Walter H. son of P. D. & J. Harner died June 10, 1858 aged 5 days.

John Michael died Apr. 9, 1874 aged 74 y. 8 m. 24 d.

Ruth wife of John Michael died Apr. 6, 1883 aged 84 y. 9 m. 11 d.

William Michael died June 6, 1898 aged 75 ys. 1 mo. 2 ds.

Rebecca J. dau. of J. & K. Spahr died May 31, 1863 aged 1 yr. 7 days.

John F. son of R. D. & S. J. Harner died July 27, 1862 aged 2 ys. 6 mo. 10 ds.

Eleanor wife of S. M. Smith died Mar. 14, 1884 aged 87 yr. 2 mo. 13 ds.

Willie T. son of Rev. J. T. & S. A. Thatcher died Nov. 26, 1870 aged 4 Months.

Mary L. wife of J. M. Chidester died July 21, 1875 aged 28 yr. 6 mo. 24 d.

Marshall W. Chidester died Oct. 27, 1881 aged 30 yrs. 5 mo. 21 d.

Mother Nancy Morton born May 8, 1804 died Feb. 2, 1887.

Alice Morton died Oct. 26, 1867 aged 74 ys. 11 mo. 28 ds.

George Mills son of J. B. & J. S. Woodward born Dec. 15, 1858 died May 8, 1862.

One grave unmarked.

William Kimberly Mar. 6, 1821 - Nov. 11, 1900. Elizabeth his wife Aug. 4, 1835 - Aug. 6, 1895.

Alvin son of Wm. & E. Kimberly died Apr. 2, 1865 aged 1 yr. 4 mo. 5 ds.

Juliet dau. of Wm. & M. Kimberly died Dec. 4, 1860 aged 12 ys. 7 mo. 4 ds.

James A. son of Wm. & M. Kimberly died Oct. 24, 1860 aged 9 ys. 1 mo. 11 ds.

Willie Kimberly infant son of W. & M. Kimberly died Dec. 23, 1858 aged 13 days.

Emily F. dau. of Wm. & M. Kimberly born Oct. 20, 1849 died Oct. 3, 1852.

Melinda Kimberly consort of William Kimberly died Jan. 30, 1859 aged 38 yrs. 4 mo. 29 ds.

Charles Hagans son of Phineas M. & Persis A. Sturgis born Oct. 27, 1847 died Feb. 11, 1853 aged 5 yr. 2 mo. 18 ds.

Mary Virginia dau. of Phineas M. & Persis A. Sturgis born Sept. 3, 1843 died Feb. 7, 1852 aged 5 yr. 5 mo. 4 days.

Howard Baldwin son of Phineas M. & Persis A. Sturgis born Mar. 23, 1849 died Mar. 27, 1852 aged 3 yr. & 4 days.

Persis Anne consort of Phineas M. Sturgis born Oct. 22, 1823 died Jan. 22, 1853 aged 29 years and 3 months.

Jennie A. dau. of A. C. & C. Leach died May 18, 1856 in the 20th year of her age.

Catherine Leach departed this life Mar. 20, 1870 aged 72 yr. 2 mos.

William Frey M. D. 1829 - 1890.

Our Mother Jane wife of Harrison Hagans died July 25, 1871 in the 76th year of her age.

Our Father Harrison Hagans died May 7, 1867 in the 71st year of his age.

Sacred to the Memory of Revd. George Hagans who departed this life June 21st, 1834 in the 73rd year of his age.

Sacred to the Memory of Persis Hagans widow of Rev. George Hagans who departed this life Oct. 10, 1846 in the 82nd year of her age.

Sacred to the Memory of Martha Hagans consort of Geo. M. Hagans who departed this life July 13th, 1842 in the 25th year of her age.

Sacred to the Memory of Sarah Ann Hagans who departed this life Oct. 15, 1845 in the 17th year of her age.
"My span of life, how short and frail, But long enough to teach this truth, That Friendship's care cannot avail, nor bribe, nor art, nor blooming youth, To shield from death's resistless power or lengthen out my span of life one hour."

Sarah dau. of D. & S. McCollum died June 24, 1862 aged 64 ys. & 24 ds.

A. C. Brandon died Sept. 23, 1863 aged 54 ys. 6 mo. 14 ds.

William Brandon died Sept. 6, 1860 aged 79 ys. 8 ds.

Mary wife of William Brandon died Mar. 23, 1870 aged 85 yrs. 9 mo. 11 ds.

Jonathan son of W. & H. Kelly died Sept. 30, 1854 aged—(under ground).

Erected by W. Graham in Memory of Col. Jonathan Brandon who departed this life February 29th, 1832 aged 74 years & 9 months.

Naomi Ann dau. of W. & M. Brandon died Jan. 24, 1846 aged 20 yrs. 10 mo. & 3 ds.

Clark McGrew born Nov. 3, 1811 died June 15, 1837 aged 25 yrs. 7 ms. & 12 ds.

Here sleepeth all that is mortal of Martha Scott born Feb. 19, 1819 died March 3, 1850 aged 31 yrs. & 12 days.

John J. son of Thomas & Martha Scott born Oct. 29, 1846 died Aug. 29, 1851 aged 4 yrs. & 10 mo.

William W. son of T. & S. A. Scott born Sept. 9, 1855 died May 6, 1856.

Thomas Scott born Sept. 9, 1813 died June 30, 1890 aged 76 yrs 9 mo. 21 ds. Sarah A. wife of Thomas Scott born Apr. 10, 1830 died Sept. 18, 1901 aged 71 yr. 5 mo. 8 ds.

Thomas W. Scott 1857 - 1916.

Frank McKee born Oct. 19, 1853 died Jan. 22, 1856 son of Wm. & Mary McKee.

Horatio S. McKee son of Wm. & Mary McKee died Jan. 15, 1880 aged 18 yrs. 2 mo. & 8 days.

Sarah J. dau. of Wm. & Mary McKee died Feb. 26, 1858 aged 1 yr. 9 mo. & 18 ds.

Mary dau. of Wm. & Mary McKee died Oct. 19, 1848 aged 3 years & 21 ds.

Wm. McKee born Oct. 13, 1822 died Nov. 15, 1889. Mary McKee born Feb. 23, 1824 died Aug. 9, 1905.

Our Brother James S. Frey died Aug. 10, 1867 in the 27th year of his age.

Virginia Bunker Frey died July 13, 1874 aged 6 mo. & 3 ds.

Caroline Irene wife of Wm. H. Frey died Dec. 14, 1880 aged 27 yrs. 18 ds.

E. M. Frey.

John Matlick 1821 - 1909. Lovina his wife 1823 - 1883. Henry C. Matlick 1850 - 1915. Nancy A. his wife 1855 - 1883. Mandy M. 1852 - 1866. Ross F. 1857 - 1883.

Isabella L. dau. of M. S. & E. Silbaugh died Oct. 1, 1882 aged 24 yrs. 11 mo. & 19 days.

William Howard son of M. & E. Silbaugh died May 24, 1880 in his 18th year.

Rody Ann dau. of M. & E. Silbaugh died Oct. 29, 1859 aged 8 yrs. & 24 ds.

Moses Sylbaugh died Sept. 2, 1898 in the 86th year of his age.

Eva Silbaugh 1818 - 1915.

David Sterling died Jan. 19, 1853 aged 22 yrs. 11 mo.

David S. son of A. J. & E. Sterling died Dec. 22, 1852 aged 2 yr. 8 mo. 22 d.

Melissa A. wife of Joseph A. Benson died Feb. 6, 1854 aged 22 ys. 6 m. & 23 d.

Rachel wife of Elijah Brobst died Jan. 16, 1851 aged 39 yrs. 11 mo. & 16 days.

Here sleeps our babe Thomas & Martha Scott Oct. 19, 1848.

Sacred to the Memory of John Scott who departed this life Oct. 28, 1828 in the 71st year of his age.

Sacred to the Memory of Catherine Scott consort of John Scott who departed this life March 25th, 1846 in the 76th year of her age.

Mary Elizabeth daughter of John & Mary Scott died Nov. 8, 1848 in the 4th year of her age.

Alcinda daughter of John & Mary Scott died Sept. 22, 1839 in the 9th year of her age.

William Henry son of John & Mary Scott died Dec. 15, 1834 in the 2nd year of his age.

Amanda Scott died March 7, 1856 aged 20 ys. 4 ms. & 9 ds.

Mary wife of John Scott May 20, 1810 - Jan. 23, 1888 aged 77 ys. 8 ms. 3 ds.

John Scott died Apr. 12, 1861 aged 53 ys. 4 mo. 15 ds.

Winfield W. son of J. & M. Scott died Aug. 12, 1867 aged 27 ys. 7 ms. 20 ds.

Martha A. Scott Jan. 31, 1842 - Apr. 14, 1904 aged 62 ys. 2 ms. 13 ds.

The children of J. W. & E. Leach, Jared C. born Feb. 2, 1845 died Feb. 18, 1845. William C. born June 11, 1846 died Feb. 15, 1853.

H. C. Hagans 1829 - 1891. Capt. Co. H. 3rd Va. Reg.

Caroline wife of H. C. Hagans died June 2, 1866 in the 36th year of her age.

Lucian L. son of H. C. & C. H. Hagans died Aug. 10, 1870 in the 18th year of his age.

Hugh son of H. C. & M. C. Hagans died Mar. 5, 1871.

Minnie dau. of H. C. & Caroline Hagans died July 14, 1874 in the 17 year of her age.

Catherine wife of Samuel Bryte died Sept. 17, 1865 in her 77 yr.

Joseph son of L. & C. Watson died April 5th, 1857 aged 6 ys. 1 mo. 27 ds.

William M. son of B. & S. J. Clingan died July 23, 1859 aged 10 yrs. 10 mo.

Ethel M. dau. of B. F. & C. Miller born June 20, 1900 died Aug. 12, 1900.

Infant son of S. T. & S. Darby died Jan. 31, 1862 aged 1 day.

Jimmie died Nov. 26, 1871 aged 6 ys. 9 mo. 3 ds. son of D. & M. Jones.

Mary J. dau. of D. & M. Jones died July 1861 aged 15 years.

Jane dau. of J. & J. Smith died Sept. 17, 1852 aged 7 mos.

Jane wife of Josiah Smith died Mar. 4, 1852 aged 35 yrs. 1 mo. 29 ds.

Jacob Smith died Mar. 30, 1860 aged 96 years & 19 days.

Deborah wife of Jacob Smith died June 19, 1860 aged 77 years & 10 mos.

James Collins born June 25, 1773 died Feb. 10, 1852.

Charles son of Andrew & Olivia Collins born Aug. 13, 1843 died Dec. 8, 1845.

Elizabeth Reynolds daugher of Wm. & Almira Reynolds born Nov. 11, 1831 died Dec. 13, 1837.

Sacred to the Memory of Phebe Jane daughter of James and Margaret Crawford who departed this life May 13, 1846 in the 26th year of her age.

Rachel dau. of J. & R. Michael died Sept. 25, 1851 aged 1 yr. 10 ms.

James Hetherington died Mar. 15, 1862 aged 61 yrs.

Amelia dau. of J. & L. Hetherington died Dec. 19, 1872 in the 32 year of her age.

William Harned Feb. 20, 1826 - Nov. 9, 1902. Mary A. Harned Oct. 10, 1830 ——.

Harry H. Scott born Oct. 10, 1869 - ————. Gertrude M. wife of Harry H. Scott born July 12, 1874 died July 26, 1901.

Emily J. Lawson died Mar. 23, 1876 aged 52 y. 5 m. 16 d.

Archibald Gribble died Jan. 5, 1872 aged 73 y. 7 m. 15 d.

Margaret wife of Archibald Gribble died Mar. 13, 1873 aged 70 ys. 1 m. & 4 d.

Marcellus K. Gribble died Oct. 16, 1866 aged 22 y. 11 m. 13 d.

Robert Ross died July 18, 1854 aged 83 ys. 5 m. 16 ds.

H. T. Spiker Co. L 6th W. Va. Inft.

Geo. W. Spiker died Apr. 22, 1880 aged 26 y. 6 m. 15 d.

Henry Spiker born Nov. 17, 1806 died Sept. 12, 1890.

Mary wife of H. Spiker born Jan. 24, 1810 died May 24, 1892.

One grave unmarked.

Willis C. son of G. D. & L. A. Wolf 1920 - 1920.

Mary E. dau. of G. D. & L. A. Wolf 1918 - 1918.

Six graves unmarked.

John Schrack Mar. 5, 1826 - Feb. 8, 1901. Catherine wife of John Schrack Dec. 20, 1814 - Nov. 25, 1889.

George Auman died Feb. 17, 1871 in the 76 year of his age.

Elizabeth wife of George Auman died June 6, 1880 aged 85 yrs. 8 mos. & 15 ds.

Peter W. son of B. & J. Awman died Oct. 20, 1860 aged 5 ys. 2 mo.

Sarah A. B. dau. of B. & J. Awman died Dec. 25, 1871 aged 3 ys. 4 mo. 29 ds.

Corp'l R. I. McClure Co. I 4th W. Va. Cav.

Phillip Sutton Co. F 11 Pa. Res. Inf.

Jacob S. Hyde Capt. of Co. B 6th W. Va. Cavalry died at Annapolis, Md. Mar. 12, 1865 aged 35 y. 6 m. 15 d.

Amanda Hyde born May 10, 1831 died Sept. 17, 1915.

Nannie E. dau. of J. S. & A. Hyde died Jan. 23, 1869 aged 8 ys. 5 ms. 11 ds.

Josie Hyde died Nov. 19, 1880 aged 21 y. 9 m. 21 d.

Sarah wife of George W. Burke died March 30, 1860 aged 40 ys. 5 mo. 23 ds.

R. B. Waddell Sept. 14, 1837 - Feb. 24, 1907.

Lucy Ann wife of R. B. Waddell Jan. 13, 1835 - Sept. 10, 1919.

John W. son of R. B. & L. A. Waddell died Nov. 5, 1862 aged 3 mos.

Infant daughter of R. B. & L. A. Waddell died Nov. 21, 1863 aged 1 day.

Ida May dau. of R. B. & Lucy A. Waddell died March 8, 1877 aged 2 ys. 10 ms. & 11 ds.

George E. son of D. & E. Myers died Sept. 2, 1866 aged 2 yrs. 9 mo. 16 ds.

John M. Waddell died 1844.

Sophia Fogle wife of John M. Waddell died 1892.

Samuel Harned died October 7th, 1849 aged 25 years ——(below ground).

William son of Samuel & Elizabeth Harned died Oct. 13, 1849 aged 2 years.

Ann Conner born March 6, 1804 died March 5, 1854.

Edward Harned died November 9th 1849 aged 49 years.

Sarah wife of Edward Harned died July 3, 1890 aged 87 years.

Virginia Ellen dau. of Wm. & M. A. Harned Sept. 27, 1854 AE 5 yrs. 14 ds.

John F. McGrew died Sept. 22, 1885 aged 40 y. 6 m. & 20 d.

James W. son of Isaac & Margaret McGrew born May 13, 1847 died Nov. 19, 1851.

Selena J. dau. of I. & M. McGrew born July 1, 1857 died July 8, 1858.

Isaac McGrew died Sept. 23, 1885 aged 78 y. 7 m. & 8 d.

Margaret wife of Isaac McGrew died July 22, 1896 aged 77 y. 10 m. 18 d.

Samuel Forquer Mar. 12, 1811 - Aug. 29, 1897. Isabella wife of Samuel Forquer Nov. 16, 1816 - Oct. 17, 1900.

Frank son of D. M. & S. C. Forquer died Nov. 24, 1890.

Ralph E. son of D. M. & S. C. Forquer born Apr. 26, 1888 died Dec. 20, 1888.

Nina M. dau. of D. M. & S. C. Forquer Sept. 4, 1900 - Nov. 25, 1906.

Lulu E. dau. of M. & S. Kemp died Sept. 10, 1879 aged 1 y. 4 m. 2 d.

Wm. Earnest son of J. E. & A. R. Bird died Nov. 15, 1891 aged 1 yr. 2 mo. 20 ds.

Oliver P. Scott 1864 - 1928.

Mollie C. Scott 1868 - 1926.

Arlie Adey 69 Co. U. S. C. A. C. Corps.

John H. Nieman May 5, 1817 - Mar. 12, 1904. Mariah wife of John H. Nieman May 23, 1828 - June 28, 1917.

George A. Nieman 1857 - 1929. Sarah C. Nieman 1862 - 1917.

Russell son of Sam'l & Sadie McGrew May 26, 1896 - Aug. 17, 1909.

James C. son of Sam'l & Sadie McGrew Dec. 13, 1892 - July 27, 1913.

Daniel Mosser 1837 - 1929, Mary V. his wife 1845 - 1920.

Elizabeth wife of Daniel Mosser died Aug. 11, 1885 aged 46 years 11 mo. & 20 Ds.

Elizabeth wife of J. W. Burk died Jan. 8, 1901 aged 42 ys. 11 ms. 6 ds.

John E. Evans died Jan. 14, 1894 aged 76 yrs. 6 mo. Susannah wife of John E. Evans ———— aged ————. Geo. E. Evans ———— aged ————. Three graves unmarked.

William Connor died July 25, 1868 aged 69 yrs. 7 mo. 23 ds.

Harrison Curry Co. L 6th W. Va. Cav.

J. M. Parsons died Oct. 1, 1869 aged 74 ys. 1 mo. & 20 D. Mary A. wife of J. M. Parsons died Nov. 11, 1880 aged 78 yrs. 7 m. & 7 D.

Susan Spindler age 78 yrs.

Mary E. Protzman Aug. 3, 1857 - June 13, 1918.

Jonathan Spindler Jan. 20, 1826 - Feb. 2, 1914.

Deborah wife of J. Spindler born Jan. 28, 1828 died July 5, 1903.

Mich'l H. Thomas Co. K Pa. H. A.

Callie A. dau. of S. & M. E. Nedrow died Sept. 19, 1888 aged 14 ys. & 15 Ds.

Birdie C. Collins Sept. 4, 1877 - Aug. 9, 1920.

Mary E. wife of Samuel Nedrow 1853 - 1916.

Ella P. Benson Aug. 1, 1856 - July 12, 1911. Infant Nov. 3, 1909.

J. Marshall Benson Aug. 1, 1856 - Sept. 16, 1927.

Joseph T. Weltner 1847 - 1928.

Charles W. Chorpenning 1886 - 1888.

Hannah L. Chorpenning 1844 - 1909

Eliza J. Shrader 1862 - 1916.
Three graves (small) unmarked.
George Silbaugh 1842 - 1917. Matilda his wife 1840 - 19—.
Charles E. McGinnis June 14, 1905 - Aug. 26, 1928.
Sarah J. wife of Jacob Brooks 1851 - 1918.
Sarah W. Brooks 1892 - 1916.
Emanuel Beeghly Nov. 9, 1827 - Aug. 11, 1912. Mary his wife May 22, 1837 ——.
Michael K. Beeghly born Aug. 30, 1798 died Sept. 23, 1876.
Margaret wife of M. K. Beeghly died Nov. 21, 1878 aged 78 y. 1 m. 18 d.

* * * *

The Gooding or Goodwin cemetery about one and one half miles south west of Hopewell Church, Grant District, Preston County, W. Va. Copied July 9, 1931.
Daniel Gooding died Jan. 1, 1874 aged 77 years.
Elizabeth Gooding wife of Daniel Gooding died March 22, 1889 aged 71 years 9 months & 16 days.
Andrew Goodwin born Aug. 15, 1833 died July 29, 1907 aged 68 ys. 11 mo. & 14 ds.
Harriet Goodwin died Mar. 17, 1931 aged 98 yrs.
Mary Holace dau. of Charles & Laura Goodwin born April 10, 1908 died Aug. 8, 1909 aged 1 yr. 3 mo. & 29 ds.
Seventeen unmarked graves among whom are those of Louise Bowman and her child, two children of Oakey Goodwin, two children of Alice and Sam Johnson, five children of Andrew and Harriet Goodwin, two children of Bruce and Pearl Goodwin, one child of Belle Lynn, and one child of Oliver Goodwin. This information furnished by Mary, wife of Judson Goodwin.

* * * *

Cemetery on land now owned by Albert Metheny, formerly the Jehu King farm and originally owned by Valentine King. About one mile from Laurel Run Church, Grant District, Preston County, W. Va. Copied July 9, 1931.
Jacob Wolf born Nov. 14, 1814 died Jan. 22, 1895 aged 80 ys. 2 mos. & 8 ds. Lieu Reiny Wolf born Aug. 12, 1820 died Oct. 13, 1888 aged 68 yrs. 2 mos. & 1 day.
Minnie O. Daughter of Adam & Harriet Wolf born April 12, 1878 died Nov. 17, 1895.
One grave unmarked.
John King Sr. died Aug. 30, 1848 aged 64 years.

Ethelinda L. dau. of W. J. & E. H. King died May 18, 1862 aged 1 yr. & 18 ds.

James King died April 29, 1865 aged 86 y. 1 mo. 24 ds.

Ema wife of James King died May 8, 1843 in her 64 Years.

Infant dau. of P. & M. Everly died Feb. 27, 1885 aged 14 days.

Infant son of P. & M. Everly died Aug. 28, 1856 aged 2 days.

Infant dau. of Henry & Martha Smith born June 1832.

Infant son of Henry & Martha Smith born Sept. 1834.

Sylvester W. son of T. & J. King died Apr. 2, 1833 aged 4 ys. 2 mo. 1 d.

Marcelles son of T. & J. King died May 28, 1835 aged 7 mo. 23 d.

Infant son of J. D. & S. Benson died Oct. 1, 1870 aged 2 y. 8 mo. & 26 dys.

Augustine Wolf died Dec. 26, 1859 aged 49 yr. 4 mo. & 15 d.

William son of B. & S. J. Michael died June 16, 1852.

One stone broken, unreadable.

Nancy A. dau. of V. & M. Shaffer died Sept. 3, 1854 aged 4 yr. 4 m. 6 d.

Henrietta dau. of A. & J. ————— died Jan. 10, 1852 AE 1 yr. 9 m. 18 d.

Deborah C. dau. of J. & E. J. Edwards died Feb. 29, 1837 aged 2 yr. 10 m. 16 d.

Twelve graves unmarked.

John M. son of M. & E. Haney died Feb. 17, 1854 aged 6 y. 7 m. 27 ds.

Mary G. dau. of M. & E. Haney died Jan. 24, 1854 aged 1 yr. 9 mo. 22 ds.

* * * *

Cemetery on top of hill near Shady Grove Church, one and one half miles northeast of Brandonville, Grant District, Preston County, W. Va. Copied July 11, 1931.

Absalom G. son of J. & B. Crawford died Jan. 19, 1848 aged 6 ys. 4 mo. 22 ds.

Eugenus J. son of Wm. & R. Guthrie died Mar. 16, 1844 aged 12 ys. 11 mo. 24 ds.

Ephriam Guthrie died Oct. 20, 1854 aged 4 ys. 4 mo. 6 d.

Mary wife of A. B. Guthrie 1819 - 1848.

Three graves unmarked.

James Guthrie 1761 - Jan. 1833.

"A Pioneer who crossed the sea, and carved a home for you and me, To all who were in want or need, Grandfather was a friend indeed".

Mary wife of James Guthrie 1764 - 1839. George son of James and Mary Guthrie 1796 - 1832.
Two graves unmarked.

William Guthrie died July 12, 1873 aged 78 ys. 10 mo. 2 d.

Rebecca wife of William Guthrie died Apr. 15, 1869 aged 68 ys. 1 mo. 6 ds.

Isabel wife of Henry Sliger born Nov. 28, 1798 died Apr. 22, 1870 aged 71 ys. 4 mo. 24 ds.

Susanna wife of J. B. Nicola died May 7, 1880 aged 44 years 11 mo. & 11 ds.

Peter Guthrie Feb. 18, 1842 - Aug. 6, 1916.

John Guthrie died Dec. 10, 1870 aged 78 years 3 mos. & 10 Ds.

Elizabeth wife of J. Guthrie died Feb. 15, 1875 aged 75 years 9 mos. & 15 Ds.

J. Wesley son of A. G. & E. J. Harshbarger died Feb. 1, 1872 aged 1 yr. 2 mo. & 3 ds.

Mary daughter of James & B. Guthrie died Dec. 23, 1872 aged 18 yrs. 2 mo. 8 Ds.

Lucretia dau. of J. & B. Guthrie died April 28, 1877 aged 17 years.

James G. Crawford died Feb. 22, 1902 aged 86 ys. 7 ms. 27 Ds.

Rachel wife of James G. Crawford died Sept. 28, 1874 aged 70 ys. 5 ms. 12 Ds.

Alexander B. Guthrie died June 2, 1877 aged 62 ys. 1 mo. 2 Ds. Anne wife of A. B. Guthrie died June 12, 1897 aged 79 ys. 1 mo. 12 ds. Abner F. son of A. B. & M. Guthrie died May 15, 1875 aged 35 ys. 1 mo. 3 ds.

Michael Beeghly died Dec. 19, 1877 aged 77 ys. 6 ms. 1 day.
Six graves unmarked.

Noah Ross died Dec. 23, 1881 aged 25 ys. 1 mo. 18 ds.

Martin DeBerry May 23, 1822 - Apr. 27, 1902.

Nancy wife of Martin DeBerry died Sept. 21, 1891 aged 70 ys. 4 mo. & 26 Ds.

Susannah E. wife of W. F. Moyer died July 4, 1896 aged 33 ys. 11 mo. 7 ds.

John H. Deal Apr. 19, 1843 - Apr. 11, 1911.

Lucy Ann Deal May 21, 1853 - Aug. 29, 1926.

Jack Deal Feb. 21, 1899 - Oct. 16, 1923.

William R. Thomas July 19, 1854 - June 20, 1921. Barbery E. Thomas July 17, 1858 - May 22, 1921. Wilbert Thomas Mar. 14, 1889 - Oct. 30, 1905.
Four graves unmarked.

Stephen Guthrie Jr. born Apr. 17, 1827 died Mch. 31, 1895.
Two graves unmarked.

S. Spencer Guthrie 1858 - 1927. Julia D. his wife 1860 - 1928.

Children of Spencer & Julia Guthrie. Ross F. aged 16 ys. 4 ms. & 3 ds. Willie H. aged 7 ys. 5 ms. 26 ds. Julia C. aged 2 ms. 1 day.

Sarah Ann wife of J. P. Barnes died Jan. 30, 1880 aged 32 yrs. 11 mos. & 19 ds.

James Guthrie Sr. died March 29, 1879 aged 72 yrs. 6 mos. 22 ds.

Barbara wife of James Guthrie died May 2, 1888 aged 67 y. 8 m. 19 ds.

John Forman born First Month 21st, 1767 died Eleventh Month 29th, 1846.

Sarah wife of John Forman born Second Month 25th, 1775 died Fourth Month 24, 1838.

   One grave unmarked.

Corp'l I. J. Light Co. C 3rd W. Va. Cav.

Benjamin Morton died Jan. 13, 1851 aged 85 ys. 3 ms. & 27 ds. Ann Hanse wife of Benj. Morton died June 25, 1845 aged 85 y. 6 mo. & 24 ds.

Clarissa A. Boger 1833 - 1918.

Children of Ezra & Jemima Turney. Christian T. July 23, 1877 - Mar. 12, 1878. Clarence I. May 21, 1885 - ——. Stephen O. Dec. 19, 1872 - Apr. 11, 1881.

Ami Stephens son of S. & R. Garner died Mar. 6, 1864 aged 8 yrs. 5 mo. & 6 ds.

Mary Jane dau. of S. & R. Garner died Mar. 13, 1864 aged 10 yrs. 7 mo. & 26 ds.

Henry Turney Mar. 20, 1808 - Apr. 22, 1872. Mary wife of Henry Turney Jan. 11, 1800 - Nov. 15, 1884.

Mary Jane dau. of S. & R. Garner died March 13, A. D. 1864 aged 10 y. 7 mo. 26 ds.

John Barnes Oct. 10, 1803 - Feb. 16, 1897.

Catherine Barnes born Nov. 20, 1807 died Mar. 12, 1887.

James H. Crawford 1875 - 1918.

   Three graves unmarked.

Emma Pearl daughter of Joseph & Catherine Sliger Aug. 15, 1895 - June 17, 1916.

Jonas Turney July 12, 1836 - Oct. 14, 1907.

George C. Turney died Dec. 28, 1910 age 22 ys. 11 ms. 4 Ds.

   One grave unmarked.

George W. Crawford 1852 - 1907. Mary A. Crawford 1858 - 1925.

Margaret Wingrove 1842 - 1910.

Quinnie dau. of W. D. & Ida M. Dennis May 16, 1895 - Nov. 20, 1918.

   One grave unmarked.

Grace dau. of Wm. D. & Ida M. Dennis born Feb. 24, 1891 died May 14, 1898 aged 7 ys. 2 mo. 20 ds.

Philip Dennis died June 5, 1897 aged 61 yrs. 9 mo. 27 ds. Mary wife of P. Dennis died Aug. 27, 1903 aged 67 yrs. 5 ms. 7 ds.

James T. son of P. & M. Dennis died Dec. 3, 1889 aged 5 yrs. 11 ms. 15 Ds.

Elias P. son of P. & M. Dennis died July 9, 1878 aged 1 yr. 2 ms. 27 ds.

Robert F. son of P. & M. Dennis died May 15, 1872 aged 1 yr. 6 ms. 18 ds.

Sarah C. dau. of P. & M. Dennis died May 9, 1872 aged 4 yrs. 2 ms. 25 ds.

Two graves unmarked.

Jacob Frankhouser age 96 yrs.

One grave unmarked.

David Dennis died June 4, 1861 aged 56 yrs. 8 ms. & 21 ds.

Catherine Dennis died April 28, 1897 aged 85 ys. 8 ms. 27 ds.

Elizabeth dau. of D. & C. Dennis died Feb. 26, 1840 aged 2 ys. 10 ms. 10 ds.

Samuel son of D. & C. Dennis died Jan. 5, 1857 aged 1 yr. 5 mo. 10 ds.

Catherine dau. of D. & C. Dennis died Dec. 11, 1857 aged 7 yr. 1 mo. 15 ds.

Amy dau. of D. & C. Dennis died Dec. 10, 1857 aged 4 yr. 10 ms. 10 ds.

Three graves unmarked.

Charles son of C. & M. C. Dennis died Aug. 2, 1865 aged 1 yr. 2 mo. 1 d.

John T. Smith 1810 - 1894. Nancy his wife 1822 - 1904. George E. 1859 - 1929.

One grave unmarked.

David Frankhouser born Sept. 25, 1805 died Jan. 10, 1898. Ruth W. wife of D. Frankhouser born May 29, 1813 died Jan. 12, 1893.

Two graves unmarked.

Lindsey H. Frankhouser 1836 - 1917.

Lewis F. Myers 1856 - 1925.

Mary A. Myers 1858 - 1924.

Edith B. Myers 1883 - 1915.

David Dennis 1840 - 1921. Harriet his wife 1855 - 1926.

Lillie May dau. of David & Harriet Dennis born Feb. 18, 1888 died May 8, 1901 aged 18 yr. 2 mo. & 20 d.

Theodore son of I. M. & M. C. Thomas aged 7 mos.

Charles C. Younkin born Mar. 5, 1911 died July 25, 1911.

One grave unmarked (recent).

Three graves unmarked.

Scott J. son of Walter & Lulu Frankhouser born & died Sept. 22, 1911.

Cora Guthrie Jan. 15, 1833 - Aug. 17, 1924.

Grace dau. of H. & L. Guthrie Dec. 15, 1892 - Feb. 14, 1893. Twin Bro. to Walter Guthrie died July 11, 1895.

Jeremiah Guthrie Sept. 10, 1852 - April 25, 1918.

Nancy A. Guthrie Apr. 12, 1859 - June 1, 1926.

Dellie dau. of Jer. & N. A. Guthrie born Sept. 17, 1893 died Jan. 22, 1895.

Infant son of Jer. & Nancy Guthrie June 10, 1902.

Infant dau. of Jer. & Nancy Guthrie Jan. 29, 1886.

Fleming C. Barnes 1839 - 1927.

Alcinda J. Barnes 1845 - 1923.

Preston T. Guthrie born July 4, 1842 died Dec. 27, 1895 aged 53 ys. 5 mo. & 23 ds.

Wm. Willet Apr. 25, 1843 - Aug. 10, 1921. Elizabeth wife of Wm. Willet Apr. 16, 1836 - Aug. 11, 1908 aged 72 ys. 3 ms. 25 ds.

Allie Willet died Feb. 26, 1888 aged 21 y. 2 m. 8 d.

Samuel Romesburg 1840 - 1922. His wife Persis A. Guthrie 1844 - 1918.

Infant of H. F. & J. M. Barnes Aug. 12, 1903.

Ometa Blanche dau. of W. F. & M. J. Frankhouser died Sept. 11, 1905 aged 6 mo. 8 ds.

One grave unmarked.

Jonas Frankhouser born Sept. 20, 1833 died Feb. 3, 1920. Ruth G. Frankhouser born May 22, 1838 - ———.

Rachel J. wife of W. F. Thomas 1847 - 1919.

Two graves unmarked (recent).

Orvel R. son of J. H. & E. P. Thomas 1909 - 1910.

Joseph H. Harshbarger 1874 - 19—. Hattie G. his wife 1881 - 1925.

W. S. Younkin June 27, 1847 - July 6, 1914. E. H. Younkin Apr. 10, 1855 - 19—.

Delma Mildred dau. of S. P. & L. M. Frankhouser June 4, 1918 - Dec. 1, 1920.

Camden DeBerry July 27, 1862 - Jan. 23, 1918. Anna his wife May 13, 1866 - ———.

Infant dau. of P. C. & E. A. DeBerry died June 2, 1890.

Jacob B. Welsh 1842 - 1912. (unplaced stone) Co. C 37 Reg. Co. A. 191 Reg. Pa. Vol.

Margaret P. Welsh 1848 - 1916.

Lillian Goodwin Smith Aug. 24, 1903 - Sept. 1, 1903.

Three graves unmarked.

D. K. Harshbarger Dec. 27, 1825 - Sept. 24, 1909.   Elizabeth his wife
Oct. 26, 1832 - Mar. 14, 1912.

Maggie E. wife of A. J. Moyers 1863 - 1928.

Mildred G. Barnes 1909 - 1922.

Russel E. Barnes Mar. 15, 1891 - Jan. 3, 1925.
Four graves unmarked.

Leander K. Guthrie 1856 - 1914.

Andrew J. Seese 1843.   Rebecca his wife 1837 - 1925.
Two graves unmarked.

William H. Smith 1842 - 1913.

Asa K. Frazee 1836 - 1917.   Rachel his wife 1843 - 1927.   Walter
1873 - 1895.
Two graves unmarked.

Darwin F. Moyers 1909 - 1917.

Charles H. Thomas Mar. 6, 1851 - Apr. 8, 1916.

Ray Thomas Feb. 17, 1899 - Feb. 15, 1916.

Joseph Guthrie 1846 - 1912.   Hannah E. his wife 1850 - ———.

John Frankhouser died Sept. 17, 1913 age 79 yrs. 5 mo. 28 ds.

Amanda Frankhouser Feb. 18, 1843 - May 15, 1915.

Clarence H. Deal Aug. 29, 1916 - Dec. 12, 1916.   Mary M. Deal
Sept. 30, 1918 - Feb. 13, 1919.
One grave unmarked.

Pearlie Grace Frazee 1886 - 1925.

Robert E. son of Mr. and Mrs. Troy Guthrie 1929 - 1929.

Edward Dennis 1887 - 1929.
One grave unmarked.

Hannah M. Glover 1860 - 1931.
One grave unmarked.

*   *   *   *

Cemetery at Albright, Portland District, Preston County, W. Va.
Copied July 11, 1931.

A. W. Collins Co. D 5th W. Va. Inft.

John A. Son of W. V. & M. Chidester died Nov. 17, 1861 aged 2
ys. 6 ds.

Zacheus son of Eugenus & Mary A. Sylpult died Apr. 23, 1863 aged
5 ys. 8 ms. 7 ds.

Teny F. daughter of Eugenus & Mary A. Sylpult died Apr. 1, 1863
aged 13 ys. 2 mo.

Col. Wm. H. King died Aug. 17, 1892 aged 65 ys. 2 ms. 4 ds. Elma
wife of Wm. King died Aug. 24, 1893 aged 45 ys. 5 mo. 22 ds.
Mary A. wife of Wm. H. King died Apr. 25, 1872 aged 40 ys.
4 mo. 11 ds.

Mary A. wife of Wm. H. King died Apr. 25, 1872 aged 40 y. 4 m.
11 d. 31 yrs a member of the M. E. Church.

One grave unmarked.

Ralph H. son of W. H. & M. A. King died Dec. 12, 1860 aged 2 ys.
11 m. 7 ds.

Ida M. dau. of G. M. & P. A. Michael died Jan. 16, 1864 aged 3
years 9 mo. & 16 ds.

Mary A. dau of J. H. M. & H. Pastem died Sept. 17, 1861 aged 2
ys. 1 mo. & 8 Ds.

Edward W. son of A. & A. Elliott died Oct. 10, 1861 aged 8 mos. &
14 Dys.

Florence L. dau. of A. & A. Elliott died Oct. 12, 1861 aged 2 yrs.
8 mos. & 27 dys.

Elisha T. son of J. & G. Hewitt died July 5, 1863 aged 19 yr. 7 m.
19 ds.   Was a private in Co. B 14 West Va. Infantry.

William D. son of J. & G. Hewitt died June 9, 1865 aged 19 ys. 8 mo.
9 ds.   Was a private in Co. E 6 West Va. Cavalry.

Three graves unmarked.

Martha E. wife of W. D. Snyder born July 2, 1817 died May 14, 1888.
Susan H. Snyder born June 14, 1857 died Sept. 13, 1883.

Three graves unmarked.

Rhoda V. daughter of Wm. O. & E. Mayfield died Dec. 6, 1871 aged
1 yr. 23 ds.

Cloyd A. son of W. H. & C. Casteel died Nov. 16, 1871 aged 1 yr.
10 mo. 22 ds.

Nathaniel Casteel born July 8, 1819 died March 31, 1883 aged 63 yrs.
8 mo. 23 ds.

Samuel Bishoff died Jan. 10, 1884 aged 75 yrs. 1 mo.

Lydia Bishoff born Mar. 15, 1810 died July 6, 1903.

Samuel E. Welch died April 6, 1882 aged 50 years.

Infant children of S. E. & P. L. Welch.

Infant son of D. & M. A. Morgan born Dec. 4, 1871. Mary A. dau.
of M. A. Morgan died Mar. 24, 1873 aged 1 mo. 28 ds.

David Morgan died June 24, 1898 aged 78 years.

Mary A. wife of David Morgan died Jan. 25, 1873 aged 56 y. 10 m.
20 d.   She joined church in Feb. 1858 and lived a consistent
christian until death.

Mary wife of David Morgan died July 28, 1868 aged 43 years 9 m.
13 d.

A. W. Chidester July 10, 1829 - May 27, 1906.

Nancy wife of A. W. Chidester died May 7, 1869 in her 41 years.

Children of A. W. & M. E. Chidester. E. Blanche June 26, 1888 -
July 1, 1890. Domer E. Aug. 4, 1893 - Sept. 5, 1894. Bruce

Apr. 22, 1883 - Apr. 24, 1883. S. Clyde July 23, 1878 - June 5, 1880.

Charles W. son of J. W. & M. J. Coburn died Sept. 30, 1861 aged 4 ys. 6 ms. & 6 ds.

Cecil C. son of J. W. & M. J. Coburn died Feb. 23, 1862 aged 8 days.

William Bishoff Oct. 3, 1811 - Nov. 7, 1881. Catherine Bishoff June 22, 1817 - Sept. 25, 1902.

One grave unmarked.

Emma dau. of A. J. & D. Welch Dec. 1, 1875 aged 18 yrs. ——(under ground).

Jennie B. dau. of A. J. & D. Welch ——(date under ground).

One grave unmarked.

(Name and dates broken off)—aged 33 yrs. 1 mo. 22 Dys.

Rachel C. wife of Isaac Elliott born Nov. 16, 1842 died Feb. 18, 1907.

Infant (marker, no name).

One grave unmarked.

John C. Crane 1841 - 1907. Mollie R. Crane 1848 - 19——.

D. W. M. Bucklew died Mar. 16, 1883 aged 10 mo. 2 wks. 4 dys.

J. V. Bucklew died Apr. 1, 1883 aged 3 yrs. 11 mo. 8 dys.

(South face of marker) Abraham Feather Feb. 16, 1818 - Mar. 29, 1905.

(North face) Elizabeth Feather Aug. 3, 1818 - Jan. 24, 1907.

(East face) Our Father & Mother James Boylan & Wife.

Abraham Feather Feb. 16, 1818 - Mar. 29, 1905. Elizabeth Feather Aug. 3, 1818 - Jan. 24, 1907.

C. B. Moore Jan. 23, 1851 - Feb. 28, 1910.

Flossie dau. of L. E. & V. B. Sylpolt born Feb. 1, 1890 died Apr. 10, 1898.

Vance Graham July 27, 1860 - Mar. 26, 1906.

Elizabeth Wable died Sept. 27, 1896 aged 82 yrs. 5 ms. 2 Ds.

*   *   *   *

Jenkins Cemetery about one mile south west of Mt. Nebo Church, in west part of Pleasant District, Preston County, W. Va. Copied July 15, 1931.

Henson Liston June 11, 1819 - Sept. 29, 1901. Elizabeth his wife Apr. 28, 1819 - July 27, 1916.

(Unplaced Govt. marker) Henson Liston. Co. A. W. Va. Inft.

Thankful J. Liston Aug. 22, 1860 - July 16, 1915.

Lillie Jenkins Nov. 18, 1867 - July 2, 1927.

Elisha Jenkins Sept. 4, 1836 - Sept. 16, 1921. Sarah E. his wife Sept. 27, 1845 - ——————.

Two graves unmarked.

Abraham Liston died May 31, 1875 aged 62 y. 2 m. 15 d.

Elizabeth wife of A. Liston died Jan. 27, 1897 aged 80 ys. 6 ms. 23 ds.

Graham Jenkins died Dec. 13, 1869 aged 58 years 10 mos. & 14 Days.

Eliza Jenkins died Sept. 29, 1881 aged 65 yrs. 5 mos. & 1 day.

Sanford C. H. Jenkins died June 4, 1875 aged 27 years 6 mos. & 22 Days.

Hester A. wife of William Wolf died July 7, 1880 aged 40 years 10 mos. & 6 days.

James S. Jenkins died Mar. 22, 1878 aged 71 y. 5 mo. 17 d.

Rachel wife of J. Jenkins died May 6, 1872 aged 69 y. 5 m. 3 D.

Jonathan son of J. & R. Jenkins died Mar. 7, 1870 aged 29 y. 7 m. 3 d.

Persis H. wife of Isaac A. Jenkins died Sept. 24, 1866 aged 25 ys. 7 ms. 2 ds.

Julia dau. of G. & E. Jenkins June 6, 1860 aged 7 yr. 5 mo. & 7 ds.

James K. son of G. & E. Jenkins Oct. 16, 1853 AE 7 y. 8 m. 11 d.

Here Lieth the —(unreadable)—in Memory of John Jenkins who wase Bourn March 27, 1754 lived in esteem in the regular Baptist church of christ and died in the Triumphs of Faithful December 24, 1834 in the 84 year of his age.

Rachel dau. of J. & R. Cale died July 25, 1855 aged 11 yr. 9 m. 14 d.

Elisha son of J. & R. Cale died Jan. 4, 1880 age 47 yr. 4 mo. 9 da.

Two graves unmarked.

Belinda dau. of Jacob & Rachel Cale died July 18, 1820 AE 3 mo. 20 ds.

Rolly Jenkins 1822 - 1905. Martha his wife 1842 - 1921.

Verlinda wife of Rolly Jenkins died March 25, 1853 aged 30 yr. 4 mo. & 13 d.

Jonathan Jenkins died Aug. 1, 1859 aged 80 yrs. 5 mo. & 13 ds.

Esther wife of Jonathan Jenkins died Oct. 7, 1839 aged 52 yrs. 9 mo. & 12 ds.

Infant son of D. & M. Graham died Sept. 11, 1839 AE 2 days.

In memory of Ludema Gibson died Sep. 8, 1833 age 25. Go home Dear friends And cease from Tears i shall Li Here Tal christ Apeals prepare for Dath what Time you Have There is no repentance in The Grave.

John Jenkins died Feb. 10 day in 1810 in the 3 year of his age.

Jacob son of J. & R. Cale died May 24, 1855 aged 4 yr. 9 mo. 22 ds.

Josiah Gibson born No. 19, 1815 died Sept. 19, 1839. Benjamin born Sept. 22, 1817 died May 31, 1834.

Levi Gibson born Oct. 1, 1787 died Dec. 10, 1862. Sarah Gibson born June 28, 1790 died Dec. 24, 1850. Lydia Liston born Dec. 26, 1826 died Aug. 15, 1850.

J. Thompson Graham Mar. 20, 1835 - Feb. 11, 1910. Lucinda Graham July 3, 1835 - Feb. 5, 1910.

Jacob Cale died Feb. 27, 1885 in his 94th year. Rachel wife of J. Cale died Oct. 14, 1884 in her 84th year.

Lumema A. Graham born Apr. 26, 1835 died Apr. 16, 1907 age 73 ys. 11 mo. 16 Ds.

In Memory of Mary Jane wife of John Cale Jr. and daughter of David Graham died Apr. 19, 1861 aged 29 yrs. 10 mo. 23 D.

David Graham died May 26, 1879 aged 77 y. 7 m. & 18 d.

Margaret wife of David Graham and Daughter of Hannah & John Gribble died March 26, 1861 aged 66 yr. 10 mo. 5 D.

Mary E. dau. of H. & E. Liston died Oct. 19, 1870 aged 23 y. & 5 mo.

John T. Gibson died Apr. 15, 1886 aged 57 y. 6 m. 17 d.

Laura J. May 29, 1869 - Dec. 1871. Louis F. May 29, 1869 - Dec. 27, 1871. Children of W. H. & Louisa J. Jenkins.

   Two graves unmarked.

James Gibson born July 31, 1833 died Nov. 28, 1852.

John M. Rodabough Sept. 1866 - Jan. 1871.

Hannah A. dau. of John & E. F. Jenkins Sept. 11, 1871 aged 8 yrs. 19 ds. Emma A. dau. of John & E. F. Jenkins died May 4, 1845.

Evan Jenkins Died Sept. 9, 1877 aged 89 y. 3 m. & 8 D.

Hanna wife of Evan Jenkins died June 12, 1866 in her 74 year.

Hanna J. dau. of E. & H. Jenkins died June 24, 1845 aged 13 ys. 2 ms. 14 d.

Annie dau. of J. & M. A. Jenkins died June 21, 1863 aged 9 ms. 6 Ds.

Jonathan Jenkins died Mar. 24, 1864 aged 43 ys. 4 m. 21 Ds.

Ruhama dau. of J. & M. A. Jenkins died Dec. 29, 1865 aged 19 yr. 4 m. 3 Ds.

Orlando son of J. & M. A. Jenkins died July 3, 1866 aged 17 yr. 1 m. 29 Ds.

George L. Clark 1855 - 1875.

John Jenkins 1803 - 1887. Elizabeth his wife 1803 - 1863.

David Graham departed this life Oct. 8, 1839 aged 76 years & 6 months.

Hannah Graham wife of David Graham departed this life Oct. 28, 1839 aged 72 years 6 mo. 27 days.

＊   ＊   ＊   ＊

   Small cemetery known as the Everly Cemetery about one and one half miles southwest of Mt. Nebo Church, Pleasant District, Preston County, W. Va. Copied July 15, 1931.

Christopher Cale died Jan. 15, 1825 in his 84 yr.

Elizabeth wife of Christopher Cale died Mar. 28, 1838 in her 83 year.

Lewis Everly died Dec. 4, 1892 aged 81 yr. 9 mo. & 29 d. (stone broken).

Eve wife of Lewis Everly died Aug. 7, 1886 aged —(broken stone, part missing).

Thomas Everly died May 7, 1882 aged 29 yr. 6 mo. 25 ds.

Elza Zweyer died Mar. 17, 1910 aged 87 ys. 1 mo. 24 Ds.

Mary Zweyer died Mar. 19, 1858 aged 10 yr. 3 mo. 17 d.

Adam Zweyer died June 30, 1833 aged 61 y. 3 m. 19 d.

Mary wife of Henry Everly died Apr. 2, 1878 aged 92 y. 1 m. 27 d.

Thomas Zweyer died May 30, 1834 aged 23 y. 6 m. 18 d.

   One grave unmarked.

Thomas Zweyer died Apr. 23, 1846 aged 4 ys. 8 ms. 21 ds.

Henry Zweyer died May 5, 1851 aged 10 ms. 1 D.

John Zweyer died Mar. 23, 1862 aged 5 ys. 10 ms. 19 Ds.

John Zweyer died Apr. 23, 1890 aged 83 y. 1 m. 11d.

Christ Zweyer born Aug. 30, 1811 died Mar. 13, 1904.

William Smith born Sept. 20, 1797 died Sept. 28, 1887 age 90 ys. 8 Ds. Catherine wife of William Smith born Dec. 4, 1793 died Jan. 1, 1883 age 90 ys. 28 Ds.

   Three graves unmarked.

Joseph Clark 1809 - 1891. Elizabeth J. 1833 - 1904.

John Cale died Mar. 2, 1882 aged 91 y. 10 mo. 22 d.

Elizabeth wife of John Cale died Jan. 30, 1843 aged about 47 years.

Thomas son of J. & E. Cale died Jan. 10, 1842 AE about 13 yr.

Mary A dau. of J. & E. Cale died Nov. 29, 1851 AE about 21 yr.

Rebecca wife of Joseph Clark died Apr. 20, 1856 aged 18 yrs. 11 Mos.

Elizabeth dau. of John & Elizabeth Cale died Aug. 15, 1861 in the 28 year of her age.

Ruth dau. of John & E. Cale died Oct. 10, 1862 aged 20 yrs. & 9 Mo.

   Two graves unmarked.

Francis M. son of A. & M. Cale died June 26, 1863 aged 1 mo. 22 days.

John son of H. & E. M. Cale born Jan. 28, 1854 died Aug. 24, 1878.

   Three graves unmarked.

Harrison Cale born Dec. 27, 1824 died Aug. 28, 1907. Emily M. Cale born Apr. 24, 1830 died Mar. 18, 1907.

A. J. Greathouse Feb. 3, 1875 - Oct. 2, 1914.

Jesse son of Wm. & M. J. Greathouse died Feb. 2, 1903 aged 10 y. 1 m. 27 D.

William Greathouse Aug. 20, 1846 - Oct. 1, 1907. Martha J. Greathouse Nov. 28, 1851 - Oct. 28, 1907.

* * * *

Three miles south of the village of Pisgah, on the abandoned L. Bircher farm, in the western part of Grant District, Preston County, W. Va. the following grave markers are located under a large tree. Copied July 17, 1931.

T. Christopher Co. E 3rd P. H. B. Md. Inft. (Govt. marker).

Frances L. wife of John Trembly died June 6, 1858 aged 58 yr. 8 mo. 29 d.

Marshall S. son of M. Christopher died Sept. 20, 1854 aged 11 yr. 3 mo. 23 Ds.

Mary wife of John Christopher died Sept. 11, 1854 aged 50 y. 5 m. 13 d.

Joshua Lawson died Mar. 7, 1854 in the 65 year of his age.

In Memory of Rachel Lawson who departed this life October 12, 1828 aged 65 years 10 months.

Five graves unmarked.

*   *   *   *

Cemetery on land owned by Abner Walls about one half mile south west of Pisgah, Grant District, Preston County, W. Va. Copied July 17, 1931.

Walter H. Michael died Nov. 8, 1909 age 48 yrs. 7 mos. 1 day. A. F. A. M.

Solomon Walls July 18, 1823 died Feb. 1, 1897.

Walter Clark son of J. E. & Mary C. Ormond born May 21, 1879 died Apr. 18, 1884. Elizabeth A. wife of John P. Ormond born Jan. 7, 1797 died Feb. 11, 1887.

Mary Miller died in the triumphs of faith Nov. 1841 aged 52 years.

Jehu infant son of H. & M. Joseph died Nov. 26, 1853.

Matilda wife of H. Joseph departed this life July 23, 1863 aged 30 yrs. 11 mo. & 5 days.

Eugene B. Walls died Aug. 9, 1893 age 43 yrs. 11 mo. 9 ds.

George Curtis son of W. S. & A. M. Walls died May 13, 1902 aged ly. 7 m. 17 d.

Doyle Grant son of W. S. & A. M. Walls died April 14, 1907 aged 6 mo. 26 ds.

Among those unmarked are the graves of Mary Ann Lawson Walls, Nancy Michael Walls, Bryson Walls, Ezra Walls, Lovena Walls, Hettie Walls, and Causy Walls. These names furnished by Mrs. Abner Walls.

*   *   *   *

Fairview Cemetery located one half mile east of Pisgah, Grant District, Preston County, W. Va. Copied July 17, and 18, 1931. Names at unmarked graves were furnished by Mr. Wm. Gibson.

Wm. McCoy Smith July 20, 1856 - Mar. 31, 1917. *Mrs. Smith.

*Winfield Smith. *Bessie Smith.

* Indicates unmarked graves.

Jonathan Gribble born Jan. 26, 1842 died June 13, 1906.

Mary F. Gribble born Sept. 21, 1846 died May 1, 1920.

Robert Furman 1852 - 1918.   Mary M. his wife 1853 - 1929.

Harmon son of R. M. & M. M. Furman born Jan. 21, 1874 died Aug. 3, 1902.

*Child of Grace Furman.

Harold W. son of W. O. & G. L. Jenkins Jan. 23, 1918 - June 17, 1918.

Lulu Pearl dau. of H. J. & A. M. Gibson 1926 - 1927.

Eli J. Walls 1825 - 1894.   Mary J. his wife 1828 - 1901.

*Oran Bircher, also another Bircher.

Icy M. dau. of J. & P. J. Bircher died Nov. 12, 1892 aged 2 yr. 9 mo. 11 ds.

Anne J. dau. of J. & P. J. Bircher died July 5, 1892 aged 9 mos.

Perry J. Rogers born Oct. 16, 1820 died May 2, 1904 aged 83 yrs. 6 mos. & 16 ds.   Elizabeth A. Rogers born Oct. 21, 1824 died Sept. 9, 1902 aged 77 yrs. 10 mos. & 19 Ds.

Mary Eva dau. of Roy & Dacie Wheeler Jan. 7, 1927 - Jan. 10, 1927.

Jesse Cale died May 29, 1899 aged 58 y. 8 m. & 27 ds.

Martha Cale died April 5, 1925 aged 80 ys. 10 ms. & 11 ds.

Lizzie King born Dec. 4, 1869 died July 31, 1906 aged 36 ys. 7 ms. 27 D.

Jesse C. Forman 1868 - 1920.   Shiloah his wife 1872 - ———.

*Freeland Forman.

Samuel Forman 1843 - 1917.   Sevilla his wife 1846 - ———.

Henry M. Rogers 1862 - 1912.   Letitia A. his wife 1862 - ———.

Theodore son of W. J. & L. J. Rogers Mar. 2, 1888 - Aug. 18, 1910.

Ewing A. Rogers born July 29, 1894 died Mar. 14, 1897 aged 2 yrs. 7 mo. & 14 ds.

*Cora Greathouse.

Levi M. Gribble died Feb. 12, 1897 in his 50 year.

*George Rogers.

William E. Rogers born Mar. 6, 1841 died Dec. 18, 1913.   Margaret Rogers June 22, 1840 died Mar. 19, 1919.

Malinda E. dau. of William E. & Margaret J. Rogers born Jan. 6, 1866 died April 11, 1889 aged 23 yrs. 3 mos. & 5 ds.

David N. son of William & Marg't J. Rogers born March 8, 1881 died March 28, 1889 aged 8 yrs. & 20 ds.   Pura M. dau. of William & Margaret J. Rogers born June 10, 1883 died March 31, 1889 aged 5 yrs. 10 ms. & 21 ds.   Lena N. dau. of William & Margaret J. Rogers born Oct. 25, 1877 died Nov. 19, 1877 aged 25 days.   Nina Rogers dau. of Malinda E. Rogers departed this life Mar. 23, 1889 aged 3 years 3 months & 23 days.   Lloyd E.

* Indicates unmarked graves.

son of J. N. & R. L. Rogers born Dec. 12, 1888 died March 25, 1889 aged 8 months & 13 days.

John T. Knotts died Oct. 21, 1888 aged 60 y. & 5 ds.

Wade son of J. O. & Maude Walls June 25, 1916 - Oct. 15, 1916.

*Mary Walls.

Nora Gay dau. of L. S. & S. A. Christopher died Oct. 30, 1897 aged 2 ys. 1 mo. 6 ds.

Marshall King Nov. 1, 1849 - May 22, 1919.

Alpheus King Jan. 9, 1822 - Sept. 23, 1915. Margaret King Mar. 20, 1818 - May 5, 1902.

Lawrence W. Kelley Nov. 12, 1877 - ———. Maggie E. his wife Feb. 23, 1873 - Feb. 19, 1923.

Irene dau. of Berthal and Earnest H. Kelley born Aug. 20, 1922 died May 1, 1925.

William Forman died April 28, 1927 aged 2 mos. 13 days.

Bessie V. dau. of Clyde & Nellie Forman Mar. 16, 1916 - Mar. 22, 1916.

Sylvester T. Clark 1859 - ———. Victoria O. his wife 1867 - 1925.

Obadiah Metheny 1848 - ———. Nancy Otto his wife 1848 - 1923.

Thurman Davis Aug. 15, 1911 - Feb. 7, 1921.

Ralph E. Metheny 1893 - 1922.

Infant son July 25, 1908 - July 29, 1908. Gerald Everett Sept. 19, 1916 - Dec. 15, 1916. Children of B. D. & Zona Spiker.

William H. Metheny May 4, 1848 - Mar. 30, 1903.

In Memory of our father John Christopher died Mar. 16, 1891 aged 76 y. 3 m. 6 d.

Deliah wife of J. Christopher died Oct. 6, 1896 aged 62 yrs. 1 mo.

S. M. Metheny Apr. 21, 1848 - Sept. 5, 1927. Mary A. wife of S. M. Metheny Nov. 27, 1847 - Apr. 11, 1905.

Mary L. Metheny Feb. 1, 1865 - July 11, 1919.

Ami F. Walls Mar. 25, 1828 - Nov. 8, 1887.

Elizabeth A. Walls Oct. 4, 1840 - July 24, 1913.

Rheufus H. son of A. F. & E. A. Walls died Feb. 27, 1871 aged 1 y. 9 m. 8 d.

Sarah E. wife of Marshall Harned died Dec. 25, 1884 aged 23 years 2 mo. & 1 d.

Hester A. King 1823 - 1920.

Dora F. dau. of J. A. & L. C. Metheny born Sept. 28, 1883 died Dec. 6, 1885.

*Jack Rogers.

Archibald G. Gribble died May 17, 1891 aged 71 yrs. 4 ms. 18 Ds. Delilah A. wife of A. G. Gribble died Feb. 3, 1856 aged 38 yrs. 3 ms. 3 ds.

* Indicates unmarked graves.

Winfield W. Gribble 1843 - 1928. Hannah M. Gribble 1844 - 1918.
John J. Gribble born June 22, 1832 died Dec. 9, 1920. Lucinda
 Gribble born Nov. 22, 1839 died Sept. 17, 1905.
Ruea M. Gribble Feb. 9, 1884 - Apr. 25, 1911.
*Mrs. Lester Christopher.
William Gail son of Lester L. & Rebecca Christopher born Aug. 12,
 1910 died Oct. 30, 1910.
*Mrs. Charles Gribble.
E. Benton Gibson 1890 - ———. Norma B. his wife 1892 - 1922.
*Homer Griffith.
George E. Spurgeon died June 2, 1900 aged 7 yrs. 3 mos. 18 ds.
Daniel B. McCollum born July 26, 1813 died Oct. 27, 1896. Anna
 McCollum born Dec. 29, 1820 died Apr. 24, 1890.
Jacob Mosser died May 1, 1883 aged 72 y. 5 m. & 23 ds. Phebe W.
 wife of Jacob Mosser died Mar. 22, 1897 aged 80 y. & 19 D.
Emma P. dau. of W. F. & S. Michael born Sept. 18, 1867 died June
 8, 18——.
John Cale born Aug. 21, 1828 died Feb. 26, 1914. Hannah H. Cale
 born Oct. 30, 1851 died Aug. 15, 1903.
W. F. Michael Apr. 24, 1827 - Jan. 20, 1910. Charlotte Michael Feb.
 12, 1825 - Apr. 19, 1906.
*Daughter of Joseph Conners.
Mattie M. Walls Jan. 27, 1876 - Mar. 13, 1923.
Lulu M. dau. of J. I. & Mamie B. Galloway Aug. 3, 1919 - Dec. 20,
 1922.
Julia Jean dau. of J. I. & Mamie B. Galloway Oct. 29, - Nov. 19, 1917.
William J. Mosser 1842 - 1924.
Rebecca J. Mosser 1860 - 1928.
Jasper N. Rogers 1861 - 1917.
William Goodwin 1834 - 1915. Rachel J. his wife 1830 - 1914.
*Bruce Hill.
Blanche Hill Haines Oct. 26, 1874 - Jan. 2, 1899.
James M. Gribble born Jan. 26, 1835 died Mar. 26, 1897.
Mary Cleo Gribble dau. of A. O. & A. B. Gribble Mar. 7, 1903 - Oct.
 30, 1918.
Harrison Gribble 1826 - 1887. Mary M. his wife 1832 - 1911.
Vasie Gribble 1875 - 1879.
James Michael born May 4, 1802 died June 11, 1880 aged 78 ys. 1
 mo. 7 Ds.
Mary Michael born Nov. 17, 1804 died Nov. 26, 1888 aged 84 ys. 9 Ds.
Sally Sept. 19, 1883 - Aug. 6, 1884. Leona Nov. 15, 1894 - Sept. 7,
 1896. Children of G. P. & C. E. Lewis.

* Indicates unmarked graves.

G. P. Lewis Mar. 17, 1858 - ———. Clara E. his wife Jan. 15, 1863 -
    May 30, 1918.
Vina Ella dau. of G. P. & C. E. Lewis Oct. 26, 1903 - Sept. 12, 1918.
Emma Olive July 14, 1890 - Feb. 28, 1903. Dau. of H. C. & M. M.
    Benson.
*H. Clay Benson.
Dolly M. infant dau. of W. & E. Wolf 1929 - 1929.
*George Bircher.
Vida M. Forman wife of Thomas Robbins 1901 - 1923.
(Glass case marker) Wesley L. Everly & Delia B. Everly.
*Mrs. Greathouse. *Mrs. Tekoah Christopher.
J. S. Everly 1868 - 1930.
Mary J. dau. of J. S. & M. A. Everly born Jan. 8, 1907 died Jan. 11,
    1907.
Henry H. Everly 1839 - 1882 Hanna J. his wife 1845 - 1919.
Emma O. dau. of H. H. & H. J. Everly died Mar. 2, 1876 aged 4 yr.
    10 ms. 17 ds.
Martha J. wife of G. W. Gribble died Nov. 12, 1871 aged 37 ys. 8 m.
    13 d.
Thomas King died Feb. 25, 1878 aged 73 y. 2 m. 2 d.
Jane King wife of Thomas King died Feb. 19, 1890 aged 83 y. 6 m.
    8 D.
William G. son of Irvin E. & Mary C. Christopher died April 9, 1889
    aged 5 years & 1 day.
*Infant of Charles and Daisy Ryan.
Irvin E. Christopher 1839 - 1924.
Mary C. Christopher 1847 - 1906.
Mary A. wife of E. B. King born Feb. 17, 1839 died Aug. 29, 1898.
John L. Everly 1837 - 1927. Co. A 7th W. Va. Inft. Hila his wife
    1840 - 1918.
Norman K. son of C. J. & E. B. Feather June 1, 1916 - Feb. 12, 1918.
*child of C. J. & E. B. Feather.
Viola Fern dau. of Edith & Arlie Forman June 13, 1921 - Jan. 30,
    1922.
Evan King Nov. 11, 1855 - May 4, 1923. Olive O. Apr. 18, 1962 - —.
Troy E. Gribble 1894 - 1928. 501 Refrigeration Plant Co. U. S.
    Army. Served in France.
Marshall E. Metheny 1897 - ———. Gertrude Ryan 1903 - 1924.
Kenneth K. Christopher 1903 - 1926.
Effie E. Christopher 1875 - 1922.
Dallas D. Christopher 1910 - 1927.
Guy B. Christopher 1892 - 1918. 1st Divn. 16th Inft. M. G. Co. A.
    E. F.
* Indicates unmarked graves.

Jehu H. Christopher 1839 - 1916.   Isabelle N. his wife 1853 - 1927.

Siota E. dau. of J. H. & I. N. Christopher died July 11, 1898 aged 15 yr. 7 ms. 9 Ds.

Junior son of J. H. & I. N. Christopher died Oct. 10, 1896 aged 11 ms. 21 ds.

Rutherford H. son of J. H. & I. N. Christopher died Dec. 16, 1891 aged 14 y. 11 m. & 16 d.

George H. King born Oct. 4, 1837 died Sept. 12, 1915.   Francis A. King born Sept. 2, 1836 died June 1, 1907.

Children of G. H. & F. A. King.   Ullysses G. King 1867 - 1878.   Ida C. King 1872 - 1878.   Nora J. King 1869 - 1871.   Marshall S. King 1874 - 1875.

Benjamin Lawson died Nov. 10, 1875 aged 83 ys. 1 mo. & 25 d.   A Soldier of 1812.

Jane wife of Benjamin Lawson died Apr. 8, 1871 aged 84 ys. 6 ms. & 9 d.

Wm. Smith 1830 - 1915.   Elizabeth his wife 1837 - 1914.

(Six graves marked) Melvina - Eliza - Charles - Minnie - William - John.

Carlos Roy son of A. L. & C. A. Lewis Dec. 5, 1919 - Feb. 18, 1920.

*Child of Mr. and Mrs. Harvey Smith.

*Child of Mr. and Mrs. Sauers.

*Child of Mr. and Mrs. Bud Golden.

Geraldine Blanche dau. of Rodd & Mary Golden Apr. 15, 1923 - Sept. 4, 1923.

John Lucian son of Rodd & Mary Golden June 23, 1921 - July 21, 1921.

George Carlus son of Rodd & Mary Golden Apr. 8, 1920 - Apr. 19, 1920.

Mary Belle dau. of Rodd & Mary Golden May 16, 1919 - May 26, 1919.

*George Golden.   *Mrs. George Golden.

George Moore Golden born Apr. 24, 1888 died Apr. 28, 1909 age 21 ys. 4 ds.

Adam Wolf 1841 - 1926.   Harriet 1849 - 1927.

(Stone uncrated) Corpl. Adam Wolf Co. C 3rd W. Va. Cav.

Lulu E. Stuart dau. of Adam & Harriet Wolf Sept. 22, 1874 - Jan. 12, 1914.

*Albert Wolf.

Silas K. Haines Mar. 1, 1831 - June 29, 1886.   Mary Haines Aug. 28, 1833 - April 30, 1906.

(U. S. Marker) S. K. Haines Co. H. 3rd P. H. B. Inft.   Mary Haines nee Yohey.

* Indicates unmarked graves.

Bruce H. son of Albert & Sarah Wolf born Aug. 2, 1873 died May 25, 1904.

*J. Smith and three children.

Adam Smith died June 10, 1891 aged 72 yrs. 5 ms. & 15 days.

Willard son of W. O. & G. A. Walls Dec. 3, 1914 - Mar. 10, 1916.

Elizabeth wife of Wm. J. King Dec. 14, 1833 - July 20, 1917.

Geo. W. Street died June 11, 1898 aged 91 y. 6 m. 28 ds.

Ethelinda wife of Geo. W. Street died Dec. 21, 1893 aged 84 y. 2 m. 29 ds.

Hannah Ella Maude dau. of Wm. C. & Emma Myers died Feb. 25, 1894 aged 8 yrs. 11 mo. 9 ds.

Robert Russell son of Wm. & L. A. Beutty born Aug. 1, 1891 died Oct. 29, 1897.

James W. son of Wm. C. & Emma Myers died Aug. 9, 1905 aged 22 yr. 9 mo. 22 ds.

Rufus C. Myers June 3, 1870 - Aug. 13, 1914.

William C. Myers 1841 - 1916. Emma K. his wife 1846 - ⸺.

*Dau. of Wm. C. & Emma Myers.

J. T. Gribble Nov. 24, 1840 - Jan. 30, 1929.

Frances Ann Gribble Dec. 23, 1849 - Jan. 22, 1930.

Thresa Mildred Rush Jan. 23, - Feb. 17, 1925.

Jemima wife of A. S. McNare nee Walls born Oct. 29, 1835 died Aug. 2, 1872 aged 36 yrs. 9 mos. 4 ds.

Dora B. dau. of A. S. & J. McNare died May 21, 1868 aged 3 ms. 7 Ds.

R. F. Walls. Alice wife of R. F. Walls. Leona Maude died Feb. 6, 1879 aged 2 yrs. 1 mo & 29 ds. Philip Benton died Nov. 17, 1900 aged 17 yrs. 3 mos. & 17 ds. Edison Evert died Dec. 17, 1900 aged 20 years 4 mos. & 11 Ds. Nevada Dell died Dec. 27, 1900 aged 22 yrs. 3 mos. & 15 Ds. Haddie wife of R. F. Walls died Dec. 3, 1900 aged 45 yrs. 5 mos. & 10 ds.

Sarah wife of Charles Walls died Jan. 25, 1874 aged 83 y. 1 mo. & 3 d.

G. W. Walls born Apr. 24, 1830 died Oct. 4, 1896. Belinda wife of G. W. Walls born Oct. 7, 1829 died Mch. 2, 1908. Estella G. dau. of G. W. & B. Walls born Feb. 9, 1872 died Sept. 13, 1896.

J. Harvey Walls Jan. 20, 1855 - Sept. 2, 1906.

Phoebe wife of J. H. Walls died Dec. 10, 1896 aged 40 yr. 6 ms. 24 Ds. Addie B. born Oct. 11, 1874 died Dec. 30, 1881. Bertha M. born Apr. 2, 1891.

John M. Galloway Apr. 2, 1840 - Jan. 14, 1920. Lydia A. his wife May 23, 1844 - Feb. 2, 1910.

Lester A. son of E. J. & E. C. Galloway died Feb. 13, 1899 aged 2 Ds.

* Indicates unmarked graves.

Carrie Oakley dau. of C. A. & M. J. Galloway Sept. 8, 1914 - Sept. 25, 1915.

Cora L. Everly died April 8, 1931 age 54 years.

Emma E. dau. of H. D. & E. M. Cupp Aug. 21, 1915 - Sept. 7, 1916.

*Child of H. D. & E. M. Cupp.

George L. Galloway May 10, 1866 - Sept. 17, 1918.

Thomas H. King 1850 - 1927.

Daniel W. O'Neal June 24, 1849 - July 1, 1913.

Samuel O'Neal 1840 - 1920 Co. B 54 Regt. Pa. Inft.

Bertha B. dau. of W. G. & O. M. O'Neal born Aug. 14, 1903 died Aug. 2, 1904.

Hattie B. dau. D. A. & Alice Ryan Nov. 29, 1901.

Daniel A. Ryan 1861 - ———. Alice A. his wife 1861 - 1916.

Vada Alice dau. of Ralph & Avis Ryan 1916 - 1926.

Mary C. wife of John E. Ormond born Oct. 22, 1838 died Dec. 25, 1901.

Harry B. son of John E. & Mary C. Ormond born Aug. 7, 1883 died Feb. 3, 1904.

*John Ormond.

Roy L. 1896 - 1898. Homer C. 1899. Children of I. S. & M. Lewis.

Guy son of I. S. & M. Lewis Dec. 16, 1892 - Aug. 18, 1912.

Sylvester Christopher 1885 - 1927.

Eldrich Roy Ryan Feb. 4, 1916 - Dec. 28, 1924.

W. Lucille Ryan Mar. 28, 1920 - May 18, 1930.

*John Wolf.   *Mrs. John Wolf.

Waitman C. Gibson Sept. 23, 1837 - Feb. 2, 1919.

Rebecca Gibson Apr. 5, 1842 - Dec. 14, 1924.

Mary dau. of Oliver B. & Martha C. Graham Feb. 5, 1910 - Feb. 10, 1910.

Rhoda O. dau. of W. C. & Rebecca Gibson died Mch. 24, 1893 aged 22 ys. 11 ms.

Elma A. Michael Aug. 10, 1849 - Feb. 17, 1924.

*P. B. Michael.

*Mr. Andy Sharpnack.   *Mrs. Samanthy Sharpnack.

*Son of Mr. and Mrs. W. R. Piper.

Rufus C. Christopher 1869 - ———. Virginia J. 1862 - 1926.

Jesse A. Christopher. Pennsylvania Pvt. 33rd Field Art. 11 Div. Apr. 15, 1926.

*George Hornby.   *Infant of Edna Hornby.

Jehu King 1851 - 19——. Mary A. his wife 1855 - 1927.

Thomas W. King 1849 - 19——. Mary F. his wife 1853 - 1926.

*Robert Foringer.   *Mrs. Robert Foringer.

Edward F. Dillow 1903 - 1922.

* Indicates unmarked graves.

L. H. Dillow 1862 - ———. Mary J. his wife 1870 - 1920.
*Eugene Gribble.
Carl Junior Sept. 1, - Oct. 13, 1918. Willis Eugene Sept. 21, - Oct. 7, 1919. Children of Mr. & Mrs. C. B. Smith.
Baby Mary dau. of I. B. & Effie Smith born & died Oct. 7, 1910.
John H. Smith 1834 - 1908. Elizabeth A. his wife 1836 - 1910.
Coral B. dau. of Chas. R. & Maggie E. Michael born March 10, 1902 died Jan. 26, 1904.
John Goodwin 1830 - 1910. Mary Goodwin 1854 - ———. William Goodwin 1874-1928.
(U. S. Marker) Jno. Goodwin Co. A 1st W. Va. Cav.
Robert L. Wilson Dec. 3, 1841 - Mar. 2, 1909. Katherine his wife Oct. 23, 1852 - Mar. 21, 1909.
Harvey C. Wilson Nov. 21, 1884 - Apr. 28, 1911.
*John Christopher son of Sylvester (Sell) Christopher.
Era June dau. of Roy & Violet Cunningham Dec. 31, 1924 - Apr. 4, 1926 age 1 yr. 3 mo. 4 ds.
*Infant of Howard Gibson.
Willis R. son of F. & V. Bishop born & died Apr. 21, 1929.
Asberry A. Christopher Mar. 5, 1859 - Sept. 3, 1927. Phebe J. his wife Nov. 23, 1861 - Mar. 25, 1921.
*Josie Christopher wife of Marshall Christopher and dau. of John Wolf.

* * * *

Cemetery at St. Peter Church, four miles northwest of Bruceton Mills, Grant District, Preston County, W. Va. Copied July 19, 1931.
James G. Spindler 1867 - 1929.
Laura B. Spindler 1866 - 19——.
Andrew Spindler born Jan. 3, 1830 died Oct. 28, 1907 aged 77 ys. 9 ms. 25 ds.
Nancy J. wife of Andrew Spindler born Sept. 5, 1837 died April 20, 1903 aged 65 ys. 7 ms. 15 Ds.
Dora A. died July 25, 1879 aged 3 mo. & 13 days.
Cora E. died Mar. 25, 1879 aged 2 years 6 mos. & 5 Ds.
Loretta wife of S. M. Barkley died Nov. 14, 1899 aged 36 yrs. 9 months & 18 days. Henry W. son of S. M. & L. Barkley died Aug. 20, 1900 aged 17 yrs. 6 months & 18 Days.
One grave unmarked.
Samuel T. Wiley May 25, 1850 - Nov. 10, 1905. Historian. Ella his wife April 9, 1859 - ———.
Eleanor Essie dau. of S. T. & Ella Wiley June 11, 1886 - Dec. 29, 1890.
Three graves unmarked.
* Indicates unmarked graves.

Agnes Thelma dau. of J. A. & M. J. Reckard Mar. 10, 1905 - Apr. 25, 1908.

J. M. Kelly 1870 - 19——. N. E. his wife 1876 - 19——. Our son J. Rufus 1897 - 1923.

Waitman T. Maust 1860 - 19——. Bessie B. his wife 1875 - 1915.

Sylvester W. Maust born April 30, 1864 died Oct. 20, 1898 aged 34 years 6 mo. 20 ds.

James H. son of S. W. & E. F. Maust died Feb. 23, 1893 age 1 yr. 6 ms. 7 ds.

Martha J. Galloway died Aug. 31, 1873 aged 41 yrs. 1 mo.

Jacob Dull died Apr. 23, 1881 in the 77 year of his age.

Mary A. Dull died April 7, 1875 in the 69 year of her age.

Minnie May dau. of Evan & Belle Moyer died Mar. 18, 1895 aged 3 yrs. & 14 ds.

Laura J. dau. of E & B Moyer died June 16, 1887 aged 1 year 11 mo. & 12 Ds.

Theodore son of P. & C. Gardner died Nov. 30, 1871 aged 1 y. 10 m. 11 d.

John H. Gardner died Nov. 7, 1891 aged 24 ys. 3 m. 12 ds.

Two graves unmarked.

Plesey C. dau. of G. W. & N. E. Seese died Feb. 17, 1872 aged 6 ms 7 ds.

Three graves unmarked.

Charles son of John & Catherine Skiles died Sept. 2, 1881 aged 11 years & 3 mo.

Mariah dau. of J. & C. Jefferys died Oct. 22, 1871 aged 3 ys. 4 ms. 22 ds.

Clinton son of J. & C. Jefferys born July 15, 1875 died Nov. 20, 1881.

Charlotta wife of J. Jefferys born Sept. 28, 1834 died Dec. 17, 1881.

Ruth dau. of J. & C. Jefferys born July 29, 1865 died Aug. 20, 1885.

Jackson Jefferys died Sept. 2, 1906 aged 75 years 3 mo. & 28 Ds.

Henrietta infant dau. of Mr. & Mrs. M. L. Gardner.

Philip Gardner Feb. 13, 1833 - Oct. 27, 1908. Christina wife of Philip Gardner Dec. 5, 1838 - ——.

Geo. W. Thornton husband of Ida Thornton died Jan. 3, 1894 aged 26 yrs. 11 mo. 1 day.

David E. Thornton 1837 - 1917. Mary H. 1842 - 1922.

One grave unmarked.

William Allen 1828 - 1918. Mary J. Allen his wife 1826 - 1901.

Cora F. dau. of Wm. & Mary Allen died June 22, 1892 aged 19 y. 2 m. 19 d.

Three graves unmarked.

John M. Spindler 1863 - 1929.

Cerena Spindler Dec. 10, 1854 - June 22, 1909.

John Spindler born Dec. 23, 1823 died Aug. 22, 1906 age 82 years 4 mo. 9 ds.

Ellen Spindler born Aug. 2, 1827 died Feb. 2, 1913 age 85 years 6 mos.

Lucinda dau. of Jno. & Ellen Spindler died Apr. 10, 1876 age 16 yrs. 5 mo. & 10 days.

Catherine wife of A. Lenhart died Aug. 16, 1875 age 43 yrs. 11 mo. & 16 ds.

Aaron Lenhart died Oct. 27, 1900 aged 74 years.

U. S. G. son of A. & C. Lenhart died Aug. 28, 1875 aged 8 yrs. 7 mo. & 16 ds.

Francis R. Adey Mar. 15, 1837 - Mar. 29, 1925.

William H. Adey Apr. 2, 1833 - Apr. 1, 1892.   Priv. Co. B 3rd Regt. Md. Vol. Inft.

Cora M. Adey Sept. 1, 1880 - July 20, 1891.

Three graves unmarked.

John Haines died Mar. 23, 1871 aged 60 ys. 5 mo. 17 ds.

Elizabeth Haines born Dec. 10, 1815 died Mar. 11, 1884.

Catherine wife of Daniel Barkley died ————————aged 62 yr. 10 mo. 9 ds.

One grave unmarked.

Martha C. wife of F. J. Lieb died July 26, 1880 17 y. 1 mo. 9 d.

Frederick J. Lieb May 2, 1850 - July 4, 1916.

Lydia wife of J. Nedrow born Feb. 14, 1826 died Jan. 18, 1873.

Joseph Kelley born July 9, 1842 died Feb. 18, 1879 aged 36 yrs. 7 mo. & 19 ds.

Harriet C. wife of Joseph Kelley born Aug. 28, 1849 died Dec. 14, 1890 age 41 y. 3 m. 16 d.

Adam Clark son of Joseph & Harriet Kelley born June 3,·1873 died Jan. 3, 1896 aged 22 yrs. 7 mo. & 2 Ds.

Four graves unmarked.

James R. son of C. M. & E. O. Sechler 1912 - 1912.

George Maust July 22, 1813 - Oct. 3, 1898, Jane wife of George Maust May 13, 1833 - June 30, 1898.

Adam Seese died Apr. 5, 1881 aged 77 years 14 ds.

Harriet wife of Adam Seese died Nov. 1884 aged 78 years.

Charles Sechler Feb. 18, 1857 - Mar. 1, 1906.   Martha B. wife of Charles Sechler Mar. 12, 1859 - ————.

Myrtle M. dau. of C. & M. B. Sechler died Nov. 5, 1895 aged 2 ys. 11 mo. 5 ds.

John Liston died Nov. 26, 1878 aged 77 ys. 3 ms. 13 ds.

Lydia E. dau. of Geo. & E. J. Laub died Sept. 15, 1881 aged 7 yr. 9 mo. 10 ds.

David I. son of Geo. & E. J. Laub born June 8, 1881 died Apr. 11, 1895.

Elizabeth wife of the late Jonathan Laub died Dec. 13, 1884 aged 65 yr. 9 mo. 3 ds.

Saloma Laub Beerbower Mar. 24, 1840 - Jan. 19, 1896.

Samuel Laub born Sept. 14, 1849 died Dec. 19, 1898.

John R. Wirsing died Jan. 20, 1891 aged 29 yr. 10 mo. & 6 Days. Evens E. Wirsing died June 13, 1891 aged 28 yrs. 2 mo. & 21 days.

John Wirsing born Nov. 14, 1821 died Dec. 26, 1900. Sarah wife of J. Wirsing born Aug. 25, 1825 died June 20, 1897.

Ida May wife of R. N. Wirsing Nov. 24, 1878 - Dec. 9, 1902.

Joseph H. Haines born Apr. 19, 1843 died June 21, 1924.

Mary A. wife of J. H. Haines born June 20, 1845 died Mar. 18, 1895.

John Myers born Oct. 17, 1834 died Mar. 11, 1898. Lydia E. wife of John Myers died June 4, 1894 in her 49 year. (Other markers same lot) Grandma - Father - Mother - Elizabeth - Charlotte - Emma - James A. - Rachel A. - Sadie E. - dau. of John & L. E. Myers died May 21, 1881 aged 4 yrs. 5 mo. & 28 days. Mary C. dau. of J. & L. E. Myers Oct. 13, 1866 aged 9 days.

John P. Speelman Feb. 17, 1830 - Sept. 27, 1905.

Catherine wife of John P. Speelman Nov. 3, 1832 - Mar. 22, 1909.

Daniel Myers 1837 - 1901. Elizabeth Myers 1841 - 1922.

Samuel L. son of Rev. D. H. & E. Myers born Apr. 10, 1869 died May 30, 1893.

William J. Barnes born Dec. 18, 1836 died Oct. 13, 1912.

Naomi wife of W. J. Barnes born Jan. 27, 1848 died Feb. 1, 1895.

Cora C. dau. of W. J. & N. Barnes born Oct. 11, 1878 died Feb. 6, 1894.

Geo. W. Seese born May 19, 1832 died Sept. 1, 1892.

Bertha A. Seese born Apr. 28, 1893 died Sept. 5, 1897.

James W. White born May 9, 1869 died Dec. 18, 1898 aged 29 y. 7 mo. 9 ds.

Eliza wife of Hugh White born Mar. 8, 1812 died Feb. 19, 1899 aged 86 yrs. 11 mo. 11 ds.

Six Graves unmarked.

H. H. Fike Feb. 23, 1828 died Nov. 19, 1898.

Lydia A. Fike Aug. 7, 1834 died Feb. 22, 1896.

Minnie A. Silbaugh 1869 - 1921.

*   *   *   *

On the farm owned by Jesse Ryan and near the house of Alva Bryte, about one half mile due south of the White School house northwest of Bruceton Mills, West Virginia, are the following grave markers. Copied June 23, 1932.

Daniel C. Raymond 1824 - 1911.

Susan A. wife of Daniel C. Raymond died Aug. 29, 1865 aged 34 ys.
7 mo. 29 ds.

Mary E. Raymond born May 20, 1832 died Jan. 17, 1897 aged 64 yrs.
7 ms. 28 ds.

*   *   *   *

The Wheeler Cemetery located on land now owned by Charles
Rexroad near the old abandoned Hazel Run Church, about one half
mile from the present St. Peter Church in northern Grant District,
Preston County, West Virginia.   Copied June 23, 1932.

Willie L. son of J. W. & N. Haines died Nov. 10, 1873 aged 4 yr.
15 d.

Charles E. son of J. W. & N. Haines died Sept. 26, 1872 aged 1 y.
7 m. 2 d.

Martha Ann dau. of C. P. & S. A. Connelly died Nov. 27, 1857 aged
4 yrs. 2 mo. 4 days.

John A. son of Alpheus & Phebe Wheeler died Oct. 8, 1856 aged
1 yr. 5 mo. 8 d.

Smith Wheeler died March 29, 1881 aged 81 years & 1 month.

Hannah wife of Smith Wheeler died March 27, 1866 aged 60 years
5 month & 11 d.

George W. Myers died Sept. 18, 1862 aged 29 years 2 mo. & 5 days.
Erected by W. H. & C. Myers.

*   *   *   *

Cemetery on the Jonas Maust farm near the Sandy Creek bridge
where Sandy Creek crosses the Pennsylvania state line in Grant
District, Preston County, West Virginia.   Copied June 23, 1932.

William W. Wirsing Dec. 25, 1853 - May 1, 1907.   Virginia his wife
May 1, 1858 - ——.

E. Chalfant Wirsing Dec. 9, 1897 - Feb. 28, 1907.

Barbara E. wife of J. M. Wirsing born Nov. 20, 1850 died July 17,
1900 age 49 yrs. 7 mo. & 27 ds.

Winfield R. son of J. M. & B. Wirsing born June 2, 1894 died May
26, 1900 age 5 yrs. 11 mo. & 24 ds.

Clara B. dau. of J. M. & B. E. Wirsing born Jan. 25, 1885 died Feb.
28, 1885 age 1 mo. 3 ds.

Vesta E. dau. of J. M. & B. E. Wirsing born Aug. 4, 1883 died Dec.
21, 1883 age 4 mo. & 17 ds.

George W. son of J. W. & G. M. Haines died Jan. 31, 1862 aged 2
yr. 9 mo. 11 d.

Sivilia Alice dau. of I. E. & Sarah Cecelia Haines born June 4, 1876
died Sept. 15, 1876 age 3 mo. 11 ds.

Laura Bell dau. of I. E. & Sara Cecelia Haines born June 20, 1886 died Aug. 15, 1890 age 4 ys. 1 mo. 26 ds.

Daniel A. son of Jonas & Rebecca Haines born Sept. 25, 1840 died Nov. 2, 1862 age 22 yrs. 1 mo. & 8 ds.

Elizabeth dau. of Jonas & Rebecca Haines born Jan. 15, 1839 died Jan. 11, 1900 age 60 yrs. 11 mo. & 27 ds.

Rebecca wife of Jonas Haines born July 24, 1813 died Dec. 8, 1900 aged 84 yrs. 4 mo. & 14 ds.

Noah F. son of Jonas & Rebecca Haines born June 13, 1831 died Aug. 23, 1900 age 69 yrs. 2 mo. 10 ds.

—————— wife of David Seese died Aug. 6, 1867 aged 29 yrs. 9 months.

Levi N. son of A. & L. A. Maust died Jan. 11, 1870 aged 1 yr. 3 mo. 5 ds.

Lenah E. dau. of A. & L. A. Maust died Oct. 29, 1875 aged 3 yr. 7 mo. 16 ds.

Jonas Maust Feb. 6, 1828 - Apr. 8, 1910. Mary Ann his wife Jan. 17, 1835 - Feb. 27, 1879.

Armour son of Jonas & Mary A. Maust Sept. 5, 1869 - Mar. 24, 1870.

George W. son of J. & M. A. Maust died Apr. 16, 1868 aged 6 mo. 23 ds.

Amanda L. dau. of J. & M. A. Maust died Apr. 25, 1857 aged 3 yrs. 19 ds.

Daniel W. son of J. & S. Maust died Feb. 7, 1863 aged 1 yr. & 11 mo.

Joseph W. son of J. & S. Maust died May 21, 1860 aged 8 mo. & 2 ds.

*   *   *   *

East View Cemetery, East View Church, near the Pennsylvania State line in Grant District, Preston County, W. Va. Copied June 23, 1932.

Joseph Reckard July 6, 1825 - June 1, 1909. Margaret Reckard Aug. 31, 1830 - June 21, 1903.

John Cupp private Company H. third Regt. P. H. B. Maryland Vol. Inft. Discharged May 29, 1865 died Nov. 20, 1910 aged 69 years.

Areana wife of A. J. Maulsby 1873 - 1927.

Mollie A. Myers 1876 - 1914.

Samuel S. Teets Apr. 30, 1869 - ——— Bertha his wife Sept. 5, 1870 - Apr. 10, 1918.

Narra P. Teets Oct. 29, 1904 - ———. Charles E. Teets Nov. 19, 1914 - ———. Ersel Teets born Apr. 27, 1910 died March 15, 1911.

John D. Emerson 1857 - 1922. Mary his wife 1860 - 19———.

Jacob V. Smith Sept. 17, 1852 - Feb. 3, 1929. Eliza A. Dec. 15, 1854 - Feb. 28, 1929.

George H. Teets 1847 - 1926. Co. F. 7th Reg. W. Va. Vol. Inft.
Lydda K. his wife 1850 - 19———.

*   *   *   *

Cemetery at Mountain Grove Church in north west part of Grant
District, Preston County, West Virginia. Copied June 23, 1932.
Leonard J. Everly Co. E. 6th W. Va. Cav. born Nov. 18, 1844 died
Nov. 22, 1909 age 65 yrs. & 4 ds.
Margaret J. Everly 1851 - 1927.
Four graves unmarked.
Rolla F. Wilhelm died Oct. 27, 1902 age 36 yrs. 2 ms. Ida A. Wil-
helm born Sept. 17, 1865.
Claude Forman 1902 - 1902. Ota May Forman 1903 - 1905.
Abraham B. Maust born Aug. 30, 1830 died June 25, 1911.
Louisa A. Maust died Sept. 17, 1901 age 68 yrs. 4 ms. & 8 das.
James Collins 1847 - 1912. Margaret his wife 1853 - 1920.
Clara Nedrow 1877 - 1920.
One grave unmarked.
Charles H. Glover 1870 - 1916.
Seven graves unmarked.
Letetia M. Spiker 1880 - 1910. B. V. & B. B. twin infants 1910 -
1910.
Six graves unmarked.
Mary Virginia dau. of Jacob & Mintie Uphold born July 30, 1914
died Oct. 18, 1914.
Roy son of Sam & Lucy Wiles Oct. 13, 1915 - Dec. 1, 1921.
John M. Wiles 1855 - 1927. Eliza Wiles 1853 - 1927.
Abraham Liston born Mar. 26, 1854 died Aug. 28, 1900 aged 46 ys.
5 mo. 2 ds.
Mary Ella dau. of A. & Eliza Liston died Apr. 11, 1889 aged 4 ys.
2 m. 12 ds.
Jeremiah Thomas son of A. & Eliza Liston died Feb. 13, 1896 aged
5 yrs. 3 mo. 23 ds.
Edward son of F. R. & M. Hileman born Apr. 12, 1906 died ———
1906.

*   *   *   *

Abandoned cemetery known as the Stuck Cemetery on the Loraw
farm on Little Sandy Creek, about two miles south of Bruceton
Mills, W. Va. Copied June 24, 1932.
Samuel Falkenstine 1800 - 1884. Anna his wife 1806 - 1864. Samuel
S. 1833 - 1909. Ashbel 1838 - 1861.
(Broken stone) Ashbel Falkenstein born April 16, 1838 died ———.
Mathias Stuck died Mar. 21, 1848 aged 65 yrs. 1 mo. 19 days. Nancy
wife of Mathias Stuck died Jan. 29, 1853 aged 65 ys. 3 ds.

William F. son of J. & A. Gensler died Dec. 1, 1870 aged 10 yr. 6 mo. 25 da.

Eliza wife of David Falkenstine died Apr. 30, 1852 aged 43 y. 1 mo. 18 d.

Samantha J. dau. of D. & E. Falkenstine died Mar. 15, 1845 aged 10 yr. 3 mo.

Margaret S. dau. of D. & E. Falkenstine died June 4, 1845 aged 4 y. 2 mo. 16 d.

Seven graves unmarked.

*   *   *   *

Old abandoned cemetery in the woods about one-fourth mile off the road on the farm of Harvey Benson, formerly the Armstrong Farm, about two and one-half miles southwest of Bruceton Mills, W. Va. Copied June 24, 1932.

Sacred to the Memory of Eliphalet Chidester died Feb. 12, 1821 aged 70 years 2 months.

Sacred to the Memory of Mary wife of Eliphalet Chidester died Feb. 14, 1833 aged 72 ys. 3 mo. 9 d.

To my Husband Andrew Chidester died May 5, 1854 aged 58 ys. 9 mo. 25 d.

Frederick C. son of I. & E. Armstrong died Apr. 19, 1857 aged 1 yr. 8 mo. 29 d.

Susan W. R. dau. of I. & E. Armstrong died Apr. 13, 1857 aged 4 yr. 5 mo. 5ds.

Lucy D. I. dau. of G. H. & C. Armstrong died Mar. 6, 1861 aged 6 mo. 25 ds.

Cassias C. son of J. & M. E. Armstrong died Sept. 30, 1854 aged 5y. 7mo. 4ds.

Isaac G. Armstrong died Apr. 11, 1866 aged 78 ys. 3 m. 10 ds.

Frances wife of Isaac Armstrong died Dec. 15, 1868 aged 76 y. 6 mo. 6 ds.

Eliphalet Armstrong died April 9th 1833 aged 19 years 8 mo. & 20 days.

Frances L. dau of B. G. & M. Trowbridge died Mar. 17, 1847 aged 10 ys. 7 mo. & 24 das.

Susanna dau. of B. G. & M. Trowbridge died Oct. 1, 1839 aged 1 yr & 9 mo.

Eliphalet Collins died July 22, 1863 aged 15 yrs. & 13 ds.

William A. Collins died Mar. 16, 1864 aged 20 ys. 7 mo. 7 d.

Henry Clay son of E. & A. Collins died Aug. 29, 1854 age 7 y. 3 mo. 27 d.

Mary dau. of I. & E. Metheny died May 14, 1843 aged 3 ys. 18 ds.

(Small field stone) April 9, 1833 Eliphalet Armstrong.

*   *   *   *

Beech Run Hill Cemetery near Mt. Zion Church in Pleasant District, Preston County, W. Va., about four miles north of Albright, W. Va. Copied June 25, 1932.

Isaac P. Morton Orderly Sergt. of Co. B 3rd W. Va. Cav. born Oct. 8, 1829 died May 10, 1892.

Mary wife of Isaac P. Morton born Oct. 5, 1829 died ——————.

Lesta M. Martin Aug. 19, 1893 - Oct. 23, 1894. Walter C. Martin May 20, 1893 - Sept. 19, 1896.

Six graves unmarked.

Rolla F. Martin Sept. 11, 1840 - Sept. 27, 1913.

Susanna wife of Rolla F. Martin June 3, 1840 - Feb. 25, 1904.

Nine graves unmarked.

Lewis Reckard Co. K 3rd P. H. B. Md. Inft.

Eva dau. of Eben & Rachel Liston died Feb. 4, 1863 age 27 yrs.

Three graves unmarked.

Elizabeth wife of Daniel T. Martin died Nov. 13, 1845 aged 26 yr. 6mo. 8ds.

In sacred Memory of Sarah Jane Metheny daughter of Peter & Eve Metheny who was born Oct. the 8th A. D. 1833 and departed this life August the 11, 1851 aged 17 years 9 mos. 3 days.

Ezra son of P. & E. Metheny died Oct. 13, 1861 aged 16 ys. 5 m 23 d.

One grave unmarked.

Peter Metheny born Jan. 9, 1805 died Sept. 21, 1896 aged 91 ys. 8 mo. 11 ds.

Eva Metheny born Dec. 16, 1809 died Oct. 18, 1888 aged 79 ys. 10 m. 2 ds.

Hobart R. Metheny May 30, 1902 - Dec. 8, 1905.

One grave unmarked.

Savilla B. wife of Perry Metheny born Oct. 20, 1838 died Oct. 21, 1901.

Polly Titchnell born Oct. 12, 1802 died Feb. 9, 1891.

James son of J. & J. Titchnell born Oct. 21, 1842 died Feb. 16, 1862.

One grave unmarked.

Isarael son of J. G. & R. Mason died Jan. 13, 1854 aged 5 ds.

Infant son of J. G. & R. Mason died Apr. 30, 1853.

William son of J. G. & R. Mason died Sept. 26, 1852 aged 6 mo. 1 ds.

Margaret Fetters Lee 1772 - 1839 wife of Dudley Lee a Soldier of 1776 - 1780. Erected by Capt. C. C. Lee.

Eight graves unmarked.

Ida A. dau. of C. W. & L. A. Martin died Oct. 3, 1877 aged 4 ms. 18 days.

William M. son of Samuel & Rebecca Martin born Feb. 4, 1858 died Feb. 5, 1880.

Two graves unmarked.

Samuel Martin born Aug. 7, 1821 died Mar. 16, 1903.

Rebecca Martin born July 10, 1824 died May 19, 1919.

George W. T. Martin 1851 - 1918. Rebecca his wife 1846 - 1925.

Georgia May dau. of D. C. & M. E. Radabaugh b. Jan. 14, 1898 d. Mar. 24, 1916.

Mary Lucretia Bell Radabaugh Apr. 19, 1919 - Nov. 15, 1927.

Geo. Dewitt Co. B. 3rd W. Va. Cav.

Nine graves unmarked.

Ebonezer son of E. & M. Liston died July 13, 1854 aged 18 ys. 2 m. 18 d.

Lydia dau. of E———— Feb. 16, 1855 aged 23 ys. 5 ms. 11 ds.

Stephen Titchnell died Mar. 6, 1857 aged 84 ys. 8 ms. 14 d.

Lydia wife of S. Titchnell died May 26, 1866 aged 81 ys. 24 days.

Elizabeth wife of Milton F. Martin died July 6, 1858 aged 23 ys. 5 mo. 3 ds.

Margaret wife of Elisha Liston died Dec. 10, 1868 in her 51 yr.

John T. Liston died Oct. 3, 1897 aged 57 yrs 9 days. Co. B 14 Reg. West Va.

M. Clark Liston born July 10, 1853 died June 27, 1890.

Lucy A. Liston born July 31, 1853 died Nov. 5, 1914.

One grave unmarked.

Nettie dau. of J. T. & Mary Liston Dec. 6 1877 - June 13, 1903.

Statia Dau. of ———————— Sept. 27, 1866 - May 8, 1904.

John T. Liston 1840 - 1897. Mary A. C. 1844 - 19—.

Charlie E. J. son of J. T. & M. A. C. Liston died Jan. 18, 1872 aged 2 ys. 4 ms 2 Da.

Seven graves unmarked.

DAVID HAGAN WAS BORN JULY 18, 1807 AND DIED JUNE 30 IN 1819 GENTLE READER LOOK DOWN & SEE AS I AM NOW SO YOU MUST BE WHO ONCE WAS SPRIGHTLY AS THE MORN BUT DEATH HAS VEIL-ED MY MORNING SUN.

Nine graves unmarked.

One marker unreadable.

J. G. Conner May 18, 1857 - ————————. Elizabeth C. his wife July 21, 1855 - Oct. 11, 1923.

Eight graves unmarked.

Joel son of J. & M. Stump died Dec. 21, 1861 aged 9 ys. 3 ms. 10 ds.

Malinda daughter of J. & M. Stump died Dec. 6, 1861 aged 7 ys. 24 ds.

Catherine dau. of J. & M. Stump died May 16, 1842 aged 3 Ms.

Mary C. dau. of J. & M. Stump died Aug. 3, 1852 aged 6 mo. 12 ds.

John Groves died Aug. 10, 1857 aged 37 ys. 1 mo. 3 d.

Charles S. Liston Jan. 1, 1875 - Aug. 11, 1901.

Junior T. son of D. J. & Dessie Wolf Mar. 3, 1899 - Nov. 10, 1918.

Dessie wife of D. J. Wolf Dau. of J. T. Liston May 4, 1875 - Mar.
20, 1906.

Mary A. dau. of E. F & L. P. Bishop Dec. 1, 1901 - Jan. 16, 1917.

Clary C. dau of D. & M. Field Oct. 9, 1853 aged 9 ys. 4 mo. 11 Ds.

One grave unmarked.

Jonathan Martin Co. A 7th W. Va. Inft.

George son of J. & M. Stump died Jan. 12, 1862 aged 2 ys. 6 ms 4 Ds.

Nine graves unmarked.

Martin Luther Martin 1860 - 1916.

Three graves unmarked.

Raymond D. Liston 1862 - ———. Mattie B. His wife 1866 - 1920.

Samuel J. Martin Mar. 4, 1842 - Mar. 5, 1904. Lucy A. wife of Samuel J. Martin Sept. 21, 1838.

Jesse Martin born Aug. 31, 1819 died June 9, 1899.

Elizabeth A. wife of J. Martin born Apr. 7, 1820 died Jan. 4, 1899.

Martha wife of J. W. Smith 1855 - 1892.

One grave unmarked.

Lucy dau. of J. & M. Stump died Dec. 14, 1871 aged 6 ys. 9 ms 4 Ds.

Elizabeth wife of J. W. Freeland died Apr. 7, 1875 aged 24 ys. 9 ms.

Ada F. E. daughter of Wm. D. & C. Titchnell died Aug. 7, 1881 age
1 year 2 mos. 28 days.

Moses W. son of Revd. D. &. A. Titchnell born Jan. 24, 1844 died
Feb. 6, 1862. Was a private in Capt. J. M. Godwins Co. 6th Va.
Regt.

Daniel H. son of Wm. D. & C. Titchnell died Aug. 18, 1878 age 2 yr.
7 mos. 2 dys.

S. D. son of Revd. D. & D. Titchnell born Oct. 12, 1837 died Jan. 28,
1862. Was a private in Capt. Sniders Co. 7th Va. Regt.

One grave unmarked.

Rev. Daniel Titchnell died May 8, 1893 age 77 ys. 8 ms. 25 ds.

Mary E. wife of G. M. Miller died Feb. 24, 1872 in her 26 Yr.

Sallie E. dau. of C. W. & M. E. Miller born Apr. 27, 1868 died Dec.
25, 1880.

Charles U. son of C. W. & M. E. Miller born Dec. 22, 1866 died Jan.
22, 1881.

John C. Stone Aug. 17, 1834 - June 30, 1923 Co. F 17th Reg. W. Va.
Vol.

Charlottie F. Stone born Feb. 12, 1834 died Jan. 16, 1902 aged 65
yrs. 11 ms. 12 ds.

Stephen Titchnell Oct. 6, 1823 - Mar. 11, 1903. Lydia Titchnell Feb.
4, 1822 - ———.

Four graves unmarked.

Minnie F. dau. of John W. & Rachel J. Titchnell died Dec. 31, 1898 aged 15 yrs. 2 mo. 7 days.

Louvenia Olive dau. of John W. & Rachel J. Titchnell died Sept. 29, 1876 aged 1 yr. 10 mo. 7 days.

One grave unmarked.

Levi Bruce son of A. G. & M. Titchnell died Sept. 22, 1878 aged 2 yrs. 4 mos. 19 ds.

Otis Marshall son of A. G. & M. Titchnell died Sept. 16, 1878 aged 10 yrs. 5 mo. 7 ds.

Osea Jane dau of A. C. & M. Titchnell died Sept. 9, 1878 aged 7 yrs. 7 mo. 16 ds.

Idella J. dau. of L. N. & E. C. Martin died May 3, 1878 aged 6 yr. 4mo. 8Ds.

Elva A. dau. of L. N. & E. C. Martin died Nov. 15, 1881 age 4 yr. 5mo. 6ds.

Lloyd O. son of J. R. & L. A. Martin born Aug. 31, 1899 died Jan. 1, 1900.

Lizzie J. dau. of H. & L. L. Liston born Nov. 21, 1893 died July 27, 1895.

Abraham Liston born Aug. 15, 1843 died Jan. 26, 1896. Co. I 17th Regt. W. Va. Inft.

Adaline wife of A. Liston born Aug. 12, 1842 died May 1, 1917.

Oscar S. McNair West Virginia Pvt. 155 Depot Brig. October 9, 1927.

Mary Etta dau. of S. E. & Elma J. Lee Dec. 9, 1903 - Feb. 3, 1916.

Infant dau. of J. A. & Pearl Nedrow Feb. 27, 1916.

J. Dillon Miller Mar. 14, 1850 - Feb. 18, 1920. Rachel his wife Dec. 20, 1847 - Mar. 27, 1925.

Jesse P. son of J. R. & L. A. Martin born Dec. ——, 1901 died Dec. 22, 1901.

Levi May Jan. 21, 1822 - Mar. 22, 1908 aged 86 yrs. 2 mos. 1 day.

Jane May Apr. 19, 1820 - June 2, 1902 aged 82 yrs. 1 mo 14 ds.

Messie M. dau of J. D. & R. E. Miller May 2, 1888 - Jan. 27, 1890.

One grave unmarked.

John Stump died Feb. 20, 1883 aged 64 yrs. 10 mo. 5 dys.

Mary wife of John Stump died Feb. 23, 1899 aged 72 yrs.

Five graves unmarked.

Lieut. Hosea Metheny Co. F 17th W. Va. Inft.

Peter Titchnell Co. H 3rd P. H. B. Md. Inft.

A. C. Titchnell Jan. 12, 1843 - Dec. 20, 1927. Martha Titchnell Nov. 29, 1845 - Sept. 21, 1912.

Three graves unmarked.

Henry Bishoff Co. F 6th W. Va. Inft.

Three graves unmarked.

Alma E. dau. of L. C. & O. F. Loraw June 14, June 16, 1906.
Nine graves unmarked.
Virginia Rebecca dau. of T. R. & Vespa I. Martin Sept. 10, 1918 -
Dec. 16, 1920.

* * * *

Small cemetery on the D. C. Radabaugh farm about one mile
east of Beech Run Hill School house, in Pleasant District, Preston
County, W. Va. Copied June 25, 1932.
Noah Titchnell born Mar. 6, 1843 died Apr. 11, 1892 Co. A 7th W.
Va. Vol. Inft.
William E. son of W. B. & R. Crane died Oct. 18, 1864 aged 6 ms.
29 ds.
Six graves unmarked.
Samuel Crane died Dec. 1, 1821 aged 59 yr. 11 mo. 6 ds.
Col. Jacob Crane died Sept. 30, 1859 age 57 yr. 5 mo. 11 ds.
Virgie B. dau of A. & M. McNear born July 25, 1874 died Jan. 22,
1878.
Alpheus McNear died May 13, 1895 age 72 yrs. 4 mos. 21 days.
Mary wife of A. McNear born April 10, 1830.
Sarah L. wife of Martin Luther Martin born Dec. 19, 1869 died May
22, 1902 aged 32 years 5 mos. 3 days.
Harlan Benton son of M. L. & Sarah L. Martin Oct. 20, 1901 - Nov.
24, 1908.
J. P. Metheny died Aug. 11, 1870 in his 32 year.
Four graves unmarked.

* * * *

Cemetery on the Sanfred Ryan farm near the Hope School house
about four miles north of Pisgah, Grant District, Preston County,
W. Va. Copied June 27, 1932.
Donald C. son of R. F. & B. J. Ryan Feb. 12, 1903 - Mar. 28, 1908.
Lou Ada dau. of R. F. & B. J. Ryan born Aug. 26, 1888 died Jan. 22,
1895 age 6 yr. 4 mo. 27 ds.
Eddie J. son of E. D. & E. Ryan died Aug. 31, 1871 aged 1 year 7 mo.
Frankie son of E. D. & E. Ryan died Jan. 15, 1871 aged 2 yrs. 11 mo
& 25 days.
E. D. Ryan Co. B 14th W. Va. Inf. Elizabeth Ryan.
Edward D. Ryan died April 8, 1887 aged 53 yrs. 7 mo. 24 days.
Elizabeth Ryan died Apr. 1, 1900 aged 66 yrs. 7 mo. 2 days.
Julia A. Wolfe died Feb. 3, 1888 aged 76 years.
Joanna Wolfe May 4, 1851 - May 20, 1905.
Six graves unmarked.

* * * *

Cemetery on Mintare Everly farm about four miles west of Bruceton Mills, Grant District, Preston County, W. Va. and near the Greenville School house. Copied June 29, 1932.

Emanuel Yohey died September 11, 1889 aged 64 years 4 month & 17 days.

David Yohey died August 23, 1898 aged 67 years 8 month & 30 days.

Five unmarked graves. The following persons were buried here: Amanda Yohey. Frances .Dickey. Fanny Yohey. Two other Children. The first person buried here was David Dickey a minister. This information furnished by Sarah Frances Haines Wolf, great granddaughter of David Dickey.

*   *   *   *

Pleasant Hill or Glover Cemetery near Glover School about four miles northeast of Brandonville, Grant district, Preston County, W. Va. Copied July 4, 1932.

Mertie C. dau. of A. & S. Glover born Mar. 30, 1873 died Apr. 4, 1873.

Four graves unmarked.

Harrison Glover May 17, 1836 - Sept. 6, 1903.

Cynthia E. Glover 1845 - 1926.

Amanda Beeghly died Apr. 28, 1887 aged 23 yr. 6 mo.

Five graves unmarked.

Ami Glover born Jan. 15, 1840 died Apr. 22, 1921. Sarah Glover born Dec. 15, 1838 died Jan. 4, 1915.

Emaline dau. of A. & S. Glover born May 3, 1864 died Sept. 13, 1877.

Amanda J. born Jan. 22, 1867 died Sept. 11, 1877. Leroy D. born Sept. 7, 1871 died Sept. 10, 1877. Children of A. & S. Glover.

Barbara wife of Wm. Glover died Aug. 18, 1877 aged 68 yrs. 9 mo. 15 ds.

William Glover died Aug. 8, 1877 aged 75 yrs. 3 mo. 11 ds.

Martha A. dau. of H. & Martin Glover Mar. 30, 1860 - Mar. 3, 1888.

Anibell dautr. of A. & C. Conneway died May 3, 1885 aged 26 yrs. 5 ms. & 17 ds.

Amos Conway died Dec. 18, 1885 aged 52 yrs. 1 mo. & 24 ds.

Catherine wife of Amos Conneway died Aug. 26, 1903 aged 73 yrs. 6 ms.

Ezra Glover 1846 - 1929. Barbara 1844 - 1883. Mary 1850 - 19—.

Barbara wife of E. Glover died Apr. 29, 1883 aged 39 yrs. 9 ms 25 ds.

Malinda A. dau of E. & B. A. Glover died Mar. 3, 1872 aged 3 yr. 6ms. 2ds.

Three graves unmarked.

Dessie Glover Dec. 24, 1892 - Mar. 1, 1893. Ada B. Glover Oct. 24 1894 - July 21, 1895.

Charles V. Glover July 11, 1896 - Sept. 8, 1896. Oliver S. Glover Apr. 12, 1900 - July 18, 1900.

Wm. D. Glover Nov. 21, 1859 - July 23, 1905.

Josiah Ditmore Nov. 16, 1847 - Aug. 11, 1924.

Malinda Jane his wife Mar. 21, 1848 - Feb. 5, 1921.

John M. Glover 1851 - 1925. Margaret his wife 1851 - 1920.

Effie A. wife of D. W. Glover Aug. 24, 1870 - Feb. 21, 1921.

Two graves unmarked.

* * * *

Cemetery near the Salem Church on the Noah Thomas Farm about four miles northeast of Brandonville, Grant District, Preston County, W. Va. Copied July 4, 1932.

George Caton 1847 - 1927. Susannah his wife 1845 - 1929.

Lyda M. Fearer May 16, 1877 - Apr. 9, 1930.

Lincoln C. son of G. A. & T. B. Caton 1915 - 1919.

Jacob Rosenberger 1848 - 1911. Mary S. his wife 1848 - 1929.

Ella Rosenberger 1870 - 1910.

John A. Teets 1858 - 1921. Sarah M. his wife 1867 - 19—.

Ezra F. Thomas 1847 - 1927. Sarah C. his wife 1849 - 1926.

Lloyd A. Maust 1895 - 1930. Co. B 13 Engrs.

Jasper son of Mr. and Mrs. G. W. Knox 1927 - 1929.

Four graves unmarked.

William D. son of T. M. & W. M. McElroy Jr. 1923 - 1923.

Edna F. McKinney 1895 - 1919.

Woodrow J. son of S. J. & F. O. McKinney May 19, 1913 - Dec. 17, 1913.

Jacob H. Ringer July 12, 1838 - Feb. 20, 1909.

Mary C. Ringer Aug. 19, 1842 - July 2, 1915.

Pleasy E. Ringer May 10, 1884 - Aug. 25, 1914.

U. Marshall Cupp 1870 - 19—. N. Alice his wife 1864 - 1922.

Two graves unmarked.

Wm. Conn Aug. 24, 1838 - Sept. 1, 1909. Ann wife of Wm. Conn Dec. 7, 1829 - Oct. 3, 1895.

M. A. Conn June 14, 1871 - Aug. 16, 1883. J. W. Conn Aug. 2, 1866 - Oct. 2, 1866.

Harry Collier died Sept. 27, 1906 aged 40 ys. 11 ms. 17 ds.

Little Helen dau. of J. W. & E. M. Wolfe Feb. 12, 1911.

Paul Wilson Wolfe Jan. 10, 1909 - Dec. 14, 1918.

Three graves unmarked.

Charles W. son of J. M. & M. J. Rishel 1889 - 1910.

Donald E. Rishel 1919 - 1920.

Five graves unmarked.

W. H. Herring Nov. 15, 1833 - Dec. 24, 1912. Margaret wife of W. H. Herring May 23, 1841 - Jan. 13, 1905.

P. W. Ringer 1858 - 1898.

One grave unmarked.

Isaac S. son of J. & M. A. Seese died Mar. 30, 1889 aged 17 ys. 9 ms. 19 ds.

Mary A. wife of J. M. Seese died Apr. 22, 1897 aged 71 yrs. 5 mo. 5 Ds.

John Seese born Apr. 9, 1814 died July 11, 1900 aged 86 ys. 3 ms. 2 ds.

Estella G. Seese 1902 - aged 9 days.

John J. Livengood Mar. 3, 1855 - June 12, 1890.

Opal L. Herring Feb. 19, 1909 - Mar. 30, 1909.

Ira Herring Aug. 12, 1887 - Oct. 30, 1887. Harry V. Aug. 12, 1887 - Mar. 22, 1905.

Wilmer H. Herring Jan. 11, 1910 - Feb. 11, 1917. Dorothy E. June 6, 1917 - June 13, 1917.

Albert F. Herring 1861 - 1921. Period his wife 1869 - 19—.

Joshua Knox 1849 - 1929. Martha C. his wife 1854 - 1905.

Infant son of H. A. & M. P. Knox Mar. 10, 1920.

John Knox died Feb. 11, 1897 aged 49 yr. 9 mo. 5 ds.

Jesse Knox died Feb. 1, 1889 aged 70 yrs. 8 ms. & 8 ds.

Mary wife of Jesse Knox died Apr. 30, 1897 aged 69 ys. 10 ms. 8 ds.

Jesse J. Knox Sept. 8, 1858 - Apr. 18, 1909.

Marshall Thomas 1860 - 1919. Mary E. his wife 1865 - 1910.

One grave unmarked (recent).

John son of I. & M. E. Wilson born Dec. 10, 1877 died Feb. 11, 1878.

Lyda wife of Jacob Thomas born Oct. 18, 1820 died July 4, 1854.

Jacob Thomas died Mar. 1, 1891 aged 63 ys. 8 ms. 4 ds.

Nancy Thomas died Aug. 23, 1911 aged 73 yrs. 8 ms. 7 ds.

Mary M. Thomas Mar. 14, 1869 - May 2, 1891.

Minnie C. wife of C. F. Fearer born June 5, 1871 died Mar. 30, 1894.

Elizabeth Thomas born Aug. 1, 1880 died Oct. 27, 1895.

Lucinda E. Dennis born Feb. 3, 1865 died Jan. 9, 1899 aged 33 ys. 10mo. & 27ds.

Isaac Thomas 1857 - 19—. Elizabeth his wife 1848 - 1927.

Etta wife of Edward Dennis 1886 - 1920.

Harvey Thomas Nov. 18, 1891 - Mar. 26, 1916.

Two infants of Wilma & Thomas Wolfe Aug. 3, 1911 - Aug. 5, 1913.

John E. Wolfe 1846 - 1921. Lyda his wife 1851 - 1924.

Infant son of W. C. & E. C. Wolfe 1911.

Benj. Coffman Co. F 15 W. Va. Inft.

Magdalene Thomas Apr. 13, 1820 - June 1, 1899.

Jacob M. Thomas died Nov. 21, 1881.

Mary consort of Jacob M. Thomas died Apr. 27, 1840.

Hephzybah consort of Jacob M. Thomas died Dec. 31, 1872.

Chester C. son of H. H. & L. Thomas July 12, 1903 - July 22, 1904.

Bruce son of D. S. & A. Thomas July 14, 1889 - Sept. 16, 1891.

Mary E. wife of Irvin Wilson born June 22, 1859 died June 30, 1889.

Etta G. Wilson July 20, 1879 - Mar. 29, 1896.

Samuel Rishel Aug. 2, 1829 - Apr. 2, 1909. Catherine wife of Samuel Rishel July 24, 1833 - Apr. 28, 1909.

Charley W. son of Samuel & Catherine Rishel Mar. 16, 1876 - June 11, 1881.

Mary A. daughter of Samuel & Catherine Rishel Jan. 24, 1864 - Apr. 3, 1872.

Virginia dau. of Samuel & Catherine Rishel Sept. 6, 1861 - Nov. 9, 1861.

Andrew Thomas May 4, 1836 - Feb. 21, 1907.

Adam Rosenberger July 5, 1812 - Oct. 20, 1893.

Sallie Rosenberger July 18, 1822 - Oct. 5, 1900.

Walter C. son of I. T. & C. B. Patton Jan. 21, 1887 Feb. 21, 1906.

Isaac T. Patton 1863 - 1920. Caroline B. his wife 1855 - 1923.

Otis W. Herring 1894 - 1918.

Pauline G. dau. of O. W. & C. P. Herring 1919 - 1919.

Martha daughter of J. C. & M. M. Ditmore 1898 - 1905.

Charles son of E. & C. Prinky Mar. 1, 1896 - Oct. 12, 1911.

Pearly May Fike born Mar. 21, 1889 died Jan. 24, 1895.

Noah Thomas 1864 - 19—. Lovina C. his wife 1863 - 1923. Ethel 1886 died Aug. 29, 1886.

Ella B. wife of Ira Thomas born July 16, 1866 died Apr. 25, 1895.

*   *   *   *

Cemetery at Centenary Church, about six miles southeast of Bruceton Mills, and in Pleasant District, Preston County, W. Va. Copied July 4, 1932.

James M. Titchnell July 17, 1862 - Nov. 17, 1924.

Sarah R. wife of James Titchnell Sept. 17, 1863 - July 16, 1917.

Wm. Wilhelm Oct. 6, 1836 - Dec. 5, 1908.

Lavina wife of Wm. Wilhelm born May 20, 1825 died June 23, 1902.

J. Wesley Groves Oct. 3, 1857 - Nov. 9, 1906.

Theodore Groves Sept. 5, 1901 - Jan. 31, 1918.

Oliver F. Miller Mar. 30, 1891 - ————. Osie O. his wife Apr. 1, 1893 - Sept. 21, 1925.

Jacob H. Sisler Apr. 30, 1850 - July 16, 1909. Mary E. Sisler June 16, 1851 - ————————.

John Q. Kelly 1854 - 1927. Minnie A. 1870 - 1930.

Ida dau. of J. Q. & M. A. Kelly Nov. 3, 1907 - Apr. 26, 1909.
One grave unmarked (recent).
Agness Blanche dau. of Chas. & Icie Groves June 25, 1909 - Sept. 24, 1909.
One grave unmarked.
William Benson May 19, 1849 - Mar. 18, 1931. Hannah Benson May 4, 1858 - Sept. 20, 1926. One grave, same lot unmarked.
Harold W. son of A. R. & Verna G. Dodge Dec. 13, - Dec. 24, 1916.
Henry C. Jackson Mar. 31, 1844 - Mar. 27, 1921. Sarah M. his wife May 14, 1848 - Aug. 20, 1920.
Wm. Carlus son of E. A. & A. M. Jackson Oct. 15, 1913 - Nov. 12, 1913.
Two graves unmarked.
Martha Maude wife of F. S. Englehart 1891 - 1918.
Jesse M. Englehart May 28, 1875 - Oct. 25, 1917.
Edith Pearl dau. of G. H. & M. Benson Nov. 22, 1890 - Nov. 17, 1912.
Two graves unmarked.
Bruce Harold Chidester July 22, 1907 - Feb. 12, 1909.
Elisha Bishoff Apr. 17, 1837 - Sept. 18, 1912.
Noah Ringer 1856 - 1931. Martha B. 1866 - 19—.
Charles F. Jenkins 1861 - 1929.
Infant son of Mr. & Mrs. B. F. Awman 1915.
William H. Cupp Feb. 7, 1840 - Feb. 26, 1912.
Pauline dau. of G. S. & T. B. Bishoff Feb. 11, 1910 - Sept. 11, 1911.
Mrs. Hannah E. Cupp died May 10, 1931 aged 85 yrs. 1 mo. 15 days.
Two graves unmarked.
Maude infant dau of R. & A. M. Otto died Oct. 10, 1886.
Alice M. wife of Kenneth Otto Oct. 4, 1866 - Aug. 3, 1904.
Mary A. Ringer born Dec. 4, 1831 died Sept. 28, 1912.
William C. Ringer died Apr. 11, 1899 age 68 yrs. 3 mos. 22 ds.
Albert Ringer Mar. 12, 1895 - Sept. 29, 1924.
Two graves unmarked.
Mary Friend June 8, 1851 - May 6, 1919.
Marvin E. Livengood Sept. 7, 1919 - Oct. 21, 1919.
Myrtle A. wife of H. A. Spindler Jan. 26, 1893 - July 12, 1922.
Cyrus C. Graham Apr. 3, 1862 - Oct. 6, 1921. Allie V. his wife May 24, 1868 - —————.
John Englehart May 2, 1852 - Jan. 13, 1921. Anna Englehart June 22, 1855 - —————.
John S. Ringer Nov. 23, 1866 - July 2, 1927. Emma J. his wife Nov. 3, 1864 - Dec. 6, 1922.
Roland L. Merriman Apr. 29, - Aug. 17, 1923.
One grave unmarked.
Melissa E. Bishoff Feb. 11, 1867 - Sept. 4, 1923.

John B. Leonard July 6, 1836 - Jan. 16, 1908.

Margaret Ellen Leonard born Apr. 7, 1853 died Nov. 26, 1927 aged 74 years 7 mo. 19 days.

Minnie dau. of J. B. & M. E. Leonard Nov. 16, 1891 - Oct. 16, 1908.

Elroy Leonard born Jan. 25, 1874 died May 11, 1928 age 54 yrs. 3 mo. 16 days.

Tillman Leonard Sept. 1, 1883 - ————. Effie Lewis wife of Tillman Leonard Sept. 5, 1906 - Dec. 30, 1927.

Three graves unmarked.

Vorman O. Sines Aug. 5, 1906 - Aug. 24, 1907.

James B. Kelly 1856 - ————. Lizzie A. his wife 1860 - 1918.

Peter Frankhouser 1819 - 1867. Mary A. his wife 1827 - 1917.

Lela dau. of I. A. & R. C. Frankhouser Feb. 10, 1900 - Feb. 14, 1900.

Little Ray son of I. A. & R. C. Frankhouser Sept. 21, 1888 - Sept. 18, 1889.

Ward W. son of I. A. & R. C. Frankhouser June 9, 1897 - Mar. 21, 1905.

Charles Wolfe 1893 - 1931.

J. C. Wolfe May 16, 1828 - Nov. 17, 1905.

Mary Wolfe Mason born Oct. 18, 1855 died Jan. 1, 1921.

Vergil son of E. R. & M. M. Bucklew Feb. 22, 1903.

Earl P. son of M. T. & R. B. Cale Feb. 20, 1902 - Aug. 12, 1904.

Henry C. son of M. T. & R. B. Cale died Feb. 15, 1899 aged 13 y. 8 m. 26 d.

George W. Ringer May 31, 1828 - May 24, 1902. Mary Ringer his wife Oct. 28, 1833 - June 24, 1924. One grave, same lot unmarked.

Harold D. Awman July 17, 1923 - July 18, 1923. Emmett W. Awman Sept. 19, 1922 - Sept. 19, 1922.

Laura S. dau. of B. G. M. & L. Awman Nov. 23, 1890 - Jan. 17, 1908.

Mary M. dau. of B. G. M. & L. Awman May 14, 1898 - Nov. 26, 1898.

Lydia D. Awman 1864 - 1930.

Benjamin Awman July 11, 1828 - Mar. 21, 1907.

Julia A. Awman Feb. 5, 1830 - Jan. 21, 1909.

Lillie J. dau. of A. & M. Strawser born Aug. 10, 1887 died Jan. 17, 1899.

Henry Chidester born Apr. 19, 1817 died Dec. 23, 1897.

Margaret Chidester born July 20, 1818 died Jan. 29, 1911 age 92 yr. 6 mo. 9 ds.

Joseph N. Miller born Dec. 14, 1809 died Feb. 6, 1902.

Mary A. Miller born Apr. 23, 1812 died Oct. 2, 1900.

W. H. Ringer Dec. 4, 1861 - Nov. 23, 1907.

Emma A. wife of W. H. Ringer born Feb. 26, 1858 died Jan. 23, 1896.

Elisha Ringer 1852 - 1932. Charlott D. his wife 1855 - 1929.

Asa C. son of E. & C. Ringer died Nov. 3, 1897 age 3 yrs. 1 mo. 16 ds.

Alfred Kelly born Mar. 9, 1823 died Dec. 19, 1903 age 80 yrs. 9 mo. 10 ds.

Christena Kelly born June 9, 1825 died Aug. 16, 1907.

Edna Pauline Spiker dau. of J. A. & Alberta Spiker Feb. 3, 1919 - Oct. 15, 1919.

Edgar R. Spiker son of J. A. & Alberta Spiker Aug. 4, 1921 - Dec. 25, 1921.

George A. Kelly 1850 - 1930.

Four graves unmarked.

Nancy wife of W. A. Miller born Dec. 9, 1836 died May 21, 1896.

Perry J. son of S. H. & J. V. McElroy born May 27, 1891 died Nov. 17, 1895.

Edith B. dau. of S. H. & I. V. McElroy died Feb. 16, 1889 age 3 mo. & 8 d.

Robert R. Spiker 1838 - 1920. Angelina his wife 1844 - 19—.

Bruce F. son of R. R. & A. Spiker died Jan. 4, 1887 aged 2 ys. 20 ds.

Nancy wife of Z. Feather born Oct. 10, 1845 died Mch. 3, 1882.

John Metzler died Oct. 22, 1883 aged 77 yr. 9 m. 17 d.

Rachel wife of John Metzler died Oct. 15, 1880 aged 72 y. 1 m. 20 d.

Sarah M. wife of J. R. Scott died Nov. 25, 1876 aged 26 yr. 6 mo. 21 dys.

Conrad Ringer died Jan. 3, 1893 aged 86 yrs. 7 mo. 27 ds.

Mary wife of Conrad Ringer died Nov. 7, 1877 aged 72 years 1 mos. & 14 Ds.

Cindivali Everly June 9, 1828 - July 21, 1908.

John H. Awman died March 3, 1879 aged 28 years 10 mos. & 23 ds.

Two infants of B. G. M. & L. Awman.

Martha R. dau. of A. & H. E. Engle died Dec. 19, 1880 aged 3 y. 6 m. 3 d.

Lidda A. wife of A. W. Ringer died May 19, 1885 aged 25 yr. 5 mo. 5 d.

One grave unmarked.

John A. Miller died Jan. 17, 1892 aged 35 yrs. 1 mo. & 5 Ds. A member of No. 117 I. O. O. F.

Catherine Wolfe 1832 - 1913.

Henry L. son of L. A. & M. E. Martin died Apr. 4, 1879 age 1 mo. 16 days.

Lucian A. Martin died Apr. 11, 1897 aged 67 yrs. 1 m. 5 days.

Mary E. wife of L. A. Martin died Mar. 9, 1876 aged 41 yrs. 4 mo. 13 ds.

Lillie G. Martin died Jan. 21, 1877 aged 1 yr. 11 m. 21 ds.

Sarah A. dau. of L. A. & M. E. Martin died Feb. 5, 1875 aged 21 yrs 7 mo. 27 days.

John Martin died Jan. 4, 1879 aged 78 y. 2 m. 7 days.

Sarah wife of John Martin died June 18, 1874 in her 70th year.
Mary C. dau. of J. E. & R. Jenkins died Jan. 28 1875 aged 16 yr. 2 mo. 7 d.
Jehu Jenkins Mar. 15, 1829 - July 28, 1907. Ruffina wife of Jehu Jenkins died Feb. 25, 1883 aged 54 y. 7 m. 6 d.
Catherine Jane Jenkins Jan. 25, 1846 - May 25, 1918.
Mary & Emma daughters of C. F. & M. J. Jenkins Mar. 19, 1893 - Apr. 2, 1893.
Albert S. son of H. J. & M. E. Ringer born Sept. 7, 1889 died July 27, 1890.
Mollie E. wife of H. J. Ringer Nov. 18, 1858 - Oct. 4, 1910.
John J. Ringer 1836 - 1928. Elizabeth his wife 1833 - 1893.
Charity wife of H. Otto died Feb. 14, 1902 aged 74 yr. 2 m. 20 days.
Herbert Otto died Nov. 19, 1893 aged 67 yr. 7 mo. 5 ds.
Isaac Otto 1850 - 1921.
One grave unmarked.
In memory of Flora B. Ringer whose body lies in Dustin, Okla. 1886 - 1911.
Geo. F. Livengood 1864 - ——. Ella M. his wife 1870 - 1922.
Three graves unmarked.
Mary M. dau. of P. F. & J. A. Sisler May 17, 1907 - June 5, 1907.
Jack - Juda - Robert sons of L. F. & P. A. Miller born Aug. 20, 1888 died Sept. 11, 1888.
Wilber F. son of L. F. & P. A. Miller died March 12, 1885 age 8 mo. 8 ds.
Geo. Rodeheaver died June 22, 1880 aged 69 y. 4 m. 5 d.
Lourana wife of Geo. Rodeheaver died Mar. 2, 1877 aged 63 yr. 9 m. 4 ds.
Albert B. son of Amanda Shaffer died Sept. 10, 1878 aged 4 mo. 4 days.
Lee P. Scott died July 15, 1875 aged 28 yr 7 m. 23 days.
Sarah A. wife of L. P. Scott died May 15, 1880 aged 29 y. 4 m. 27 ds.
Lillian O. dau. of L. P. & S. A. Scott died Mar. 16, 1875 aged 8 m. 14 ds.
John D. Rigg 1833 - 1906. Catherine A. Rigg 1839 - 1914.
Thomas L. Rigg 1862 - 1904.
Ida M. Rigg 1864 - 1871.
Chas. H. B. Rigg 1866 - 1881.
Bertha C. Rigg 1870 - 1881.
Wm. S. Rigg 1868 - 1881.
Virgil Bruce son of G. W. & M. E. Bishoff born Mar. 15, 1893 died Oct. 8, 1893.
David C. son of G. W. & M. E. Bishoff born Mar. 10, 1899 died June 2, 1899.

Allen son of A. & M. Shaffer died Sept. 2, 1872 aged 17 yr. 5 mo. 18 ds.

Alexander Shaffer Feb. 13, 1831 - Feb. 8, 1892.

Amanda E. Shaffer Nov. 2, 1858 - Oct. 26, 1907.

Victory May dau. of W. N. & S. J. Lynch died May 31, 1881 aged 3 yr. 3 m. 12 ds.

Kata Ann dau. of W. N. & S. J. Lynch died June 4, 1881 age 3 yr. 4m. 16ds.

Charlota Bell dau. of W. N. & S. J. Lynch died June 2, 1881 aged 5 yr. 10 mo. 12 ds.

Charles R. son of W. N. & S. J. Lynch died Oct. 19, 1888 aged 3 yrs. 14 ds.

Mary L. Rexroad born Dec. 16, 1853 died Aug. 4, 1892.

Virginia Livengood 1855 - 19—.

David S. Livengood 1849 - 1929.

One grave unmarked.

Gertie M. dau. of D. S. & V. Livengood died Dec. 28, 1891 age 4 y. 8 m. 22 d.

Theodosia dau. of D. S. & V. Livengood died Mar. 8, 1882 aged 29 days.

Two graves unmarked.

Maude E. dau. of E. S. & J. C. Livengood July 9, 1881 - Aug. 12, 1919.

Clarence L. son of E. S. & J. C. Livengood Sept. 29, 1876 - Jan. 26, 1881.

Edgar C. son of E. S. & J. C. Livengood Feb. 17, 1874 - Feb. 2, 1881.

J. Loyd son of E. S. & J. C. Livengood Dec. 11, 1871 - Feb. 28, 1888.

Wm. V. son of P. & E. R. Ringer died Feb. 14, 1881.

Seven graves unmarked.

Nitia M. dau. of A. S. & I. V. Chidester died Aug. 24, 1886 aged 6 m. 22ds.

Ida V. wife of A. S. Chidester Oct. 26, 1859 - Feb. 4, 1912.

Ashbel S. Chidester 1861 - 1925.

Amaziah Chidester died Jan. 23, 1898 aged 54 yrs. 5 ms. 15 ds.

Elizabeth Chidester born Feb. 17, 1823 died Mar. 3, 1905.

Wm. Chidester Aug. 30, 1821 - May 2, 1896.

Evelyn M. dau. of I. N. & Lizzie M. Chidester 1905 - 1915.

Three graves unmarked.

Geo. W. Jeffers 1853 - 1925. Martha his wife 1855 - ——.

Cora A. dau of G. W. & M. M. Jeffers born Sepr. 20, 1876 died Jan. 1, 1891.

Ida V. wife of B. G. Miller died Mar. 18, 1894 aged 34 yr. 8 mo. 3 da.

*   *   *   *

Cemetery near Cuzzart Church in the eastern part of Pleasant District, Preston County, W. Va. Copied July 4, 1932. Parnell Cemetery.

Two graves unmarked.

Eugene infant son of J. C. & P. L. Feather Feb. 1, Feb. 12, 1925.

Matthew son of S. E. & M. A. Feather Dec. 12, 1889 - July 3, 1910.

Gay D. son of B. F. & R. C. Smith 1918 - 1918.

Seven graves unmarked.

Ida E. dau. of H. C. & M. E. DeBerry 1902 - 1921.

Two graves unmarked.

Annie M. Sphar wife of C. A. Sphar born May 28, 1879 died May 14, 1929.

C. C. Sphar son of C. A. & Annie Sphar b. Dec. 25, 1910 d. May 22, 1919.

Four graves unmarked.

Dexter E. son of S. & E. Feather June 21, 1921.

Cyrus Shaffer Jan. 5, 1846 - Feb. 27, 1917.

One grave unmarked.

Peter Strawser born Mar. 14, 1833 died Dec. 10, 1906.

Mary wife of Peter Strawser born Sept. 12, 1836 - ——————.

Annie Ruth dau. of W. F. & D. M. Schnopp May 29, 1919 - Feb. 25, 1920.

Infant of C. R. & M. R. Kelly May 16, - May 21, 1917.

Oran Harold 1925 son of Mr. and Mrs. C. C. Ringer.

Three graves unmarked.

Charles A. Rodeheaver 1872 - 1919. Emma M. his wife 1880 - 19—.

One grave unmarked.

Sons of E. K. & Nancy V. Miller. Martin L. Oct. 21, 1886 - Feb. 3, 1905. Earl U. Jan. 16, 1888 - Nov. 11, 1901.

Dessie dau. of G. & V. Spiker July 30, 1887 - Aug. 17, 1888.

Infant daughter Sept. 16, 1893 - Oct. 3, 1893. Jasper V. Dec. 2, 1898 - Apr. 23, 1904 children of H. E. & S. A. Strawser.

Pearl A. Strawser died Feb. 27, 1902 age 16 ys. 5 ms. 28 ds. Jesse C. Dec. 5, 1887 - Apr. 29, 1900.

Dellie M. Sept. 6, 1884 - Oct. 1, 1884. Infant May 5, 1890 children of A. & M. Strawser.

Two graves unmarked.

Philip Schnopp 1851 - 19—. Mary J. his wife 1861 - 19—.

Joseph R. Schnopp Dec. 5, 1918 - Oct. 19, 1921.

Benjamin P. Schnopp Nov. 28, 1920 - Dec. 27, 1920.

Twenty-four graves unmarked.

Here lie the body of Susan Mah Feather a wife of J. Feather died in her 19 year 1825.

Dessie M. dau. of J. A. & M. J. Rechart died Sept. 15, 1899 age 4 ms. 16 ds.

Laura E. dau. of J. A. & M. J. Reckart died Jan. 28, 1879 age 2yrs. 1mo. 10ds.

Pearl dau. of J. A. & M. J. Reckart died Dec. 27, 1885.

Children of E. M. & M. E. Livengood. William O. died Oct. 2, 1898 age 2 y. 7 ms. 14 ds. Alverda J. died Jan. 8, 1881 aged 5 yrs. 11 mo. 21 ds.

F. M. Livengood Jan. 19, 1848 - ——. Martha E. Nov. 7, 1848 - Nov. 26, 1917.

Samuel S. Livengood died May 30, 1896 aged 73 ys. 8 mo. 9 ds.

Mary J. Livengood died Feb. 2, 1906 aged 79 ys 4 ms. 15 ds.

Marshall W. Ringer 1856 - 19—. Isura B. his wife 1866 - 1919.

Lawrence L. Ringer 1883 - 1920.

Three graves unmarked.

Amanda J. wife of J. A. Reckart Dec. 30, 1857 - Oct. 20, 1909.

John Schnopp 1849 - 1923. Berthenda C. his wife 1858 - 19—.

Two graves unmarked.

Winfield Scott Crane 1864 - 1923. Allie May Crane 1866 - ——.

Abbey Reta dau. of W. S. & A. M. Crane Aug. 7, 1900 - Sept. 15, 1914.

C. M. DeBerry 1879 - 1922. Julia his wife 1884 - 19—.

Mabel Ellen born & died Jan. 5, 1915.

Two graves unmarked.

Ora Otis son of H. N. & E. E. DeBerry born May 18, 1899 died Oct. 22, 1900.

John H. Smith 1857 - 1919. Elizabeth Smith 1855 - 1917.

Mary J. wife of E. A. Hartman died Dec. 29, 1887 aged 32 ys. 3 m. 27 ds.

Lucinda wife of Jonas DeBerry born Mar. 5, 1830 died Aug. 13, 1893.

Jonas DeBerry born Sept. 18, 1828 died Sept. 30, 1884.

Samuel F. son of Jonas & Lucinda DeBerry born Sept. 4, 1872 died Aug. 18, 1891.

George Spiker died Nov. 17, 1890 aged 78 yrs. 11 mo. & 3 ds.

Nancy wife of George Spiker died July 29, 1884 aged 64 yr. 7 mos. & 1 D.

James DeBerry born July 26, 1833 died Sept. 25, 1919.

Grace E. M. dau. of James & Louisa DeBerry born Feb. 1, 1887 died July 23, 1888.

Joseph S. son of James & Louisa DeBerry born Jan. 12, 1875 died Jan. 28, 1875.

Maria Guthrie died April 17, 1884 aged 60 ys. 5 mos. 6 ds.

William Guthrie born Apr. 1, 1819 died Feb. 19, 1909.

Catherine wife of George S. Beerbower died March 18, 1858 aged 39 ys. 11 mo.

Archibald DeBerry died March 21, 1860 aged 70 yrs. 6 mo.

Mary wife of Archibald DeBerry died Dec. 28, 1846 aged 49 yrs. 8 mo. 27 ds.

Infant son and dau. of W. B. & R. R. Rodeheaver.

Robert E. Rodeheaver Dec. 3, 1854 - May 20, 1876.

Wm. B. Rodeheaver July 8, 1824 - Aug. 10, 1903. Rachel R. Rodeheaver Apr. 22, 1832 - Oct. 12, 1878.

Mary A. Sphar born Sept. 11, 1838 died March 31, 1912.

M. M. R.

Two graves unmarked.

Lydia E. wife of F. F. Spiker 1869 - 1929.

One grave unmarked.

Shipley A. Sphar Oct. 10, 1874 - June 5, 1917.

Jas. B. Rodeheaver born July 2, 1833 died Apr. 12 1897.

Nine graves unmarked.

Ezra A. Rodeheaver Apr. 19, 1905 - Aug. 17, 1917.

One grave unmarked.

Infant son of Jacob & Martha E. Reckart June 20, 1881.

Jacob Reckart Apr. 21, 1841 - ————. Martha E. his wife Sept. 25, 1858 - ————.

Rufus R. Rodeheaver Sept. 16, 1845 - ————. Sara J. his wife Nov. 16, 1851 - Jan. 24, 1921.

Fuller Rodeheaver June 3, 1881 - ————. Rachel S. Jan. 28, 1886 - Dec. 21, 1917.

Wm. A. Crane 1852 - 1921. Laura B. his wife 1865 - 19—.

Laura E. dau. of J. C. & E. Reckard born Feb. 17, 1887 died May 29, 1888.

Samuel Strawser 1866 - 1928. Melissa his wife 1875 - 19—.

Nine graves unmarked.

Lucy A. dau. of Cyrus & Jane Shaffer Aug. 25, 1904 - Apr. 11, 1906.

Four graves unmarked.

Daniel W. Teets born July 24, 1850 died March 10, 1859.

Three graves unmarked.

J. P. Rodeheaver June 12, 1828 - Aug. 10, 1904.

Wm. Wolfe 1831 - 1911.

Abigail wife of T. A. J. Parnell born Jan. 6, 1825 died Sept. 14, 1858.

Three graves unmarked.

Antony Wolfe died May 12, 1843 aged 44 yr. 5 mo.

Mary Otto died Feb. 18, 1855 aged 81 yrs. 11m. 7 d.

Daniel Wolfe died June 15, 1873 aged 79 yr. 3 mo.

Anney wife of Daniel Wolfe died Jan. 13, 1864 aged 67 yrs.

Two graves unmarked.

Marshall DeBerry 1855 - 1872. Sarah Adaline DeBerry 1865 - 1871.

Jacob DeBerry 1831 - 1898. Christena DeBerry 1828 - 1879.

Harrison Teets 1848 - 1928. Virginia his wife 1868 - 19—.

Jas. F. Teets died June 1, 1919 age 14 yrs.

Sarah E. S. dau. of Jas. & Louisa DeBerry born Feb. 18, 1872 died Apr. 24, 1890.

Mary C. Spiker died Sept. 15, 1895 aged 50 yrs. 2 m. 3 d.

Vesby G. ——————— Apr. 6, 1897 - Dec. 12, 1897.

Eugene F. son of J. & N. Liggett June 24, 1927 - Oct. 10, 1927.

Shadrick Casteel born May 6, 1853 died Feb. 28, 1911.

Della May dau. of S. & R. Casteel born May 18, 1883 died Aug. 19, 1885.

Lona Pearl Miller Jan. 16, 1889 - Aug. 29, 1898.

Cecil Wayman son of N. L. & C. A. DeBerry born Sept. 10, 1899 died Oct. 16, 1900.

Two graves unmarked.

Herbert A. son of H. M. & S. E. Casteel Aug. 6, 1804 - Aug. 16, 1904.

Two graves unmarked.

John Guthrie Dec. 28, 1846 - June 15, 1917. Emma Guthrie June 27, 1840 - May 16, 1930.

Elizabeth V. Pysell 1915 - 1922. Eleanore L. Pysell 1924 - 1925.

*   *   *   *

Cemetery at the Old Brick Church near Little Sandy Creek about four and three-fourths of a mile southeast of Brandonville, and in Grant District, Preston County, W. Va. This burial lot is on an abandoned road and by the ruins of an old brick church and apparently has not been used since 1914. Copied July 4, 1932.

Simon Z. Miller died Oct. 11, 1870 aged 29 ys. 8 ds.

Phillip Strauser died Sept. 4, 1877 aged 74 ys. 10 m. 8 ds.

Martha Strauser wife of Phillip Strauser died Apr. 19, 1877 aged 83 y. & 3 m.

Stephen Guthrie born Mar. 26, 1801 died Nov. 28, 1888 aged 87 ys. 8 mo. & 2Ds.

Barbara Guthrie died Apr. 22, 1873 aged 72 y. 10 m. 27 ds.

Justus G. son of S. & E. Guthrie died Jan. 22, 1873 aged —— mo. 7 ds.

Vespa V. dau. of W. & M. Browning died Jan. 14, 1865 aged 3 y. 5 mo. 15 ds.

Zana E. dau. of Z. & I. Miller died July 30, 1870 aged 2 ys. 10 m. 12 ds.

W. Marshall son of J. M. & H. Frankhouser died Nov. 12, 1865 aged 4 ys & 8 ds.

L. Seymour son of J. M. & R. Frankhouser died Nov. 1, 1865 aged 2 y. 4 m. 17ds.

Marcellus son of P. & M. A. Frankhouser died Feb. 26, 1864 aged 14 y. 6 m. 5 d.

Charles E. son of J. C. & L. Wolfe died Mar. 18, 1854 aged 5 mo. & 15 ds.

Eugenius G. son of J. C. & L. Wolfe died Apr. 12, 1852 aged 1 mo. & 22 ds.

Lucinda wife of J. C. Wolfe died Jan. 19, 1874 aged 43 y. 10 m. 27 d.

Laura J. dau. of J. C. & L. Wolfe died November 14, 1880 aged 20 years 6 mos. 12 days.

John A. McGinnis grand son of Mary Deal died Mar. 18, 1881 aged 11 yr. 1 mo.

Mary wife of Jacob Deal born Aug. 13, 1818 died Oct. 23, 1893.

Peter Frankhouser died Mar. 3, 1893 aged 93 ys. 1 mo. 21 ds.

Catherine wife of Peter Frankhouser died Nov. 25, 1878 aged 77 yrs. & 2 ds.

Daniel Frankhouser died Jan. 22, 1873 aged 81 yr 1 m. 24 ds.

Elizabeth wife of D. Frankhouser died Nov. 25, 1876 aged 85 yr. 10 m. 11 ds.

Nicholas Frankhouser died Jan. 29, 1852 aged 86 yr. 8 mo. 25 ds.

Susanah wife of Nicholas Frankhouser died Mar. 20, 1853 in her 85 year.

Joseph Frankhouser died Oct. 27, 1867 aged 58 yrs. 5 m. 23 d.

Sarah wife of Joseph Frankhouser died Feb. 10, 1885 aged 73 yr. 9 mos.

Samuel P. son of H. & L. A. Frankhouser died Oct. 17, 1895 aged 25 y. 8mo. 23ds.

Pennelton B. son of H. & L. A. Frankhouser died Nov. 2, 1876 aged 8yr. 2m. 14d.

Henry Frankhouser 1839 - 1914. Louisa his wife 1846 - ——.

*   *   *   *

Small Cemetery of the Russel Smith farm about one-half mile east of the White School house in the northern part of Grant District, Preston County, West Virginia. Copied July 6, 1932.

David Shafer died Dec. 11, 1871 aged 58 y. 4 m. 6 ds.

Joseph Pringey died May 1850 aged 38 yrs. 9 mo. 9 ds.

Margaret Pringey died Mar. 12, 1863 aged 49 years 10 mo. & 7 days. C. - P.

Ross son of J. & M. Pringey died Sept. 17, 1851 aged 15 yrs. 5 mo. 8 ds.

Frederick Pringey died Jan. 3, 1863 aged 22 yrs. 9 mo 24 days.

Sarah Benson died Mar. 30, 1852 in the 66 year of her age.

Mary Ann wife of John Guseman died Nov. 21, 1856 aged 27 years 7 mos. 13 days. Infant son of J. & M. A. Guseman born Apr. 14, 1856.

*   *   *   *

Abandoned Cemetery on the east bank of Big Sandy creek just above the dam at Clifton Mills, Grant District, Preston County, W. Va. Copied July 6, 1932.

John Harader Snr. died Dec. 28, 1806 aged 78 years.

Mary wife of John Harader died Sept. 17, 1829 age about 75 years.

Daniel Harader Jr. died Feb. 6, 1834 aged 18 y. 1 mo. 26 ds.

Elizabeth wife of John Mosser died Oct. 21, 1812 aged about 22 yr. - J. H. -

John Harader died Jan. 23, 1840 aged 52 yrs. 3 mo. 4 ds.

Mary wife of John Harader died Jan. 8, 1863 aged 79 yrs. 9 months 26 days.

A.- B. 1845

Catherine A. wife of George Rishel died Aug. 10, 1880 age 69 yr. 2 mo. 10 da.

Elizabeth dau. of G. & C. A. Rishel died June 13, 1850 aged 10 y. 11 mo. 11 d.

W. H. H. - W. Y. Dec. 24, 1850.

William F. J. son of P. J. & M. Brown died Mar. 30, 1851 aged 4 mos.

Susan wife of John Summers died May 22, 1872 aged 42 yrs. 2 mo. 22 ds.

Mary dau. of John & S. Summers died Jan. 4, 1872 in her 18 year.

John Mosser died June 28. 1875 aged 87 yrs. 3 mo. 28 d.

Susanna wife of John Mosser died Apr. 4, 1868 aged 69 y. 10 mo. 15 ds.

Sarah dau. of J. & S. Sommers died Mar. 10, 1865 aged 6 y. 2 m. 24 ds.

Cordelia A. dau. of D. & E. F. Mosser died Mar. 4, 1872 aged 1 yr. 10ms. 24ds.

Fred Spindler died July 29, 1859 aged 62 yr. 7 mo. & 2 ds.

Daniel Harader died Mar. 2, 1863 aged 77 yr. 5 mo. 28 ds.

Mary Harader died Jan. 9, 1876 aged 85 yrs. 7 mo.

Margaret wife of George M. Thomas died Dec. 13, 1881 aged 66 y. 3 m. 9 da.

George M. Thomas died July 5, 1901 aged 87 yr. 11 ms. 11 ds.

Nancy wife of Harrison Spurgeon born Feb. 20, 1819 died Jan. 13, 1885 aged 65 yrs. 10 ms. 23 ds.

John W. son of J. & P. Beeghley died Oct. 28, 1873 aged 14 yrs. 22 days.

Thomas D. son of B. & R. Kemp died Apr. 4, 1872 aged 1 yr. 10 mo. 22 ds.

Christena wife of J. Rishel died July 21, 1868 aged 72 ys. 3 m. 21 ds.
George Rishel died Sept. 11, 1880 aged 71 ys. 3 mo. 17 days.
Don Cameron son of G. & S. Caton died Dec. 25, 1886 aged 6 yrs.
    9 mo. 10 ds.
Rebecca C. Caton died May 5, 1894 aged 19 yrs. 1 mo. 23 days.

*   *   *   *

Cemetery on the O. T. Cuppett farm, formerly the Levi Teets
farm, about one mile east of Clifton Mills, Grant District, Preston
County, W. Va. Copied July 6, 1932.
William M. Collier ——————. Sadie C. wife of Wm. M. Col-
    lier died Nov. 28, 1916 aged 45 yrs. 1 mo. 23 days.
Walter C. Collier Jan. 8, 1887 - July 21, 1908.
One grave unmarked.
Mary Z. wife of W. M. Collier died Feb. 1, 1891 aged 30 y. 9 mo. 21d.
Belva C. dau. of W. M. & M. Z. Collier died June 12, 1899 aged 10y.
    8m. 9ds.
Jackson Collier died Feb. 23, 1883 aged 54 ys. 1 mo. 28 ds.
Mary Collier wife of J. Collier Aug. 27, 1828 - June 9, 1905 aged 76
    yrs. 9 mos. 12 days.
Edna M. & Oscar E. son & dau. of H. F. & Mary A. Mosser Sept.
    18, 1908 - Sept. 26, 1908.
Hampton F. Mosser 1884 - 1919. Mary A. his wife 1880 - 19—.
Jessie M. dau. of S. A. & R. M. Maust Dec. 16, 1899 - Jan. 13, 1904.
Harold Ray son of L. H. & L. B. Mosser died Dec. 9, 1896 aged 3
    yrs. 11 mo. 24 d.
Jessie C. Silbaugh 1888 - 1920.
William Caton 1850 - 1919. Mary E. his wife 1858 - 1913.
Sixteen graves unmarked.
John M. son of L. & E. Teets died Feb. 17, 1872 aged 3 yrs. 11 mo.
    23 ds.
Allen S. Cuppett June 1, 1852 - Aug. 10, 1915. His wife Elizabeth
    Dec. 13, 1849 - ——————.
Seven graves unmarked.

*   *   *   *

Cemetery on the Wilkenson farm about one and one-half mile
north of Brandonville, Preston County, W. Va. Copied July 6, 1932.
Samuel Fike died Feb. 11, 1892 aged 62 yr. 9 mo.
Malinda wife of Samuel Fike died June 8, 1899 aged 44 yrs. 6 mo.
    10 days.
Mary A. dau. of S. & M. M. Fike died Nov. 21, 1871 aged 1 yr. 7 mo.
    & 17 da.
William H. Fike died Apr. 19, 1875 aged 21 days.

Jacob son of S. & M. M. Fike born Mar. 29, 1879 died Mar. 30, 1879.

John Fike son of Jacob & Mary Fike died Feb. 26, 1869 aged 48 ys. 24 ds.

Huldah wife of H. Mosser died Aug. 22, 1861 aged 24 yrs. 5 ms. 27 ds.

Jacob Fike

Mary wife of Jacob Fike died June 27, 1850 aged 57 yrs. 4 mo. 29 days.

*   *   *   *

Miller Cemetery about one mile west of Valley Point, in Pleasant District, Preston County, W. Va. Copied July 7, 1932.

Thomas Morgan 1869 - 19—. Nora Ellen his wife 1877 - 1924.

Marcellus Miller Sept. 8, 1873 - June 12, 1908.

James A. Miller 1852 - 1929. Catherine his wife 1845 - 1923.

Wesley C. Miller Jan. 9, 1887 - July 22, 1905.

John R. son of J. A. & G. Miller died July 12, 1895 aged 19 yrs. 10 mo. 11 ds.

Eliza B. dau. of J. R. & M. Miller died Sept. 11, 1896 aged 30 ys. 10 m. 21ds.

Mary Miller Sept. 1, 1828 - Aug. 31, 1907.

John R. Miller Sept. 12, 1830 - Jan. 25, 1906.

J. Marshall Miller Nov. 26, 1854 - Aug. 31, 1907.

Five graves unmarked.

Solomon S. Miller Feb. 12, 1841 - July 3, 1895.

Infant son of S. S. & H. Miller born died Nov. 6, 1888.

Two graves unmarked.

Marshall W. Miller 1871 - 1932.

Three graves unmarked.

William H. Hartman died Oct. 16, 1885 aged 42 ys. 10 mo. 27 Ds.

Harriett Hartman Apr. 16, 1837 - May 20, 1926.

Virginia R. dau. of W. H. & H. Hartman died Aug. 5, 1893 aged 17ys. 7m. & 2ds.

One grave unmarked.

Infant son of Wm. H. & H. Hartman Nov. 23, 1877.

Infant dau. of Wm. H. & H. Hartman born & died Sept. 23, 1871.

Martial A. son of Wm. H. & H. Hartman died Nov. 18, 1869 aged 15 d.

Infant son of Wm. H. & H. Hartman born & died Nov. 24, 1867.

Solomon Miller born Mar. 25, 1803 died May 17, 1896.

Rachel wife of S. Miller born Jan. 28, 1806 died Dec. 5, 1879.

J. G. J. Liston born Mar. 24, 1828 died Dec. 29, 1900 aged 72 yr. 9 m. 5 d.

Elizabeth Liston born Nov. 11, 1825 died May 10, 1908.

J. L. Bryte 1856 - 1910. Lydia his wife 1855 - 19—.
Five graves unmarked.
Harriet J. Smith died Apr. 21, 1890 aged 33 yrs. 5 ms.
Mary B. dau. of J. A. & G. Miller born Feb. 27, 1856 died Apr. 18, 1858.
James A. Miller born Sept. 20, 1831 died Nov. 22, 1890.
Clarissa A. wife of J. A. Miller born Nov. 2, 1833 died Feb. 8, 1919.
Wilbert Liston May 4, 1857 —————. Elizabeth his wife Mar. 8, 1847 - Jan. 13, 1917.
One grave unmarked.
Ludema Liston Apr. 11, 1844 - Sept. 4, 1927.

*   *   *   *

Cemetery on the J. Benton Graham farm about three and one-half miles southwest of Valley Point and in Pleasant District, Preston County, W. Va. Copied July 7, 1932.
Three graves unmarked.
Mary E. wife of Ezra Forman Feb. 22, 1844 - July 9, 1907.
One grave unmarked.
Curtis B. Forman Nov. 25, 1872 - Apr. 11, 1875.
Three graves unmarked.
Preston Willie Johns born June 27, 1880 died June 1, 1903, aged 23ys. 11m. 4ds.
Samuel Dorsey Johns born June 4, 1871 died Jan. 7, 1905 age 33 ys. 7 mo. 3 ds.
John Johns Oct. 15, 1837 - June 16, 1916. Mary Margaret his wife Nov. 26, 1840 - —————.
Noah H. Steerman Mar. 2, 1878 - Aug. 8, 1920.
Wm. D. Lougee Dec. 26, 1844 - —————. Nancy M. Lougee Dec. 16, 1844 - Jan. 15, 1923.
Jacob F. Martin born Jan. 16, 1806 died Oct. 26, 1885.
Margaret wife of Jacob F. Martin born Aug. 18, 1812 died Dec. 11, 1884.
Ten graves unmarked.
Almira J. dau. of J. & E. Jones died Apr. 2, 1858 aged 9 ys. 4 ms. 8 ds.
Lewis son of J. & M. Forman died Jan. 6, 1853 aged 15 yrs. 4 mo. 15 ds.
Richard son of J. & M. Forman died Oct. 8, 1854 aged 17 ys. 1 mo. 17 ds.
Cyrus son of J. & M. Forman died Mar. 10, 1858 aged 12 yr. 1 mo. 7 ds.
Jonathan Forman died Apr. 10, 1870 aged 58 yrs. 3 mo. 1 day.

Margaret wife of Jonathan Forman died Apr. 10, 1876 aged 67 ys. 11 mo. 24 ds.

Charles son of J. & R. Graham died Mar. 15, 1871 aged 5 ms 11 Ds.

James W. L. Graham died Jan. 19, 1872 aged 7 ys. 4 ms. 14 Ds.

One grave unmarked.

Jasper Graham died Dec. 20, 1886 aged 56 y. 1 m. 2 d.

Carrie B. dau. of F. D. R. & S. F. Graham Dec. 14, 1904 - Nov. 10, 1907.

Infant Mar. 17, 1892.

Rachel V. wife of J. Graham died Mar. 23 1897 aged 53 ys. 7 ms. 22 ds.

Willie A. son of Jas. & R. V. Graham born Mar. 28, 1877 died Feb. 10, 1891.

Ora A. dau. of Jas. & R. V. Graham born May 8, 1887 died Jan. 27, 1889.

One grave unmarked.

Randolph Protzman born Apr. 16, 1848 died June 24, 1903.

Isaac N. Forman died May 14, 1876 aged 47 y. 3 m. 13 d.

John R. Forman died Apr. 8, 1871 aged 71 ys. 5 ms. 3 Ds.

Martha wife of J. R. Forman born Jan. 19, 1804 died Feb. 10, 1887.

Richard Forman died Aug. 18, 1848 aged 75 years.

Mary wife of Richard Forman died Sept. 21, 1864 aged 85 yrs. 8 ms. 15 days.

Seven graves unmarked.

Richard F. Harned June 2, 1829 - Apr. 13, 1908.

Sinda V. Harned Aug. 25, 1834 - Dec. 26, 1922.

Gay son of J. S. & L. E. Harned born Jan. 21, 1897 died Jan. 27, 1897.

Jonathan Harned died Apr. 8, 1858 aged 76 yrs.

Eve wife of H. Harned died Sept. 11, 1858 aged 68 ys. 5 ms. 21 Ds.

Infant dau. of R. F. & S. V. Harned died Oct. 23, 1858.

William J. son of R. F. & S. V. Harned died Mar. 19, 1860 aged 3 ys. 5mos. 2ds.

Jasper N. son of R. F. & S. V. Harned died Feb. 2, 1870 aged 6 ys. 11ms. 24Ds.

John G. Harned July 31, 1833 - Feb. 5, 1910 aged 76 yrs. 6 mos. 5 Dys.

Roamma wife of J. G. Harned Jan. 26, 1825 - Feb. 18, 1906 aged 71 ys. 22 ds.

William S. Harned born Jan. 12, 1825 died Feb. 25, 1914 aged 89 ys. 1mo. 13Dys.

Martin L. Frankhouser Sept. 10, 1839 - Nov. 16, 1915. Julia A. his wife Sept. 29, 1842 - Mar. 14, 1912.

Melissa May dau. of M. L. & J. A. Frankhouser June 26, 1878 - July 9, 1900.

One grave unmarked.

Saloma wife of W. Frankhouser died Sept. 1, 1882 aged 33 ys. 10 ms. 22 ds.

Edward N. Harned 1859 - ———. Rebecca his wife 1866 - 1927.

Russell A. son of E. N. & R. Harned born May 13, 1896 died July 4, 1897.

Infant son of H. & M. A. Seal born Feb. 20, 1878 died Apr. 8, 1878.

Henry Seal Dec. 10, 1829 - ———. Martha Seal July 18, 1838 - Jan. 8, 1919.

Rhuea V. Harned wife of Chas. H. Seal 1879 - 1914.

Hannie A. wife of J. R. F. Harned Feb. 8, 1872 - July 2, 1906.

Belva I. dau. of J. R. F. & Hannie A. Harned Dec. 16, 1893 - July 18, 1906.

Infant son of J. B. F. & I. G. Liston Mar. 25, 1903.

Jonathan Graham Apr. 8, 1828 - Feb. 23, 1909.

One grave unmarked.

I. N. Forman Sept. 14, 1856 - ————. May E. his wife Dec. 26, 1855 - Aug. 13, 1919.

Paul Keith Forman died Jan. 7, 1930 aged 11 mos.

Kenneth born & died Apr. 10, 1919. Lucille Virginia Sept. 14, 1920 - Oct. 6, 1920. Children of Earl & Gladys Forman.

Two graves unmarked.

Benjamin Wilson born Oct. 15, 1824 died Aug. 12, 1902.

*   *   *   *

Cemetery on land formerly the Jesse Forman farm, three and one-half miles northeast of Valley Point, in Pleasant District, Preston County, W. Va. Copied July 8, 1932.

Isaac N. Graham 1860 - 1929. Elizabeth J. his wife 1856 - 1932.

Jehu Forman 1849 - 1927. Malzena 1861 - 19—.

One grave unmarked (Child of Bert Forman).

Infant son of J. Addison & Emma R. Graham May 14, 1921.

Luela M. dau. of M. F. & L. Martin died Mar. 4, 1877 aged 6 ys. 5 ms.

Jesse Forman died July 14, 1857 aged 52 yrs. 1 mo. 12 ds.

Susannah wife of Jesse Forman died Jan. 20, 1880 aged 66 y. 3 m. 20 d.

Ephraim Forman 1846 - 1931.

Mary E. wife of Amon Forman died May 21, 1892 aged 41 ys. 2 ms. 5 ds.

Amon Forman born Feb. 8, 1841 died Feb. 8, 1919.

Ora wife of Amon Forman Mar. 13, 1870 - July 4, 1905.

Seven graves unmarked.

Hannah Graham Collins Mar. 18, 1826 - June 9, 1919

Catherine wife of S. Graham born April 7, 1803 died Feb. 25, 1886.

Sterling Graham died Oct. 17, 1866 aged 71 y. 11m. 17 d.

James S. son of S. & C. Graham died Sept. 10, 1862 aged 24 ys. 5 m. 6 d.

Huldah wife of Abner Liston died Apr. 7, 1879 aged 44 y. 3 m. 27 ds.

Abner Liston born Mar. 13, 1842 died Nov. 21, 1903. Huldah Liston born Dec. 11, 1836 died Apr. 7, 1879. Bythynia Liston born July 16, 1861 ————.

Obediah A. son of A. & H. Liston Dec. 1, 1899 aged 23 y. 11 ms. & 26 d.

Six graves unmarked.

John Bryte died Sept. 18, 1839 in his 60 yr.

Easter wife of John Bryte died Sept. 30, 1871 on her 82 yr.

Margaret dau. of S. & G. Graham died Sept. 7, 1845 aged 10 m. 20 d.

Seven graves unmarked.

James Soverns died April 28, 1851 aged 48 years.

Eugenius son of J. & G. Soverns died Feb. 6, 1866 aged 26 yrs. 6 mo. 5 ds.

Nine graves unmarked.

Jeremiah son of H. & L. Smith died Mar. 21, 1855 aged 1 yr. 11 mo. 5 ds.

*   *   *   *

Locust Grove Church cemetery about four and one-half miles southeast of Brandonville, and in Pleasant District, Preston County, W. Va. Copied July 9, 1932.

Mary Jane Kelley Nov. 21, 1855 - May 29, 1929.

*   *   *   *

Cupp Cemetery on the Victor Cupp farm about three miles southeast of Brandonville, and in Pleasant District, Preston County, W. Va. Copied July 9, 1932.

Catherine Barb wife of Jacob Barb born Feb. 25, 1802 died Oct. 15, 1876.

Leonard Cupp born April 8, 1776.

Susanna Cupp died Mar. 11, 1853 aged 78 yrs.

James J. Benson died Mar. 23, 1890 aged 80 y. 2 m. 18 d.

Sarah Benson died Apr. 23, 1909 aged 87 y. 11 m. 7 d.

Catherine J. dau. of J. & S. E. Benson died Oct. 1864 aged about 3 years.

Mary E. dau. of J. & S. E. Benson died Dec. 1859 aged about 3 years.

Allen son of J. & S. E. Benson died Dec. 1854 aged about 3 years.

Infant son of J. & S. E. Benson died Dec. 1845.

Lizzie B. Fike dau. of M. V. & C. E. Cupp Jan. 17, 1876 - Mar. 25, 1905.

Leslie V. her son Feb. 10, 1905 - Apr. 10, 1905.

Lydia A. wife of A. H. Parson died Feb. 27, 1866 in her 19 year.

Henry Teets died Jan. 17, 1883 aged 73 years.

Elizabeth wife of Henry Teets died May 26, 1892 aged 79 ys. 3 mo. & 7 Ds.

Peter H. Fickey 1848 - 1909. Keziah F. 1846 - 1917.

John A. son of Peter H. & (Keziah Fickey died Jan. 25, 1893 aged 21 y. 11 ds.

Joseph C. Fickey died Oct. 7, 1910 aged 27 ys. 3 ms. 15 ds.

About forty graves unmarked.

*   *   *   *

INDEX

NOTE: *Look for name with various spellings*

———◆———